W9-AUD-971

HOPE
After Faith

HOPE *After* Faith

AN EX-PASTOR'S JOURNEY FROM BELIEF TO ATHEISM

Jerry DeWitt

with Ethan Brown

Da Capo Press
A Member of the Perseus Books Group

Printed in the United States of America. For information, address Da Capo Press, 44 Farnsworth St., 3rd fl., Boston, MA 02210.

Editorial production by *Marra*thon Production Services. www.marrathon.net

DESIGN BY JANE RAESE
Set in 11-point Palatino

Library of Congress Cataloging-in-Publication Data is available for this book.

ISBN 978-0-306-82224-7 (hardcover)
ISBN 978-0-306-82250-6 (e-book)

Published by Da Capo Press
A Member of the Perseus Books Group
www.dacapopress.com

Da Capo Press books are available at special discounts for bulk purchases in the U.S. by corporations, institutions, and other organizations. For more information, please contact the Special Markets Department at the Perseus Books Group, 2300 Chestnut Street, Suite 200, Philadelphia, PA 19103, or call (800) 810-4145, ext. 5000, or e-mail special.markets@perseusbooks.com.

1 3 5 7 9 10 8 6 4 2

To my beloved late grandfather, my Paw-Paw,
Paul Gordon Williamson

Contents

Skepticism is my Nature,
Freethought is my Methodology,
Agnosticism is my Conclusion,
Atheism is my Opinion
and Humanism is my Motivation.

HOPE
After Faith

Prologue

He that descended is the same also that ascended up far above all heavens, that he might fill all things. And he gave some, apostles; and some, prophets; and some, evangelists; and some, pastors and teachers; For the perfecting of the saints, for the work of the ministry, for the edifying of the body of Christ.

—Ephesians 4:10–12

JUST AFTER MY FIFTEENTH BIRTHDAY, I bought my first car, a two-door 1982 Pontiac Grand Prix. It was the spring of 1984, and my paternal grandfather, John Owen DeWitt, had just passed and I used the portion of his estate that he had left me, five thousand dollars, to purchase the Grand Prix. It didn't matter that I'd purchased the Grand Prix at a used-car dealership near my home in Rosepine, Louisiana, because that early 1980s moment represented perhaps the peak of cool for the Pontiac brand. In 1977, the Pontiac Trans Am starred along with Burt Reynolds in the action film *Smokey and the Bandit*. My Grand Prix seemed just as cool to me as Reynolds's ride. From its long, narrow dashboard to its imposingly large, three-spoke steering wheel, it was saturated in blue: a monochromatic color scheme interrupted only by the wood-grain accents throughout the interior. For my inaugural drive in the Grand Prix, I decided to make the fifty-mile trip from Rosepine to Sulphur, Louisiana, where I hoped to reunite with my beloved fourth-grade teacher, Ms. Blair, at Maplewood Elementary. As I pulled into the Maplewood Subdivision I drove by my old house, one of the only places I'd ever lived as a child where I'd had so many neighbors, all of whom lived in a proximity unimaginable in pastoral Rosepine. I remembered the trouble-making neighbors across the street—two middle-school boys armed with pellet guns—who shot out the back-window glass of a station wagon owned by my next-door neighbor on a freezing winter's morning. I recalled one glorious night of trick or treating, where all I had to do was just walk out of the house for seemingly endless opportunities for candy, a stark contrast from the country life in which I had no choice but to pile into my mom's car to stop at even a single house.

When I arrived at Maplewood Elementary, I walked up to the door of Ms. Blair's classroom and peered through a narrow window at the top of the door. Ms. Blair saw me at the door and, to my surprise, instantly recognized me. Seeing Ms. Blair again rekindled the appreciation I had for the tremendous energy and love that she had invested in me, a painfully shy, mildly dyslexic fourth grader. Even as I struggled with basic reading and vocabulary, Ms. Blair saw potential in me. In fact, Ms. Blair not only recognized what I *could* be; she saw what my strengths already were. She told me that I possessed a powerful sense of intuition and encouraged me to use that gift at every opportunity. "Go with your gut, Jerry," she'd say. "Go with your gut." That day, just outside Ms. Blair's classroom, however, we simply engaged in the business of catching up: we asked about the health of each other's families and vowed to stay in touch.

Over the next year, Ms. Blair and I continued to stay connected from afar through birthday and holiday cards; sometimes I'd even take the Grand Prix for a spin to Sulphur just to see her. Then, just before Easter Sunday in 1986, Ms. Blair offered me an exciting and completely unexpected invitation: she asked if I'd accompany her and her husband, Roger, and the youth group from their church, the Southside Assembly of God, to attend Jimmy Swaggart's camp meeting in Baton Rouge. A camp meeting is a large-scale religious service in which worshippers travel to a specific site to hear preachers deliver the word of God. The packed roster of preachers at a camp meeting promises a nearly nonstop succession of services and speakers and, as it slowly proceeds over several days, emotions of the attendees and their praise of God reaches a fevered pitch. The camp meeting is particularly important among Pentecostals in the rural South and Southwest, as the phenomenon has its roots in the frontier Christianity of the 1800s.

I'd never been to a camp meeting before Ms. Blair's invitation and I'd most certainly never seen Swaggart live. While Swaggart is now inextricably linked to a 1988 prostitution scandal that hastened his downfall, back then Swaggart was still a rock star among Pentecostals, particularly in his home state of Louisiana. I loved that Swaggart and his cousin Jerry Lee Lewis both came from the same black-dirt, backwoods Louisiana village, Ferriday, about 130 miles northeast of my hometown, DeRidder, in the southwest section of our state. As a young Pentecostal, I was struck by the fact that while Swaggart and Lewis represented seemingly opposite sides of a spiritual dichotomy—the sacred and the profane—both men were propelled in their careers by the power of music. Growing up in DeRidder, the TV in our living room was always tuned in to Swaggart's Sunday-morning telecast. I loved hearing Swaggart's honky-tonk piano playing blasting from the TV and savored his brilliance in having a full orchestra back him, which gave his down-home music a proud, majestic pomp. But it was the style with which Swaggart preached that affected me most. I would watch, awe-struck, as Swaggart prowled the stage, holding a leather-bound Bible open in one hand, with half of the great book hanging loose, its red bookmark swaying in the air. Swaggart shook his Bible with such authority and passion that when he looked directly at the camera and pointed his finger in the viewers' direction it felt like he was preaching right there in our living room. As a withdrawn, anxiety-ridden adolescent, the confidence and certainty of Swaggart made me think, *That's the person I want to be.* And as a teenager slowly finding my faith in the world of Pentecostalism, I admired Swaggart for both his roots as a traveling evangelist and for refusing to turn his back on his most hardscrabble of beginnings—even after building his megachurch in Baton Rouge and launching a groundbreaking televangelist career, which at its early 1980s peak boasted more than 250 TV stations featuring Swaggart's telecast. Swaggart had built an empire from dirt—could I do the same?

When Ms. Blair, her husband, Roger, and I arrived at the camp meeting at Swaggart's Family Worship Center on Bluebonnet Avenue in Baton Rouge in April of 1986, every expectation I had for the event was instantly fulfilled. The Family Worship Center had a long, sloped glass exterior that was more five-star Four Seasons Hotel than Pentecostal church. Inside, near the sanctuary, there was a mosaic of the world's continents painted on the walls that made me feel as though I had walked into the United Nations building. Closer to the sanctuary, the words of Mark 16:15—"And he said unto them, Go ye into all the world, and preach the gospel to every creature"*—were inscribed on the walls. The global imagery and the words from the Gospel of Mark sent an unmistakable message: we were all at the very center of Christ's global mission.

It was a mission that I couldn't help but feel drawn to. The idea of changing the world for the better coincided with my youthful desires to create a utopia. I was both naïve and ambitious enough to believe that I could make the world a better place and perhaps even bring about world peace. It was not necessarily an idealistic craving: I was raised in an extraordinarily chaotic environment, so peace had always been an objective of mine. The chaos I experienced at home and the yearning I felt for a more harmonious familial life imbued in me a love for humanity and a desire to lessen

*The *King James* version of the Bible has been used for all biblical quotes.

its suffering. My feelings of empathy, in turn, made me captivated by the idea that the Prince of Peace, Jesus Christ, could bring about peace through his present-day kings and priests: the faithful Christians who filled Swaggart's church. That day, I felt like a Catholic walking into the Vatican for the first time. I truly believed I was at the center of the world.

When services began that Friday night, I was struck by the sheer size of the sanctuary that held nearly eight thousand faithful–it was like attending a major sporting event inside a church house–and Swaggart's masterful, precise control of the camp meeting proceedings. It was the first time I'd ever seen a telephone on a church stage, which enabled Swaggart to deliver directions to those outside of the camera's frame. More than once I watched Swaggart leave his command chair–carpeted in a lush, velvety red and positioned on the stage, which had a futuristic, almost otherworldly octagon shape–and sprint to a corner of the stage in order to provide forceful instructions to the gentleman running the soundboard. It was difficult to witness Swaggart's occasional fits of cruelty to the soundboard staff whenever a problem with the sound frustrated him, yet I intuitively understood the enormous pressure Swaggart felt to have this extraordinarily large spectacle go off without a hitch.

I was awed and left breathless by the camp meeting. I'd never seen a service with so much showmanship and style. The lavish sanctuary stood in outsized contrast to my all-too-humble church at home in DeRidder, a small brown-brick building with blue carpeting, outdated wood paneling, small Sunday-school rooms and no baptistery. During Swaggart's camp meeting, I witnessed many things that I had never seen before except in this place, during these services. Our preachers wore old worn suits–*their* preachers sported expensive colored-coordinated suits, right down to matching scarves in their suit-jacket pockets. Our church's choir was comprised of everyday folks possessing average, unremarkable voices but Swaggart's choir seemed to be populated with singers each worthy of his or her own major-label record deal. Indeed, the soloists at the camp meeting were the very faces that I had seen and heard all throughout my childhood and adolescence on TV–the "devil box" to Pentecostals–in our living room every Sunday morning. Our church had lights; their church had lighting that bathed the Family Worship Center in warm white hues that made the deep-red carpeting on the stage seem nearly bloodlike in its intensity. Our church had worn out speakers hanging on the walls with wires poking out the sides; their church had a professional sound system with speakers pointing in every direction and barely visible, thinly cabled microphones dangling from the ceiling that came to a rest right in front of the ecstatic faces of the choir members. To the best of my memory, Swaggart's church was the only church I'd ever seen with a complete, professional drum set on the stage, much less one housed within its own Plexiglas booth in order to control the sound professionally.

But I wasn't simply impressed by the big budgets and professionalism of Swaggart's brand of Pentecostalism; I was completely taken with the messages delivered during the camp meeting. In one of the morning services, one guest preacher, an older man in his fifties with gray hair who sported a light-blue suit and spoke in a booming baritone voice and swung his arms and prowled the pulpit as he spoke, told a completely captivating story about a spring that could not be capped. He explained that a resort hotel development company had purchased a piece of land for a new hotel project and, unbeknownst to the developers, the property possessed a natural spring. Contractors hired by the developers made numerous efforts to cap the spring, all to no avail. When the foundation concrete slab was poured, it appeared as though the spring had finally been capped. But once the slab had settled, the spring cracked through the concrete and flowed to the surface. The contractors then brought in foundation specialists and the slab was repaired and sealed, which, the developers believed, would make the slab even stronger than before.

Satisfied that the spring had finally been capped, the resort was raised and its wide, spacious floors were carpeted. But then moisture from moved through the slab and saturated the carpeting until finally the spring flowed freely again. Experts were brought in once again to attack the problem: this time, they removed the carpeting, resealed the foundation and replaced the floor with water-resistant tile. The resort opened for business and, as time passed, guests checked in and enjoyed the facility. With the problem of the spring seemingly resolved, it was nearly forgotten by the developers. But the hidden source of the spring, the preacher explained, was far larger than even a great hotel could ever be. Supported and driven by the hidden aquifer, this "little spring that could" willed its way, inch by inch, back through the slab, the sealant and even the waterproof tile. The hotel's foundation was eroded by the free-flowing spring, causing a foundation failure far beyond the scope of any repair. The spring, the preacher thundered, was once again fulfilling its natural destiny and the developers realized, finally, that they had been beaten by it. So instead of continuing to try to staunch the spring's flow, they created a fountain for it in the very center of the hotel. "If we as Christians continue to allow the Holy Ghost to push us upward and onward in our lives," the preacher concluded, "eventually our devotion will become a fountain in which the spirit of God flows freely."

The story of the spring provided a profound lesson about the power of devotion to Christ. But the parable had another, more important meaning for me. By age sixteen, I was already aware of the obstacles that lay ahead for me and I carried with me that day both a longing for significance in my life and a profound sense of being lost. Not lost in the Christian sense, mind you, but lost as in living without direction in my life. To me, the natural spring was an "overcomer" and *I* wanted to be an overcomer. "Sometimes in life," the preacher said, "life's obstacles get steadily harder. And so, just like the spring, our progress can seem blocked and that God has forgotten about us. But these are just worldly obstacles that get in our way as we attempt to live for God. Once we allow the Holy Ghost to flow through our lives, we will surmount them."

Later that day, as Ms. Blair and I sat together in the middle column of seats in Swaggart's church, about two-thirds of the way back, a man in this thirties seated a full column to our right began to speak in other tongues. As he spoke, his voice became louder and louder–it was passionate, throaty, desperate, brokenhearted–and he began to get the attention of those seated around him. There is a communal phenomenon that takes place in a Pentecostal service when one person speaks in tongues loudly or uniquely enough to draw the attention of his fellow faithful. Once the congregants closest to him become quiet and begin to listen to the speaking in tongues, it draws the attention of those further and further away. The silence then radiates out from the person speaking in tongues, like the ripples caused by a rock thrown into a lake. At Swaggart's, the man's words actually hushed the thousands-strong crowd. "Do you know what's going on?" Ms. Blair whispered to me. "Yes," I said sheepishly, but I really had no idea what was happening. What I didn't know then, and what I would later learn, is that the quieting of the crowd followed by speaking in tongues meant that a message from God was coming. It was an incredible phenomenon to behold: the sound of an almost deafening noise in praise of God and then silence as the crowd awaited the word of God–dubbed by Pentecostals as "interpretation" of tongues–coming from that man. As one section after another of Swaggart's church quieted, it was like a wave in a football stadium: a wave of devotion spreading slowly across the soaring sanctuary. Then he spoke. "Thus sayeth the Lord," the man intoned in an authoritative and certain voice that sounded much like that of a general addressing his troops, "I am raising up an army of young people to take the gospel to the nation." Ms. Blair turned to me and said, "Do you want to pray?" I did. Right there, in our seats in Swaggart's sanctuary, Ms. Blair led me through the sinner's prayer.

After Saturday-night services, I rode with the Blairs back to Southside Assembly of God Church in Sulphur. It was just after midnight when I groggily slumped into my Pontiac Grand Prix to make the drive back to Rosepine. After turning the ignition key, I popped in my white-colored cassette tape of Swaggart's stirring 1981 live album, *One More Time . . . Live.* "Glory! Glory! Hallelujah!" Swaggart cried on the opening track, "Since I've laid my burdens down!" Just then, I realized that I had driven to Sulphur listening to Billy Joel–and driven back listening to Jimmy Swaggart. I'd traded one piano man for another.

I arrived back at my grandparents' home just before daybreak. I quietly slid through the backdoor, slinked down the narrow hallway that led to their bedroom and stood over my grandmother. Still under Swaggart's spell, I shook Grandma, who was asleep in her narrow, single bed framed with thick metal side rails, awake. She was startled when I shook her but as she opened her eyes, she gave me a warm, welcoming smile. "Maw-Maw," I said, "I got saved." Grandma was the matriarch of our family, the religious leader of our entire clan. I should have known better than to think Grandma would consider my sudden moment of becoming saved legitimate. But back then I was young and naïve about Pentecostal doctrine, which requires that one repent, be baptized in water and baptized in the Holy Ghost with the "evidence" of speaking in other tongues. *All* of these requirements must be met in order to be saved, Pentecostals insist, citing John 3:5 that one "cannot enter into the kingdom of God" without them.

It was an innocence compounded by the spiritual high of the Swaggart service: I truly felt saved and born again. "Did you speak in tongues?" Grandma asked, seemingly tapped into my deepest subconscious. "No," I softly replied. I hadn't spoken in other tongues so, of course, my experience at Swaggart's was illegitimate in her eyes. I walked out of Grandma's room that morning feeling like the meaning of the camp meeting had collapsed. All I could do was wander listlessly into my bedroom to prepare for bed. That night, I started a tradition that I would carry on throughout much of my life: I knelt down by my bed and prayed until I fell asleep.

CHAPTER ONE

God Loves Everyone

Three passions, simple but overwhelmingly strong, have governed my life: the longing for love, the search for knowledge, and unbearable pity for the suffering of mankind.

—Bertrand Russell

THOUGH I WAS BORN AND RAISED in DeRidder, a deeply religious small town of about eight thousand residents dominated by Pentecostals that's the parish seat of Beauregard Parish in Southwest Louisiana, my spiritual journey that began at Swaggart's on that spring day in 1986 was far from assured. On September 17, 1969, I was born to Linda Williamson DeWitt and David Wayne DeWitt at Beauregard Memorial Hospital, a small, single-story redbrick hospital on South Pine Street in downtown DeRidder. I was one month premature but the birth itself was uneventful, excluding the unusual means of transportation for me that day: Mom brought me home on a tiny pillow because I weighed all of five pounds.

Back then, Mom was a housewife who tended to the family home, an old barn that had been transformed into an rambling residential property on rural Ikes Road on the outskirts of DeRidder. Standing at barely five foot five and with her smiling, round face,

Mom was a warm, approachable presence who focused all of her energies on caring for her home and raising her new son. Dad was Mom's physical and emotional opposite. He was a long, slender five foot ten: when he went to bed the sheets barely covered his arms and legs. And with his dark, slicked-back hair he had the look of a greaser. Indeed, that's just who Dad was. Dad was once an airplane mechanic with the air force but, by the time I was born, worked as a plumber's apprentice under his father, John Owen DeWitt. Dad's somewhat lessened station in life was due in large part to his hard partying ways: his passions were riding motorcycles, hanging out in bars in nearby Leesville and drinking with friends wherever friends and family would have him. To the chagrin of all who knew him, Dad enjoyed his hobbies–drinking and riding in fast cars and on motorcycles–often at the same time. Dad's many moments of misbehavior were legendary: he drunkenly did donuts in the mayor's front yard, sped down Ikes Road while standing on the seat of his motorcycle and drag raced with friends on Ikes Road, a stunt that so infuriated my family that my great-grandfather angrily pumped off a shot at him from his shotgun.

Dad was a born daredevil who possessed frighteningly backward beliefs about what it meant to be a man–and to raise a man. When I was an infant, he refused to allow my mother to give me a pacifier. To Dad, a pacifier would just make his son weak. Dad insisted that he be allowed to spank me when I was just one week old. And Dad prevented my mom from rocking me to sleep. He believed that I should be left to cry myself to sleep because that would help make me a man. Dad's rough style of parenting could be as daredevil driven as the stunts he pulled off on his motorcycle. One night, Dad came home drunk and when he stumbled into the kitchen and then fumbled through the cupboard for another drink, he shattered a glass on the kitchen floor. "It needs to be cleaned up, David," Mom insisted. "Jerry might get at it." Dad not only ignored Mom's plea to clean up the shattered glass, he lifted me up and tried to stand me up *in* the shards. Mom stopped Dad that night but the message from Dad's behavior was unmistakable: he was going to do whatever it took to make his baby son tough. To Dad, the process of toughening me up yielded a side benefit: it tortured my mother. He resented my mom's tenderness as though she were his own mother and could be unfathomably cruel to her. When I was an infant, our family lived in Houston, Texas, for a brief stint and one night my dad had plowed through all the spare cash at home on beer. When Mom went to the mom-and-pop grocery store around the corner to buy milk for me, she begged the store's owner to give her the milk on credit, which he refused to do, compounding the humiliation.

Dad's behavior was devastating to Mom but it would soon turn self-destructive. During the late afternoon of August 27, 1972, he climbed into his plumbing truck with one of his closest friends, J. E. Bailey–a six-foot-tall, massively overweight man with seemingly superhuman strength, ironically nicknamed "Tiny"–and headed out to Anacoco Creek just north of Rosepine to drink and shoot their pistols back in the woods along the creek. Just before sunset, Dad and Tiny were good and drunk and had depleted their ammunition. Tiny clambered back to Dad's truck to retrieve some more bullets but when he dug around in the cab of the truck he discovered that they'd reached their last rounds. "I'm not gonna shoot these 'cos we're on our last rounds," Tiny shouted back to Dad. "I know you like to keep your guns in the truck loaded." There was an uncomfortable silence and then Dad called back to Tiny, "No, that's okay, go ahead and shoot 'em. I'm not gonna need 'em anymore." Tiny shrugged his shoulders and ambled back to the creek to join Dad, who was seated on a tree stump nursing a beer. Tiny loaded his pistol, pumped off a few more shots and then he and Dad climbed back over the creek embankment and back into the truck. The pair then headed south toward Rosepine on rural Hawks Road and jumped onto Highway 171 until they hit Memorial Road, where Dad dropped off Tiny at his house. Dad rejoined 171 but instead of heading straight into DeRidder as he always did, he circled town on rural Highway 112. I would learn later that Dad took the circuitous route that night to avoid the cops. Dad was far too drunk to drive and he knew it. Just before midnight, as Dad neared DeRidder, his truck veered off Highway 112 and struck the railing of a bridge. The force of the collision crushed Dad's chest against the truck's steering wheel and the crash left Dad's truck stuck to the railing, jackknifed in the middle of Highway 112, and vulnerable to oncoming traffic. As Dad lay injured in his vehicle, a scrap-iron truck coming from the opposite direction plowed into him, which turned a loose piece of metal pipe in Dad's cab into a dangerous, airborne projectile. The pipe slammed into Dad's head and when the ambulances arrived, the EMTs surveying the grisly scene knew that Dad was unlikely to survive. That night, Dad died in the very place where I was born just three years earlier: Beauregard Memorial Hospital. We'll never know if Dad would have survived had the truck not plowed into him; the injury he sustained to his chest when his truck hit the railing could have been enough to kill him.

I was barely talking when Dad was killed, so I only have one memory of his funeral. And to be honest, I can't even say that the memory is truly mine. But it feels like it is. What I recall is sitting in a truck with my mom's brother, Fred Williamson, and desperately wanting to join my family inside Beauregard Funeral Home but being prevented from doing so. With few memories of my dad and being just three when I lost him, his death was a slow burn. I'd ask my mom where my dad was or I'd say, "All I want is a dad." Mom, meanwhile, was experiencing a ferocious grieving process. We moved into the back bedroom of the home of my grandparents, Paul and Stella Williamson, in Rosepine, a much smaller town than DeRidder in nearby Vernon Parish. One afternoon my mother tearfully struggled over an old steamer trunk packed with Dad's old belongings. Mom couldn't bear the sight of this vivid reminder of Dad but she discovered that she couldn't ignore it, either. So that day I watched as Mom shut the closet door and then, visibly uncomfortable with her decision, reluctantly opened it again. To Mom, the notion of closing the bedroom's closet door meant shutting the door on her life with Dad. Mom eventually settled on leaving the closet door ajar and the wooden steamer trunk with metal handles stood as a permanent memorial to Dad.

Mourning, fortunately for Mom, didn't last long. In 1973, about a year after Dad passed, Mom married a car salesman named George William Deason. The two had met in the parking lot of a local Ford dealership. Our family has long joked that Mom went out shopping for a car and came home with a husband. George was imposingly tall, had a redbone complexion, and was draped, head to toe, in gold: he sported a gold chain, rings and a gold nugget watch. He was every inch the car salesman. He'd drive around town in the latest Ford to roll off the assembly line and drank and spent money so voraciously and so generously that he was never without company. On weekends, George held court at huge, boisterous family gatherings that were all about who could tell the tallest tale or hold the most liquor. Mom didn't mind that George was at heart such a social animal, but she was deeply unnerved by the Mardi Gras atmosphere that prevailed at the Deason family functions. It was clear, even to me as an adolescent, that there was a disconnect between the DeWitts and Deasons. So Mom resisted the natural order of things and kept me from taking George's last name; she wanted the DeWitt to remain in me. I didn't resent Mom for refusing to integrate me fully into our new family because the Deasons scared me to death. I was intimidated by crowds and found their family events, which were dominated by loud music and heavy drinking, to be terrifying.

Once Mom married George we were constantly on the move, life changes driven by George's strong entrepreneurial spirit. George always had a deal in the making and a new place to go to seal the deal. In one of our homes, an old, badly insulated wood-frame structure in Rosepine that was freezing in the winter, I suffered from colds and earaches constantly. One of my first true memories is laying my head in my grandmother's lap with her pressing a warm washcloth against my throbbing ear. I had tonsillitis and an earache and Grandma was praying for me–and speaking in tongues. I felt goose bumps cover my body as Grandma spoke in tongues that day, a feeling I'd later attribute to the presence of the Holy Ghost. My sickliness as a child was also manifested in more serious medical conditions. When I was five, I was diagnosed with two heart murmurs. The steady drumbeat of horrible news about my health kept me keenly aware of the reality of death at the very youngest age. There was no doubt in my mind that I was going to die at any moment. I never had the child's perception of immortality–to me, life itself was fatal. I saw my fears reflected in the worry and concern on the faces of my family. The same year I was diagnosed with the heart murmurs, my grandmother brought me to church and sat me in a straight-back chair in front of the altar. As I sat in the chair, Grandma performed a traditional laying on of hands, with her hands joined by the hands of her fifty fellow congregants. Instead of comforting me, this act of healing unnerved me. *They must really believe I'm gonna die,* I remember thinking as I was covered in hands.

Mom knew just how scared I was of the murmurs so when I was five and she scheduled an appointment with a cardiologist in Houston, she kept the visit a secret. While preparing for the trip to Houston, we stopped at a mall in Lake Charles, Louisiana, where I thought we were just buying toys to bring back home until an aunt pulled me aside, pulled a pair of one-piece Spider-Man pajamas from the rack at a department store and said, "Jerry, do you think you'd enjoy these pajamas to sleep in at the hospital?" I ran screaming into the comfort of Mom's arms. "We're just going to Houston for testing," Mom said soothingly. In Houston, the cardiologist told us that the murmurs needed to be monitored but would not require painful cardiac catheterization. It was a miracle. Indeed, it was the first miracle I had ever experienced. God had intervened to save me–and I owed Him. And so, even though I was just five years old, I grasped what my life's purpose was: I was meant to preach. Back at home in Rosepine, I played church with my Deason cousins. I truly inhabited the role; I scolded my cousins for cussing in the highest and mightiest of language. "Get off your high horse," they snapped back at me. I turned red with embarrassment. *I might not be that good at this,* I thought to myself and resolved not to play preacher again.

My first forays into school–in kindergarten class at Rosepine Elementary at age six–were just as awkward. An almost innate sense of inadequacy dogged me from the very beginning. The other kids intimidated me. They knew things I didn't know. They were more athletic than I was. They were loud and chaotic. I was quiet, still and introspective. I also experienced a sky-high level of separation anxiety from Mom. Whenever Mom dropped me off for school in the morning, I'd walk down the sidewalk alone in tears until one of the teachers took my hand and led me into the classroom. But even then the tears didn't stop. I didn't take my eyes off the hands of the clock in class all day; with the passing of each second my mood improved because I knew that I was that much closer to going home. My fear of school became so overwhelming that it literally made me sick. I missed dozens of days of school, forcing Mom to get a doctor's note to the school to explain all the absences. The days I made it to school were preceded by pitched battles between Mom and me in which I pleaded with her to avoid school altogether. Just about every morning, I'd hide under the kitchen table and come out only under the threat of a whipping. It was a fear that was driven by my very early obsession with mortality. Whenever the PA system clicked on at school, my heart would jump–an announcement over the PA only meant one thing: *something had happened to someone.* I believed that I was literally holding the world together with my worry. My worry was the glue that kept everyone alive. The sense of duty to worry about my family was relieved only when I saw Mom's car in line in the parking lot outside school.

I found solace and a sense of belonging outside of school with my maternal cousins Gary and Mike Walley. Their dad, Grover, was in the dirt business and when we were all small he had bought a huge hill near DeRidder. It took Uncle Grover years to cut up and sell its dirt, a delay that allowed us to transform the hill into a wonderland of adventure for little boys. We jumped our bicycles off the hill, leapt from its hilltop and raced an old wagon down its sides. The rickety wagon we rode in, which just had well-worn, broken wooden slats to sit on, deeply frightened Gary whenever we sped down the hill. But I found that I was able to steel my nerves during the steep rides and, there, on that dirt-covered hill, I found my niche: I was a daredevil. It was a trait that I inherited from Dad and I grew into it far beyond Uncle Grover's hill. At home, I'd construct long, sloping ramps made of plywood that I'd use to leap into the air and, while airborne, swivel my handlebars and back wheel of my bike. When Evel Knievel achieved superstar status in the mid-1970s, I mimicked the canyon-jumping chopper king by putting out Mom's potted plants in a row in the driveway and leaping over them on my bike.

Being so close to kin was a saving grace for a painfully shy kid like me. So when I was eight years old and George moved our family to Sulphur to take a sales job with Donaldson Ford, I was devastated. Though Sulphur is just forty-eight miles southwest of Rosepine, it's in a different parish, Calcasieu, that's solidly in Cajun country. It felt as though we'd moved to another planet. When Mom enrolled me at Maplewood Elementary in Sulphur in the midst of the third grade, I was surrounded by schoolmates with French Cajun surnames like Fuselier, Fontenot and Lejune, an unfamiliarity that only drove me deeper into a shell socially. It didn't help that Mom's relationship with George continued to be uneasy; that they were expecting their first child together in November of 1978 did little to ease the tensions between the two.

When my mom gave birth to my half-sister, Britany, on November 17, 1978, I was left at home with my grandmother during the delivery. George returned from the hospital quiet and alone that afternoon, a somber state that, even though I was just nine years old, deeply unnerved me. As I stood in the doorway of Mom and George's bedroom and watched him pack a suitcase, I saw tears well up in his eyes. I was right to have trusted my gut instincts: something *had* gone wrong. As George zipped up a black suitcase, he began to cry, which was followed by a dam break of tears. "Nothing's wrong with your momma," George said, his voice cracking under the strain, "but your sister's been born with Down's." I didn't know what Down's was but George's devastated emotional state–I'd never seen him cry before–made me realize that something was terribly wrong with my new sister. When Mom brought Britany home, she was a baby just like any other baby. But the stress of caring for a special-needs child slowly widened the fault lines that already existed in Mom and George's marriage. Where once their arguing had been occasional and mild, now it was regular and intense.

With Mom and George struggling at home and Maplewood Elementary an unfamiliar and unforgiving place for me, I didn't feel comfortable anywhere. But as fourth grade began and I was enrolled in Ms. Blair's class, I finally found a sense of friendliness and familiarity. Ms. Blair was tall, slender and had long, brown hair; she wore the long dresses that are a staple of Pentecostal dress but, in a big break from a stricter Pentecostal tradition, wore makeup. Ms. Blair carried herself elegantly but what I truly loved about her was that she controlled her classroom so completely. For me, school was a nightmare of noise and chaos. Watching kids scuffle with one another and get thick globs of ketchup and mustard on their faces as they fought in the lunchroom was such a traumatic sight for me that, to this day, I still refuse to put condiments of any kind on my hamburgers. Ms. Blair's class was a refuge from the chaos of my classmates even though I hardly excelled in my studies. Indeed, just before winter break that year, when my French teacher handed out handcrafted awards for each student that were color coded by grade, I watched with dismay as student after student rose from behind their desks to pick up awards for As, Bs and Cs, in yellow, orange and purple. When my name was finally called, I was handed an award made from black construction paper. It was, my French teacher scolded me as my classmates looked on, an F for incomplete. I was mortified as I walked back to my desk with the sad-looking award in hand; Ms. Blair, meanwhile, was in tears. She was furious with the French teacher–but heartbroken for me.

After the French class debacle, the administration at Maplewood Elementary insisted that I repeat the fourth grade but Ms. Blair, always in my corner, intervened and agreed to tutor me in hopes that I wouldn't be held back. But I was held back anyway and did half the fourth grade again at Maplewood and then, because George moved us back to Rosepine, finished out the year at Rosepine Elementary. The changing of schools midyear would be difficult for any elementary school kid but the transition came at the worst possible moment for me socially: just before the move I'd finally found my niche at Maplewood Elementary. I'd convinced Mom to allow me to hold a dance in our den and, to help me prepare for the event, she'd purchased a disco ball, strobe light and a slew of disco records including Walter Murphy's "A Fifth of Beethoven," the Bee Gees' "You Should Be Dancing" and Rick Dees's "Disco Duck." Our den was packed with fourth graders striking disco poses who were thrilled and envious that Mom had allowed me to transform the house into a nightclub. I became known as a make-it-happen kid, a new identity I was just thrilled with but one that didn't survive the move back to Rosepine.

At Rosepine Elementary and later, Rosepine Junior and Senior High, I befriended a bevy of outcasts including a schoolmate and close neighbor named Randal Jackson. Randal's family was poorer and more dysfunctional than mine but with the death of my father so early in life, my world seemed just as turbulent as his. And Randal and I bonded because we both lived just off Highway 171. During the summertime, we'd rise before the oppressively humid

Louisiana heat settled in, to walk the nearby railroad tracks to McKee's grocery store where we'd buy microwavable sausage links and a pair of Cokes. Back at Randal's house, we'd feast on our small meal of sausages and Cokes and talk about space travel and *Star Trek*. So instead of developing socially, I hung out with the outcasts like Randal and developed intellectually. I read Carl Sagan's *Cosmos* and became fascinated with the sheer size and scale of the universe. My Sagan fandom, in turn, made me long to be an astronaut one day, a career that seemed like the ultimate mix of identities, from showman to daredevil to intellectual.

But my hopes for such a sparkling future were dashed just the day before I started the seventh grade. That morning, all the seventh-graders-to-be assembled in the cafeteria of Rosepine Junior High to receive their class schedules. Schedules were based on interests like football or band but because I was so intimidated by school, I hadn't chosen *any* electives. As we all sat around the cafeteria tables, Mr. Ashworth, the school principal, read off a roster of names. "Band to the right," Mr. Ashworth shouted over the din of restless seventh graders, "football to the left." All that remained was the few, like me, who weren't interested in either sports or band. "And all of you *nothings*," Mr. Ashworth practically snarled, "go to classroom number two." It was a truly life-changing moment that solidified the fact that I wasn't a good fit for higher education, let alone NASA. But I wasn't about to allow Mr. Ashworth to define me. Inspired by Mr. Ashworth, I dubbed me and my friends the "nothings." I had been a daredevil, a party promoter, a science geek and now my new identity was defending the nothings.

The isolation I felt in school is what made the experience at Swaggart's camp meeting, where I was saved while surrounded by thousands of my fellow Pentecostals, so transformative. I was an outsider who had at last found acceptance, a spiritual embrace far more profound than any recognition I could receive among my classmates. So the morning after the last of the services at Swaggart's, I rose early and, undeterred by my grandma's disapproval, told anyone who would listen–friends, family, neighbors–about my experience of becoming saved. But, like my grandma, they were all deeply conservative Pentecostals who refused to recognize my experience. Crushed by their rejection, I felt like I had to turn to outside Pentecostalism for spiritual fulfillment. Fortunately, my girlfriend at the time, Joetta Foshee, a redhead with a fair complexion who resembled a Southern Belle but whose outspokenness was pure Yankee, was a Baptist eager to have me visit her church, Ludington Baptist in DeRidder. "If you're going to be a church person now," Joetta lectured me, "come with *us* to our church." Joetta sought to get me saved and, within a week of my return from Swaggart's, I began attending church with Joetta and her family. In the Baptist denomination, one is saved when he or she accepts Jesus Christ as their personal savior via the sinner's prayer. Even if this is done in private, the new believer must still stand in front of the church and publicly profess his or her faith, at which time they are welcomed into the church family. So I made a profession of my faith and got baptized at Ludington Baptist that week. To my Pentecostal grandmother, of course, this wasn't being baptized the right way. But I would not be swayed by my grandmother's beliefs this time–I wanted a life of deep spiritual meaning and, more importantly, I wanted to feel the same way I'd felt at Swaggart's.

I was encouraged in my exploration of Baptist faith when Ludington Baptist's pastor, John Vest, suggested that I attend a discipleship course there. A discipleship course is essentially a class on the basics of Christianity and the course was a big part of the Ludington Baptist's orientation for new members of the church. When class began during the summer of 1986, I was the only student in the once-per-week session that was held in the parsonage across the street from Ludington Baptist. I didn't mind being Pastor Vest's sole student because he was kind, mild mannered and made it a point to smile all day. "Christians," Pastor Vest said, "can be such sour pusses." I also loved the textbook for the class, *Survival Kit for New Christians*, which featured scripture on flashcards covering everything from Romans 5:10–"For if, when we were enemies, we were reconciled to God by the death of his Son, much more, being reconciled, we shall be saved by his life"–to, toward the end of the class, Matthew 28:18–20: "And Jesus came and spake unto them, saying, All power is given unto me in heaven and in earth. Go ye therefore, and teach all nations, baptizing them in the name of the Father, and of the Son, and of the Holy Ghost: Teaching them to observe all things whatsoever I have commanded you: and, lo, I am with you always, even unto the end of the world. Amen."

As much as I savored Pastor Vest's clear, simple lessons in scripture, however, I quickly became dissatisfied with what I believed to be a too literal chapter-and-verse approach to Christianity at Ludington Baptist. One afternoon during the discipleship course, I asked Pastor Vest about speaking in tongues, which brought a dismissive rebuke. "That," Pastor Vest said impatiently, "does not belong in our day; that was done away with in the time of the apostles." I couldn't be angry with Pastor Vest for his stance on speaking in tongues, which reflected Baptist doctrine. But I had learned at Swaggart's that ecstatic expressions of praise were what truly moved me; I just knew that I wasn't going to be moved by Pastor Vest. So I quietly dropped out of his class just before the end of the summer of 1986, hungry for spiritual nourishment elsewhere.

That's just what I found at the Sonshine Christian Book Store in the Park Terrace Mall in DeRidder. One afternoon, while searching for a black-leather Bible that resembled the great book that Swaggart held aloft at the camp meeting, I stumbled upon the Thompson Chain-Reference Bible, a reference-packed study version of the Bible boasting a unique system called "chain topics" devised by Dr. Frank S. Thompson. When I researched the word "baptism," the Thompson Chain-Reference Bible offered a long chain of New Testament references, from Matthew 28:19 to Acts 19:5: "When they heard this, they were baptized in the name of the Lord Jesus." My obsessive scripture study sparked by the Thompson Chain-Reference Bible kept me from leaving the Baptist faith, much to the chagrin of my Pentecostal family. In DeRidder, there was a Hatfield-McCoy-style feud between Pentecostals and Baptists and to my family, I was on the wrong team.

Just how different the Baptist faith was from my Pentecostal beliefs was starkly reaffirmed for me during a Wednesday-night prayer meeting at Ludington Baptist. I arrived just after six o'clock that night, and as I looked at the white tiled floor I felt like the church was as antiseptic as a hospital room. I tried to refocus myself by kneeling, alone, by the last row of pews and praying out loud. "Jesus!" I cried, "I come to you." I was lost in prayer. As I wailed, I rested my elbows on the seat of the pews for support.

Then, all of the sudden there was a *taptap-tap* on my right shoulder. It was one of the deacons, an older man with dark-brown hair parted on the left side and wire-rimmed glasses from under which his large nose protruded. "Son," the deacon scolded, "what are you doing?" I didn't know what to say, other than the truth. "I'm praying," I replied matter-of-factly. "Get up," the deacon continued, still angry. "We're all gonna pray in a little bit." Being disturbed while in prayer was unheard of in my family's tradition and I was furious. As I rose from my knees, I noticed that the deacon was sporting a gold nugget watch and a wedding ring with a massive inlaid diamond, which, to my Pentecostal upbringing, were entirely too worldly to be worn by someone of serious devotion. Of course, it was hypocritical of me to judge the deacon's expensive jewelry after I had just thrilled at Swaggart's flashy style, but after being interrupted in prayer by the deacon I was consumed by the idea that everything about the Baptist faith was wrong.

When the deacon and his wife took a seat on the pews a few rows in front of me and the prayer meeting began, I cast a scornful eye at his wife's equally large wedding ring. Then, Pastor Vest offered up a prayer for a sister in the church suffering from cancer. When he read this prayer aloud, there was sense of dread and a lifeless seriousness that settled upon the prayer group. It felt as if it were a cold winter's night outside and someone had opened a window wide enough to allow a chilling breeze to invade the warm room. On the one hand, I was impressed by the compassion and empathy being expressed by the members of Ludington Baptist's prayer group, and yet I was also saddened that fervent prayer, healings and miracles were tools that were absent from this church's tool chest. I couldn't help but wonder, *Would this cancer sufferer have a better chance of survival if her prayer request had been received by a Pentecostal prayer group*?

After that cold, solemn prayer meeting I concluded that the Baptist faith was simply not for me. As impressed as I was with the scriptural savvy of Pastor Vest, it was clear to me that the Baptist denomination was not my home and would most likely never be a good fit for me. The Baptist services I attended lacked the energy, emotion and enthusiasm that I had grown accustomed to and naturally perceived as the deepest expressions of devotion and sincerity. Excluding attending church services, I found it difficult to appreciate how the Baptists were living lives any different from those "of the world." I, after all, wasn't on a quest to normalize my religious experience or to balance it with real life. Instead, I was driven by an uncontrollable desire to bring the God of the Bible, with all of his mighty manifestations, into my everyday existence. For me, nothing less than a spiritual adventure equivalent of the apostles' would ever be satisfactory.

So in the fall of 1986, I returned to my family's church, the Church of the Lord Jesus Christ. I attended services with my grandmother and at first it was awkward for me to participate in worship. I'd grown accustomed to the milder, much less expressive form of praise at Ludington Baptist and had to slowly reacquaint myself with the ecstatic style of the Pentecostals. At church, I slowly, haltingly raised my hands into the air and then, desperate for inspiration, prayed and asked God to fill me with the Holy Ghost. But nothing of the kind was happening, so I added a nightly prayer to my weekly worship in which I would go into a closet at my grandmother's home and literally spend hours in prayer seeking the baptism of the Holy Ghost. One night, I was home alone and sat by a table near the bay window and prayed. A storm was brewing and wind whistled through the window. I thought of the book of Acts, chapter 2:

> And when the day of Pentecost was fully come, they were all with one accord in one place. And suddenly there came a sound from heaven as of a rushing mighty wind, and it filled all the house where they were sitting. And there appeared unto them cloven tongues like as of fire, and it sat upon each of them. And they were all filled with the Holy Ghost, and began to speak with other tongues, as the Spirit gave them utterance.

It was the original reference to speaking in tongues in the New Testament and the verses filled me with a bold and determined spirit. Over the next several days, my nightly prayer brought an overwhelming desire to say syllables that didn't make sense to me. I heard syllables in my mind and then, suddenly, I gathered the courage to *say* those syllables. *If I hear those syllables,* I thought, *I'm going to say them. I'm not going to be embarrassed*. I went back to prayer and the syllables came to me again and this time I said them out loud. It was like a rush from the top of my head to the bottom of my feet, a bolt of energy flashing through me. As I spoke, the syllables came more fluidly and seconds later I spoke in complete sentences in a language I didn't recognize.

The following Sunday I went to church and, instead of sitting down in the pews submissively, I stood up at the front near our pastor, Brother Lloyd. When he put his hands on my shoulders, I immediately began to speak in tongues. I rushed back to my seat and was so overwhelmed with tears and emotion that I could only hear the sound of hands furiously clapping, followed by Brother Lloyd's praise. "Brother Jerry," he proclaimed, "has spoke in tongues!" It was a bellwether spiritual experience for me, but I was still far from achieving my goal of bringing God's reality into my everyday life. I began thinking about my next step on this path, which naturally seemed to be preaching. But while I'd long had an adventurous spirit that often masked my thoughtful, introverted nature, there was nothing natural about me taking the pulpit. I was still uncomfortable with speaking in public and, because of my reading and spelling difficulties, I was uncertain about my ability to deliver sermons. So I returned to the sort of ferocious Bible study that I had engaged in at Brother's Vest's with the purpose that biblical understanding would open up a conduit for the Holy Ghost. Soon afterward, my Bible lessons formulated into sermons. It seemed as though every time that I studied the Bible I'd develop a sermon, though I still lacked the ability to put together a fully developed message. My intense focus on the Bible, in turn, led to feverish dreams about preaching. Night after night I would dream that I was standing on a stage delivering a message about the great revival that was soon to come. I promised the congregations of my dreams the great outpouring of the Holy Ghost as promised by Pentecostal doctrine and referenced in the book of Joel: "And it shall come to pass afterward, that I will pour out my spirit upon all flesh; and your sons and your daughters shall prophesy, your old men shall dream dreams, your young men shall see visions."

Many nights I awoke from such dreams, slid out of the bed, grabbed my Bible pen and notepad from the nightstand and quickly made notes from the messages that I had just heard myself preach. Often these messages would be centered around the idea that we should either live a life of devotion in order to bring God's presence into the world or demonstrate God's reality in the world by loving our neighbors as ourselves. My jotted-down notes from these dreams forced me to address the issue of ministry with my pastor.

One afternoon that fall, I drove out to Brother Lloyd's home in Evans, Louisiana, a tiny, rural town along the Louisiana-Texas border about twenty-five miles from DeRidder, to a doublewide mobile home trailer sitting on a slab where his house used to be. I knocked on the trailer door and Brother Lloyd, who was shoeless and dressed in blue coveralls, came to the door. "I feel like I'm called to preach," I told him. "Every time I read the Bible I'm seeing messages." Brother Lloyd replied with a dispassionate, "We'll see," and then turned around and shut the front door behind him. I wasn't offended by Brother Lloyd's lack of enthusiasm for my plans to become a preacher: to Brother Lloyd, the ministry was brutally hard and if I wasn't truly called, then it simply would weed me out.

As I traversed the tumultuous path of my spiritual quest, a new girlfriend, Kristi Craft, who I'd met at the Church of the Lord Jesus Christ, comforted me. Kristi was an attractive brunette, about two years my junior, with a great sense of humor and a deep, warm laugh that often shook her entire body. Kristi was also an in-your-face flirt who demanded attention, and I was very eager to give it. I quickly fell head over heels in love with Kristi and was certain we'd get married one day, so I willingly left her virginity unchallenged in anticipation of that fateful day. Undoubtedly, our physically romantic restraint would have come as a great surprise to many within our little church family. Prurient rumors abounded about our youthful engagements, even to the extent of detailing exactly where they were supposed to have taken place behind the church. None of the rumors were true, a fact I deeply regret to this day.

Late that fall, Kristi and I were sitting on the living room floor in her parents' home on Eighth Street in DeRidder when her father, Jerry Craft, a retired Louisiana state trooper, joined us in the living room. "DeWitt," he said, taking a seat on the couch, "tell me about your daddy." As I began to tell the story of losing my father, Mr. Craft put his hands on my shoulders and stopped me. "I worked your dad's wreck," he said sadly and then turned and went to the bedroom. At that very moment, my relationship with Kristi—and our sure-to-be married life together–seemed all the more fated. The connection between my father and Mr. Craft also provided fresh inspiration to me for my preparation in delivering a first-ever sermon at the Church of the Lord Jesus Christ.

There was something circular and conclusive about Kristi sitting next to me as I prepared to preach my first sermon. It seemed as if the circle of life was rising to a peak of consolation and repayment. Up until this point there had been numerous and significant losses in my life, but now the tide was turning and I was about to embark upon a grand adventure of oceanic proportions. Kristi reminded me of the father that I had lost, the father-in-law that I was hoping to acquire, a father who had worked to save *my* father's life, and the heavenly father whose master plan had allowed all of this pain but had also provided this consolation and the promise of a brighter future. Then the voice of Brother Lloyd interrupted my thoughts. "In a few minutes," he told the congregation, "we're gonna get Brother Jerry to give us a sermonette." I'm sure he saw the horror come over my face. All I could do was raise my hand as though I was in school. "Yes, Brother Jerry," Brother Lloyd said sternly. "Can I go in the back and pray," I meekly asked Brother Lloyd. "Yes, you can," Brother Lloyd replied, "but hurry up."

I ran back into the Sunday-school classroom, a blue-carpeted room with walls covered with images of Bible stories and Jesus himself. In the center of the room there was a large wooden table surrounded by folding chairs. The short distance from the sanctuary to the Sunday-school room allowed the music from the service to penetrate the walls and the hollow-core door; I was able to hear every beat and every word. The sound of the choir gave me great comfort because for a moment I was afraid that I would walk back into the sanctuary and the congregation would be waiting on me. So I sat down calmly at the table for a moment of prayer and reflection and heard the words "seed of David" in my mind. I then dropped the Bible onto the tabletop and it fell open to the passage where the apostle Paul talks about Christ being the seed of David and the word of God being incorruptible. *The seed of David,* I thought. *That's it.* I gave thanks to God and marked my place in the Bible.

I strode back to the sanctuary full of confidence and then, without any hesitation or fear, began to preach to the congregation about the seed of David. I told the congregation about how special we all are—that Christians are descended from a royal lineage. "We are kings and priests," I said. "We are the rulers of life. We're able to overcome anything and endure anything because of where we come from. Because we're the seed of David; like Christ, we are the lineage of David, born of the Holy Ghost. We are the lineage of Christ. We carry his spirit within us."

As I laid the groundwork for my ministry, I reconnected with Ms. Blair. Since Swaggart's camp meeting, our correspondence had transformed from casual, friendly birthday and Christmas cards to deep discussions about doctrine. Whenever I felt overwhelmed by the conflicts between Ms. Blair's Assembly of God church, the Baptist faith that I briefly adopted or my family's Pentecostalism, I'd reach out to Ms. Blair for grounding. One day she told me an incredible story that bound our two families together and reinforced my deep faith in God. My grandfather John Owen DeWitt was a presbyter, essentially a pastor to other pastors, in the Assembly of God denomination. Ms. Blair's father, Brother Fontenot, was pastor of Southside Assembly of God, which was in my grandfather's district. When Sister Fontenot—Brother Fontenot's wife and Ms. Blair's mother—was pregnant, she had a medical emergency. In Ms. Blair's telling, the baby was trapped in one of her mother's fallopian tubes. Brother Fontenot called for my grandfather to travel to the hospital and pray for a miracle. During their moment of prayer, they felt that God's spirit was present, which gave them hope that the baby had been divinely repositioned. When they asked the doctor to reexamine Sister Fontenot, the doctor said that, indeed, the baby had moved out of the fallopian tube. Both the baby and Sister Fontenot would survive. That baby was Ms. Blair.

I thought about how prayer had brought Ms. Blair to the world and had become such a profound presence in my life. It was Ms. Blair who kept me afloat during my troubled grade-school years and it was she who led me to the moment where I was saved at Swaggart's. None of this would have happened if it had not been for the prayers of my grandfather for her mother. It was, I knew then, a circle of faith—of faith in God and in family. Ms. Blair's story came just as I preached at the Church of the Lord Jesus Christ for the very first time and it made me even more convinced, if that was even possible, that I was on the right spiritual path. I resolved to dedicate my life to the ministry. I could see no other path after realizing just how interconnected Ms. Blair and my family were—a divinely guided and orchestrated connection spanning entire generations.

> *Study to shew thyself approved unto God, a workman that needeth not to be ashamed, rightly dividing the word of truth.*
>
> **—2 Timothy 2:15**

As I approached graduation at Rosepine High School, my younger cousin Gary Wayne Walley had already gotten the Holy Ghost. Gary was a heavyset, baby-faced teenager but he carried himself with a striking seriousness that lent him a preacherly authority. Indeed, by our senior year in high school, Gary had begun ministering at a deep-in-the-woods church on the outskirts of DeRidder called Three Pine Apostolic. The church was so named because it sits in the middle of a piney, wooded area off Highway 112, about five and a half miles from DeRidder's center. To DeRidder residents, Highway 112 was simply known as Sugartown Highway because it headed east toward Sugartown, a tiny unincorporated community in Beauregard Parish fifteen miles from DeRidder. To me, Highway 112 was the place where my father lost his life and, at just three years of age, I faced my first and earliest test of faith. Three Pine, an old, white wood-frame shotgun with a shingled roof resting on concrete blocks, was a quintessential Pentecostal "church house" in both appearance and in atmosphere for our part of Louisiana. To faithful Pentecostals in DeRidder, however, it was seen as a cult because of the church's dictatorial style, which was led by Brother Hebert, a short, stocky man who felt sure that he was the second coming of Jimmy Swaggart. Back then, Brother Hebert required that his congregation possess a near-fanatical devotion both to him personally and to Three Pine. Pentecostals in our area whispered about the time that a husband at Three Pine was left by his wife because he was deemed "backslid" (or insufficiently faithful) by the congregation. Brother Hebert also preached doctrines that were not part of the mainstream Pentecostal platform; for example, he insisted that during the end times the church would actually go through the tribulation period whereas most Pentecostals believed that the church would be "raptured" (or caught up to heaven) prior to the tribulation. So I was terrified of Three Pine. It also certainly didn't help that Three Pine seemed to be hiding out there in the woods from the rest of civilization.

Gary had his own ministry at Three Pine and we bonded over the fact that we were both high school students who already had their own ministry. We also shared a civics teacher in high school named D. A. Keel. Mr. Keel, coincidentally, had just begun attending services at Three Pine and he agreed to have a prayer meeting and Bible study in his civics class every morning. That's where I learned to preach: right there in Mr. Keel's classroom. Every morning, Mr. Keel would ask Gary and me to stand up in front of the classroom and deliver impromptu messages inspired by whatever Bible verse we were studying that morning. Under Mr. Keel's careful watch, we'd open our Bibles, read a passage and then preach—on the spot, with no preparation—from it to our fellow students.

One morning, we opened our Bibles to Matthew 1:1–16, which laid out the multigenerational genealogies of Christ. From Matthew, I preached that Christ, as the son of David and the son of Abraham, was the promised seed, the promise to the world, because the promise made to Abraham was that his seed would bless all nations. David, similarly, was the king of Israel, which would make Jesus his descendant, the heir. I preached that through Abraham and the Abrahamic promise, Jesus was the spiritual messiah and that through David, Jesus was the *physical* messiah.

In Mr. Keel's class, Gary and I preached in a pugilistic style that was more akin to a political debate than a sermon. I'd preach from scripture and then, sensing a flaw in my argument or an exhausted idea, Gary would jump in and offer his interpretation of the text. One morning, I opened the Bible to Ephesians 1:13–"In whom ye also trusted, after that ye heard the word of truth, the gospel of your salvation: in whom also after that ye believed, ye were sealed with the holy spirit of promise"–and preached to the class that one is sealed with the Holy Spirit of promise *after* they believe, in contrast to mainstream Christianity, which teaches that one is sealed with the Holy Spirit *when* one believes. I insisted that it wasn't good enough for one to believe that they are sealed with the Holy Spirit of promise–that the person must provide supernatural evidence of that fact, demonstrated in an act like speaking in tongues. It was a perfectly Pentecostal message of an acts-driven faith and though I was just a high school senior under Mr. Keel's tutelage, I was refining my messages and growing stronger as a preacher every day.

At the same time, I preached at the church my family attended, the Church of the Lord Jesus Christ. I'd preach once a week, at 7:00 p.m. on Wednesdays, a small service with thankfully only a faithful few in attendance. As a teenage preacher, my immaturity and naïveté were often on embarrassingly vivid display. One night, as I preached a message about giving our heart completely to God, I made a fumbling attempt to connect the message to the congregation. One churchgoer, Sister Schaffer, had just been diagnosed with a serious heart ailment. So I said that the devil could have our physical hearts because God had our spiritual hearts. I then turned to Sister Schaffer and said, *"Isn't that right?"* The horrified look in her eyes told me, rightly, no.

As high school graduation neared in the spring of 1988, I was delving deeper and deeper into my faith, which led to confrontations with the secular aspects of my life. My cousin Gary and I belonged to an organization called the Future Farmers of America (FFA) that teaches rural farming skills to high school students, much like a 4H Club. As FFA members, Gary and I would judge cows at regional fairs. We'd examine the cows and assess their hip size, color or the sheen of their coat. It was as innocent a country, noncontroversial hobby as one could imagine, but being the strident Pentecostals that we were, Gary and I managed to get into a fierce religious debate with our agriculture teacher, the very appropriately named Bill Churchman. Mr. Churchman was an Episcopalian and he was an odd man out in our world of Pentecostals and Baptists. At the time, Gary and his church, Three Pine, were in the midst of a revival and Gary insisted on the importance of the revival over everything else, including Mr. Churchman's classes.

With a revival, what you're trying to do as a preacher is build enthusiasm among the congregants and rev up momentum every night, until the atmosphere becomes so ecstatic and electric that it literally opens up a channel for the Holy Ghost. In contrast to the strict doctrine that governs Pentecostal life, during a revival there is a freedom of worship in which congregants are encouraged to embrace whatever form of worship they want to engage in, whether it's jumping, running or swaying–all to the music *and* the message. The congregants, in turn, invite family and neighbors to worship. So by the end of the night's service, during altar call, a practice in which congregants come forward to the altar in order to make a spiritual commitment to Jesus, the front of the church is packed. Those at the very front of the church are standing and leaning at or near the pulpit, weeping and repenting of their sins, asking God to forgive them of their sins, asking God to save them. There is almost a wailing of supplication. The congregants are so moved by the Holy Ghost that they speak in tongues until there is a slow building of jubilation, like a slow rolling thunder from a distance. As more and more of the congregation experience some form of ecstasy, that feeling fills up the entire church. With each night's service, that feeling of ecstasy grows until the spirit of revival spills out from the church and into the community, energizing the community with the Holy Ghost. As a preacher at a revival it is your job to evangelize to the congregants and then they, in turn, evangelize to their community.

The revival at Three Pine that spring conflicted with an FFA banquet. Gary wasn't about to miss the revival, so he told Mr. Churchman that he simply would not be able to attend. Mr. Churchman was furious that Gary would be absent from the banquet and during agriculture class he lectured Gary and me about how disrespectful and needless *our* type of devotion was. "If you have to have *that* much reviving," Mr. Churchman said in a schoolmarmish voice, "then something must be seriously wrong with the both of you." It really ticked me off that Gary was treated that way and Mr. Churchman's condescending attitude only steeled Gary's resolve. So we all boycotted the banquet.

The boycott had unintended consequences for me: Gary insisted that I attend his revival because I was skipping the FFA banquet. "If you boycott the banquet," Gary warned me, "then you have come to the revival." I had a strong aversion to Three Pine; like many Pentecostals in the area, I felt that it was a cult, not a church. But without the FFA banquet as an excuse, and out of respect for Gary's brave confrontation with Mr. Churchman, I had no choice but to attend the Three Pine revival. The revival had a wild energy that can only be described as resembling an aerobics boot camp; Brother Hebert paced behind the pulpit and the congregation ran, leapt and jumped across the sanctuary praising God. But with the air of superiority among the congregants and its suspicion of outsiders, I felt that they merely worked themselves into a frenzy with no real spiritual benefit.

Tensions were also growing with my own church, the Church of the Lord Jesus Christ. As other Pentecostal churches in the DeRidder area became more liberal in their dress code, Brother Lloyd went in the opposite direction by advocating a far more strict style of dress. In the Pentecostal church, women are not supposed to cut their hair or trim their bangs and they are encouraged to wear dresses that often reach their feet. Men, similarly, are forbidden to have facial hair and encouraged to wear long-sleeve shirts. But as I neared graduation in the late 1980s, Pentecostal men were beginning to sport short sleeves and women wore shorter and more casual dresses. Some Pentecostal women wore blue-jean skirts while others donned flamboyant, frilly and flashy prom-style dresses. Brother Lloyd was stubbornly pushing back hard against the social changes surrounding him; he was attempting to turn back the clock to a moment of deeply conservative dress in the Pentecostal world. *This is about as futile as chasing a snake through the grass,* I remember thinking as I stood with Brother Lloyd one afternoon that spring by the pulpit at the Church of the Lord Jesus Christ. After all, just down the street there was a Pentecostal church–First United Pentecostal Church, known as "First Church"–boasting a softball team that pulled in perhaps the largest number of worshippers in the area during Sunday services. Brother Lloyd, of course, managed to turn First Church's popularity into an indictment of its too liberal doctrine; the softball team was just too "worldly" and its mushrooming membership was simply proof that too many Pentecostals didn't want to live right.

With high school graduation come and gone and a hot Louisiana summer on its way, the sense of life change in the air was nearly tangible for me. But back at Brother Lloyd's Church of the Lord Jesus Christ, he continued to preach well-worn, socially conservative messages in which he lambasted the Pentecostal community as all too liberal. During one Sunday-morning service, Brother

Lloyd preached to a packed house and put his own congregation in his crosshairs. "All of you mothers who set your babies in front of that one-eyed devil–television–as a babysitter," he thundered, "should be taken out and horse whipped!" Brother Lloyd's flock had long been accustomed to his fire-and-brimstone condemnations of everything he deemed to be ungodly, but even by his ultraconservative standards this message was shocking and was greeted by a mix of nervous laughter and embarrassment with just a quiet, murmured smattering of "Amens."

Though I remained an associate pastor under the strict tutelage of Brother Lloyd, I managed to maintain my friendship with Ms. Blair, who embraced a much more open, liberal brand of Pentecostalism. Unlike more traditional Pentecostals, Ms. Blair wore makeup and cut her hair. Her husband, Roger, similarly, had a moustache and beard. To outsiders, facial hair on a man or a woman going to the local salon to get her hair cut might seem like trivial, uncontroversial acts that have little to do with the sincerity or purity of one's faith. But in the tradition-bound world in which I was raised, the Pentecostalism of Brother Lloyd and Ms. Blair were diametrically opposed to one another. As Brother Lloyd's associate pastor, my relationship with Ms. Blair was consorting with the enemy. That fear that I was doing so deeply wrong in Brother Lloyd's eyes kept my stomach in knots whenever Ms. Blair and I met for coffee or lunch.

My feelings of alienation from Brother Lloyd were only heightened during the spring of 1989 when he brought Brother McMahon, an elderly Pentecostal preacher and retired logger whose hands were as calloused as an elephant's hoof, to preach at the Church of the Lord Jesus Christ. I was furious at Brother Lloyd's decision to bring Brother McMahon to *our* church, which I felt robbed me of opportunities to preach from our pulpit. During one Sunday-morning service late that spring, Brother McMahon began preaching against the Assembly of God, the very denomination the Blairs belonged to. Brother McMahon railed against what he believed to be the wrongness of the Assembly of God's Trinitarian style of baptism, in which one is baptized in the name of the father, the son and the Holy Ghost. Pentecostals, by contrast, believe in a "oneness" doctrine in which one is baptized in the name of Jesus *only*. To Brother McMahon, the Assembly of God approach to baptism was evidence of its inferiority: their form of baptism was wrong and ours was right. "We ain't got no half-brothers," Brother McMahon snarled that Sunday morning. To Brother McMahon, if the Assembly of God members didn't baptize the right way they should not baptize at all. Brother McMahon's condemnation of Ms. Blair's faith hit me like a perfectly thrown right-hand hook. My head actually jerked backward when Brother McMahon made his "half-brothers" remark. Looking back at it now, my reaction to Brother McMahon's message was my first step toward an embrace of universalism. I knew then that I was finished with the sort of Pentecostalism that dismissed some Christians as only partly worthy. *You know, Brother McMahon, you're right,* I remember thinking. *There are no half-brothers. We are all brothers.*

As I discovered a sense of universalism and slowly moved away from the doctrinal rigidity of Brother Lloyd's church, my personal life was about to undergo a profound change. On a chilly December day in 1989, I stopped by the Brookshire Brothers–an East Texas–based grocery store chain housed in a quintessential country store building in DeRidder with a glass front, metal awning and blacktop parking lot–to visit with a church friend named James Fletcher who I'd converted from Baptist to Pentecostal. James worked in Brookshire Brothers' produce section and as I walked through its crowded aisles and passed by the break room, I saw out of the corner of my eye a skinny young Pentecostal woman with long, dark-brown hair wearing a red long-sleeve work blouse and a tight black skirt. She had just come off break and was standing on her tiptoes to put her purse into her storage locker. Curious, I stopped by the break-room door and asked her for her name. "Kelli," she said nonchalantly. I didn't want to press her any further because I'd ambushed her during her break. And besides, I knew that she was a Pentecostal girl and that was more than enough to pique my interest.

Two days later, I stopped by Brookshire Brothers again in hopes of finding Kelli. This time I spotted her counting change in the front office. I was so nervous and so young, too–I had *no* idea how to approach women–that I fumbled at making even small talk. "If you'll stop counting your change," I said, "and listen to me . . ." I trailed off. I didn't know what to say; I just wanted her attention. Kelli half-heartedly listened to my ill-conceived pitch for her attention and said nothing in response. I suspected that she was completely uninterested in me, a feeling confirmed by Kelli's continuing to count quarters as I made fitful attempts to restart the conversation. All I could do was leave Brookshire Brothers feeling embarrassed and chastened by my lame pickup lines.

But I was undeterred. The next day, I returned to Brookshire Brothers and approached Kelli yet again, this time at the cash register near the exits. I noticed that she blushed when she set her eyes on me, which at least gave me the sense that I was having some sort of effect on her. We nervously talked about a date and Kelli suggested that we go to church with her best friends, Rhonda and Shonda Johnson. Rhonda and Shonda were teenage sisters who looked like Pentecostal Doublemint twins: both had light complexions and long brown hair. I knew that Kelli's plans for the church date, at the United Pentecostal Church in Sugartown, meant that I'd never be alone with her. Sure enough, that's exactly what happened. All four of us went to church together on Sunday afternoon and the services were just horrible. Attendance was abysmal–there couldn't have been more than a handful of people in its pews–and its elderly pastor, Brother McManus, grumpily groused about how nobody wants to live for God. Brother McManus's message was as canned and clichéd as that well-worn story some old folks tell about how they used to walk uphill both ways in the snow to go to school every morning. Worse, Kelli and I didn't share a single moment together without the Johnson twins, even after services when we all carpooled together to the DeRidder Dairy Queen. Over a late dinner of chicken finger baskets, however, I grew more hopeful about my chances with Kelli when she agreed to go on a real date, this time without Rhonda and Shonda.

That Friday, I drove out in my Grand Prix to pick up Kelli at her home in Pitkin, Louisiana, about twenty-five miles from DeRidder in Vernon Parish. The drive to Pitkin from DeRidder involves long, winding highways like Highway 112 that traverse densely wooded areas dominated by tall pine trees and pass a rough landscape of downed barbed-wire fences, old homesteads and barren trailer parks where it seemed that not even a blade of grass was allowed to live. That night, it was so dark out on the roads to Pitkin that I felt as though I was floating out in the universe, completely lost. It didn't help that this first true date with Kelli was making me so overcome with nervousness that my sweat-covered hands slid off the steering wheel during the half-hour drive. As I neared Kelli's home on Fullerton Blacktop Road, just outside the center of town, I'd hoped that the visibility would become much better. But all I could see on the desolate, gravel-covered road was the occasional beacon of a yard light every few miles.

When I finally pulled my Grand Prix over onto a gravel parking space in front of Kelli's house, it seemed as though I'd driven into an open field. I was surrounded by acres of land and I could only make out the interior of the house: brown paneling in the living room, a lamp next to a recliner, the outline of a couch with a floral cover. And just a few yards in front of me was Kelli's dad's white two-door Ford LTD. But as I stepped from the car and into the dark country night, I feared that I might not have even stopped at the right house. So I called out, "Is this the Swain residence?" instead of knocking on the front door. A few moments later, Kelli's dad, who with his six-foot-tall frame and bulky overalls with white long-sleeve shirtsleeves rolled up underneath had the imposing presence of a burly farmhand, walked out onto the battleship-gray porch in bare feet. "Is this the Swain residence?" I asked again, in a voice sounding even more desperate and meek. I stood next to my Grand Prix, which had its driver's-side door flung open to cast a light on the darkness, convinced that I wasn't *anywhere* near where I was supposed to be. "What's left of it," Mr. Swain called back with a laugh. He then invited me inside and, sitting in the living room, I realized that the Swain home was so difficult to find because it was a small farmhouse on a sprawling property comprised of forty acres of land.

After exchanging the briefest of pleasantries in the living room with Kelli's parents, Kelli and I drove out through the woods toward Alexandria, Louisiana–a larger, more cosmopolitan town than DeRidder or Pitkin–about fifty miles away. The long trip to Alexandria was uncomfortable at first but Kelli shattered the ice by repeating a joke told by her boss at Brookshire Brothers, Mr. White, complete with the H-word: "hell." I was turned on. I loved that Kelli told the joke and repeated the curse word without even thinking twice about it. Kelli's unashamed cursing made me feel as though we were both living on the edge. It may sound silly now, and indeed it probably is, but as a young Pentecostal preacher in rural Southwest Louisiana, the H-word *was* the edge. When we made it to the outskirts of Alexandria, I suggested to Kelli that we eat at a local Mexican restaurant. It was exotic cuisine for the both of us; soon after our plates were put down at our table, Kelli burned her finger on a plate bearing fajitas.

I fell in love with Kelli on that first date and like young men in love everywhere, I spent much of my days trying to spend every possible moment with my new girlfriend. It wasn't difficult to devote all of my attention to Kelli because I was a young preacher without a day job. Yet my faith endeared me deeply to Kelli's parents. In the weeks after our first date, I spent many nights in the Swain home discussing biblical passages with her mom and dad. Mr. Swain loved simple, strong messages–like "If it was ever wrong, it's still wrong"–and Mrs. Swain was fascinated by the fact that Pentecostalism took its doctrinal cues from the early church, such as Paul offering thanks for his gift of speaking in tongues in 1 Corinthians 14:18–19: "I thank my God, I speak with tongues more than ye all: Yet in the church I had rather speak five words with my understanding, that by my voice I might teach others also, than ten thousand words in an unknown tongue." I realized very quickly that the bonds I'd so easily forged with Kelli, and perhaps even more importantly with her parents, meant that she was going to be the person that I should spend the rest of my life with.

So I spent much of March of 1990 laying the groundwork for a marriage proposal to Kelli. After Sunday-morning services one week, I asked Kelli's parents for permission to have their daughter's hand in marriage. Mr. Swain, typically, grunted jokingly, "What can I do about it?" while Mrs. Swain broke down in tears, though not of the happy kind. Her oldest daughter, Karen, had eloped and my proposal simply meant that she had lost another daughter to yet another man. When Mrs. Swain composed herself, she happily granted her permission for me to marry Kelli. By the middle of March, all that was left was for Kelli to say yes. I didn't even need to buy an engagement ring–we Pentecostals didn't do rings because rings meant worldliness, a love of the physical world that we soundly rejected. One night at the very end of March, I asked Kelli to join me out by Fullerton Mill Pond, a large, almost lakelike body of water on land that once boasted a successful sawmill, the Fullerton Mill; the kind that made all of these small Southwest Louisiana communities possible. It wasn't the unromantic place for a marriage proposal that it sounds: that night the moonlight reflected off the black pond, which was surrounded by towering pine trees and a pretty, winding, nearly two-mile hiking trail. Standing by the pond, I asked Kelli to marry me, and she softly uttered, "Yes." The simplicity of Kelli's reply didn't mean that we were unemotional about spending our lives together. Indeed, we'd been having conversations for weeks beforehand about marriage; the sort of "things are going so well why don't we make this permanent" talk that many young couples in love have with one another. It just made sense for us to get married. And we had bonded in part because of our mutual love for *Star Trek*, specifically Mr. Spock, the "very logical" Vulcan who promulgated logical thinking at every possible turn. For Kelli and me, marriage was the logical thing to do.

After Kelli accepted my marriage proposal, we set a wedding date soon afterward: April 30, 1990, our three-months' dating anniversary. We'd met and become engaged in a matter of months and the planning for the wedding moved at the same lighting speed as our relationship. I quickly asked Brother Lloyd if we could get married in an empty church house that he owned in Evans. It was a practical, far-from-pretty wedding place: with its metal exterior and roof, glass doors and concrete floors it resembled, and had all the appeal of, a Dollar General. But its imposing, near-industrial size meant that it could accommodate hundreds of guests–which was appealing to me because I hoped to have a huge wedding–and it was a neutral location. Neither Kelli nor I wanted to have the wedding in our family church, lest we offend each other's family. Perhaps best of all, I am ashamed to admit now, as a child of the 1970s, I felt there was something homey and comforting about the church house's dark-oak wall paneling. But as much as we loved the space, Kelli and I knew that we had a huge amount of work to do on the Evans church to make it even barely presentable. The sanctuary itself was dusty, its pews were old, there was an unfinished plywood stage upon which Brother Lloyd was to marry us and thick rolls of carpet lay scattered across the floor. In each corner of the church there were high stacks of plywood that made the space look much more like a construction site than a church. Indeed, Brother Lloyd's Evans church was a construction site; he had brought work on the church to a halt when he realized that he would prefer to focus on a smaller house of worship in DeRidder.

Our wedding plans were seemingly unromantic but they were driven by the simple fact that Kelli and I were broke. I was an unemployed young preacher and Kelli was still a clerk at the

Brookshire Brothers grocery store. Our finance-driven practicality was even reflected in the date of our union, April 30, an off date on Brother Lloyd's busy schedule. The Monday wedding would also give us the weekend to make the Evans church presentable. So on a weekend that most brides and grooms would spend primping and preparing themselves for their wedding, Kelli and I tackled a top-to-bottom cleaning of the Evans church. We mopped the floors, put the pews into proper position and moved the construction supplies out of the sanctuary and into the Sunday-school room. By Saturday night, Kelli and I were covered in construction dust and exhausted from our weekend of cleaning, so we headed over to Brother Lloyd's house next door to tell him that we'd finished the job. While we were at there, however, his son Shane began to mercilessly tease Kelli and me. Shane warned that after the wedding he was going to pick me up and throw me into the pool. Then he joked about messing with the wiring on my car so that Kelli and I couldn't leave for our honeymoon that, reflecting our scarce resources, was set for Baton Rouge. If we managed to get the car going, Shane warned, he'd hide in the car and ambush us on the drive to Baton Rouge. I knew that Shane's joking was sophomoric and shouldn't have bothered me. But Shane was a dedicated prankster: I didn't put it past him that he might actually pull off one of his threatened pranks.

The specter of finding Shane hiding in my car on my wedding day mortified me. My nervousness about Shane's teasing and pranking was magnified by my age—I was just twenty—and the seriousness with which I approached my faith. I wanted my wedding to be as filled with the Holy Ghost as any church service that I had ever attended. So Shane's pranks didn't just threaten to sour my wedding day—they were actually an act of sacrilege. Shane's teasing that day made me feel so desperate that I contemplated threatening him with physical force. But a five-foot-five, 130 pound just-out-of-his-teens guy like me was certainly no match for the hulking Shane, who was a bulky, muscled six foot two and to me resembled Hercules. Shane, I thought then, was so stinking big that there was *no* threat–at least no threat coming from me–that could make him behave himself.

So when we left Brother Lloyd's house that night, I hatched a prankster-proof plan for our wedding. We'd get married at Kelli's family church, Fullerton Pentecostal, instead of Brother Lloyd's empty Evans church and move the date to Sunday, a last-minute change from the planned-upon Monday. It was a decision that made Shane's sabotage impossible but it brought our nuptials uncomfortably close, just hours away.

That night, Kelli and I contacted Brother Malcolm, the pastor of Fullerton Pentecostal, about having our wedding immediately after Sunday-morning services. Brother Malcolm, a short, stocky man with a craggy face and squinty eyes who reminded me of Hoss Cartwright from *Bonanza*, agreed to our proposal. We then gently informed Brother Lloyd that we no longer needed his church but were mindful not to tell him that we'd changed plans because of his son Shane's teasing; that would have devastated him.

The next morning, as Sunday-morning services began at Fullerton Pentecostal Church, Kelli and I were joined by a small gathering of family. Kelli had wanted a small wedding and she got her wish that day, because no one outside of our immediate families was even aware that it was happening. I, on the other hand, wasn't happy with the last-minute change to Fullerton. Its exterior, a white wood frame with asbestos siding, was somewhat charming, a quintessential old sawmill-town Pentecostal church, but its interior was depressingly run-down. It had a reddish-brown carpet, old wooden pews and a broken-down drum set on a stage. The church didn't even have stained glass. Fullerton was far from an ideal choice but it was the best, and only, option that Kelli and I had left.

That morning, as we waited for the ceremony to begin, the congregation slowly streamed into the building and eyed my presence with curiosity and anticipation. To the congregants, the presence of a young preacher and his family meant that a revival was about to begin. They had no idea that a wedding was about to take place instead. To keep the wedding a secret and to politely usher out uninvited guests, our families remained at Fullerton all the way through Sunday school. Afterward, we visited with the congregants one by one by one as if we were just socializing after Sunday-morning services. After the small talk died down, we watched them exit Fullerton Church until the only uninvited guest left in the building was Kelli's aunt Donnie. It hurts me even now to describe Aunt Donnie as an uninvited guest because I was so fond of her: she was a heavyset, middle-aged woman with a big smile and booming voice who played the piano like she was trying to put out a fire. When Aunt Donnie played piano at a church service there was no need for a microphone–her voice and piano playing not only filled the room, they nearly overwhelmed it. It was no surprise, then, that the larger-than-life Aunt Donnie chatted away with our families and refused to leave after we attempted to exhaust her with the most mundane of chatter. By noon that Sunday, as we stood outside Fullerton Church talking with Aunt Donnie and waiting for her to run out of steam, we abandoned our effort to gently ease her out of the church. "If you want to see a wedding today," Kelli and I told Aunt Donnie with a wink, "just keep talkin'." She squealed with excitement and in that moment became our only uninvited guest.

With the wedding just minutes away, Kelli and I scrambled to a white-and-mustard-yellow-colored singlewide mobile home trailer on Fullerton's property, which the church used as a parsonage, to change into our wedding clothes. I put on a black, two-button Haggar suit that I'd just bought from JC Penney's, the first real suit I'd ever owned after a lifetime wearing cheap, casual sport jackets. Kelli, who had her hair pulled back into a bow, wore a slender, form-fitting long-sleeve white wedding dress made by her mother. We then slowly, nervously walked up the church's steps. As we entered Fullerton Church's foyer, Aunt Donnie played a wedding march on the piano and Brother Malcolm stood at the pulpit. Because the wedding was planned so spontaneously, particularly after the last-minute venue change to Fullerton Church, we hadn't had a rehearsal or even asked for any specific Bible readings. So when Kelli and I arrived at the altar, Brother Malcolm stepped down off the stage, got down onto the floor with us, opened his black-leather Bible, asked for God's blessings and read the traditional wedding vows. Brother Malcolm didn't even preach a message that day. All Kelli and I said was "I do." Excluding Aunt Donnie's wedding march, there was no music at all. It was just as plain Jane a wedding as you could possibly ask for. As the wedding concluded, I breathed a sigh of relief that it had all run so smoothly. I was relieved that we'd avoided the pranking of Brother Lloyd's son Shane. But then, toward the end of the ceremony, when Kelli and I posed for pictures, her sister Karen got up on the stage and made faces at us. She was just trying to make Kelli laugh–she crossed her eyes and stuck her tongue out–but her behavior infuriated me, just as Shane's threat of pranks had angered me the day before. Thankfully, the entire ceremony was over quickly; we didn't even have a march out.

As the wedding service ended, Brother Malcolm delivered a blessing on our marriage. "God, guide Kelli and Jerry," Brother Malcolm said. "And Kelli and Jerry, let the love of God be central to your marriage. Marriage is not just a commitment to each other. There is a third person in the marriage, Kelli and Jerry, and that person is Jesus. You owe just as much to Christ as you do to one another. And in making a commitment to each other you are to treat him or her the way Christ would have treated your spouse. Make a commitment to involve Christ in every detail of your marriage, and in return for making that kind of commitment to Christ you will receive blessings from God, and those blessings will be in the form of healthy children, financial success and protection from temptation."

Brother Malcolm laid his hands on Kelli and a familiar feeling came over me: the presence of the Holy Ghost. I began speaking in tongues—a fluid rush of syllables that was otherworldly yet recognizable as an attempt at language, like Pig Latin—and our families prayed and raised their hands ecstatically in worship. It was like a revival in miniature. After the teasing and silliness of Kelli's sister Karen, it seemed as though we had returned the service to its spiritual center, sanctified our marriage and brought the Holy Ghost into the ceremony so we could receive God's blessings.

When the wedding was over, our families left the church together and followed Kelli's parents back to their home in Pitkin. As Kelli and I drove down Fullerton Blacktop Road that afternoon, I remembered my trip to Kelli's house for our first date just three months earlier. I felt so lost searching for Kelli's home in the darkness. But now it was daylight. I'd found love and, for that moment, I felt that I'd been found. At Kelli's parents' home, we feasted on a lunch of fried chicken and cornbread prepared by my mother-in-law. I loved her down-home cooking—she complemented her fried chicken with peppers and onions from her garden—and sitting down to a postnuptial meal on string-back chairs around a big, wooden kitchen table just added to the hominess.

After lunch, Kelli and I changed out of our wedding clothes and piled into an old, beat-up four-door 1980 Buick LeSabre that my mother had donated to Kelli and me. Though our wedding had passed without incident, I was still concerned that Shane might pop up somewhere, so I actually checked the LeSabre's backseat before we pulled off. Our plans for the honeymoon were incredibly simple: we'd make the three-hour drive to Baton Rouge and get a hotel room there. Because we were so broke, Kelli and I made reservations at a Red Roof Inn in Baton Rouge. But as we approached the city limits we decided that we'd splurge on something a little nicer and booked a room at a Hampton Inn. After checking in and unpacking our belongings in our tiny hotel room, I called my grandmother to tell her that we'd arrived safely. Kelli thought that was a momma's boy thing to do and, worse, that the call to my grandmother was encroaching on *her* time. It was hard to argue with Kelli, but for me and my grandmother the drive to Baton Rouge might as well have been a cross-country trip. Later that night, we played a round of miniature golf. The next morning, we rose early and had our first breakfast as a married couple at a Baton Rouge Shoney's, a feast for me because I'd always loved their breakfast bar. We checked out of the Hampton Inn around noon–we only had enough money for a one-night stay–and headed back to DeRidder in the LeSabre.

If our wedding and honeymoon were unromantic, our first home as a married couple–my grandmother's home in Rosepine–was far from an ideal place for newlyweds. I attempted to make things more comfortable before we made the move. I'd spent the last few years in the small middle bedroom in my grandmother's house and while Kelli and I honeymooned, my grandparents rearranged the house so that we could have the big bedroom in the back. But neither Kelli nor I was disappointed in how our new life together was turning out. We hoped that we'd be traveling the country evangelizing, so the close quarters at my grandma's wouldn't matter much. Our plan was to schedule revivals at as many churches as possible and because we didn't feel called to just the South, we believed that we'd canvass the entire country spreading the word of God. Kelli and I were both very naïve about the number of revivals we'd be able to schedule and assumed that we wouldn't be at home in Rosepine for long.

Our hopes for a life on the road evangelizing about Pentecostal faith seemed realized soon after our wedding, when Brother Lloyd asked me to accompany him to a camp meeting at a huge church in Pontotoc, Mississippi, set for May of 1990. Though Pontotoc is a small town of about five thousand residents near Tupelo, the birthplace of Elvis, attendance for the camp meeting was expected to be in the hundreds. Our expectations for our life together were raised even further by the nearly six hundred dollars in cash we were given by relatives as a wedding gift. Back then, six hundred dollars was a princely sum for me. I thought that I would never want for money again. I couldn't believe how great a start Kelli and I were off to. When we arrived at the church in Pontotoc that May, after an exhausting, nearly eight-and-a-half-hour drive, my spirits soared; it was a massive structure reminiscent of an old Catholic monastery. Behind its hard stucco exterior there were dorms, hallways and corridors that resembled a series of catacombs, and a church cafeteria.

The camp meeting began on a still-cool Friday night in May with a message from Brother Lloyd. "We're gonna make it," Brother Lloyd preached. "My friends, Jesus has never failed anyone." Brother Lloyd's preaching style was very much that of an encourager who delivered a populist "all of our boats will be lifted" message. But Brother Lloyd was also able to move beyond such generalist messages to connect deeply to the everyday experiences of Pentecostals. "I remember when I'd just gotten the Holy Ghost," Brother Lloyd continued. "I was carpooling to work with a group of drinkers. One of the guys in my carpool would shake a beer can and pop the top so the spray of beer would hit me in the back of my head. Now, friends, if that had happened before I'd gotten the Holy Ghost"–Brother Lloyd paused for dramatic effect–"there would have been trouble between me and him. Friends, we can modify our behavior and God can guide us in our quest to live right. But only if we live a more devout life. We can achieve the victory, friends. Are you ready to get to that place?"

In the Pentecostal world, having "the victory" means maintaining devotion to God. The faithful in the sanctuary nodded their heads in agreement with Brother Lloyd; that night, it seemed that the victory was at hand. After he delivered his message, Brother Lloyd turned to the piano player and asked him to play "Amazing Grace" softly in the background. As the piano player riffed on "Amazing Grace"–Pentecostals are like natural jazz musicians who are able to endlessly improvise on a song–Brother Lloyd prayed under his breath. These were not prayers of supplication but of praise and worship. "I love you, Jesus," Brother Lloyd whispered. "Lord, I surrender to you."

Brother Lloyd then ministered to individual members of the congregation. "Brother," he said sternly to one middle-aged man, "you there with the blue tie, would you stand up?" The man slowly rose from the pews. Because he was already so moved by Brother Lloyd's message, he had tears in his eyes and hands raised into the air. "I see in the spirit that you are going through hard times," Brother Lloyd continued. "I see that someone in your family is suffering and that the doctor has said it is terminal." Brother Lloyd wanted the man to know that God was aware of his struggles and that awareness should strengthen his faith. I had seen Brother Lloyd provide prayer and comfort in our weekly church services in DeRidder, but witnessing him minister at a church so far away from home gave me hope that I could do the same when I went out and ministered.

As the revival continued that Friday night, the mood in the church became increasingly ecstatic and worshipful. Miracles, it seemed, were close at hand. I surveyed the huge crowd assembled in the sanctuary and was impressed by the many young people—teenagers and grade school kids—sandwiched together dancing ecstatically in between the pews and the stage, all very much in spiritual tune. I was so moved that I went up into the balcony in order to take in the scene before me. As I stood on the balcony watching Brother Lloyd's service, I began to cry. It felt miraculous to me to witness the young folks all harnessing the monumental power of God. The moment instantly harkened back to the time at Swaggart's church when the congregant rose in inspiration and spoke in tongues and gave an interpretation. I remembered the message preached at Swaggart's church—*I am raising up an army*—and as I watched hundreds of churchgoers at Pontotoc dance, sway and raise their arms in praise to the Lord under Brother Lloyd's divine guidance, it seemed that God *was* raising up an army.

The next day, Brother Richie, a pastor at the Pontotoc camp meeting and the MC of the event, took the reins of the revival from Brother Lloyd. Brother Richie had an archetypal Pentecostal look: a big-barreled chest, huge hands, thick glasses and slicked-back black hair. Brother Richie was highly respected by Brother Lloyd; he was one of the few guest preachers allowed to take to the podium to deliver a message. Brother Richie delivered a grace-oriented "God loves everybody" message and afterward one of the young pastoral assistants told me that he wanted to see me in the pastor's office. As a young preacher, I was thrilled at the possibility of a one-on-one encounter with Brother Richie and rushed to meet him in a church office. There, I found Brother Richie, who had commandeered the pastor's office, sitting behind an imposing desk. "Thank you for driving my dear friend Brother Lloyd to Pontotoc," Brother Richie intoned. "I'd like to give you something." He rose from behind his desk, slid his hand into his front pants pocket and pulled out a hundred-dollar bill. The gift completely stunned me. As a twenty-year-old preacher, the mere thanks from Brother Richie was more than enough of a gift for me, so the hundred-dollar bill left me speechless. I walked out of the office in tears, praying and thanking God for this great man's thanks and for his unbelievably gracious gift. The long, costly, nearly five-hundred-mile trip from DeRidder to Pontotoc had made me realize that the six hundred dollars in wedding money was far from a fortune. I'd suddenly become aware that money could slip away so easily and the hundred-dollar bill from Brother Richie felt like God paying me back.

Just after our meeting concluded, Brother Richie took to the stage again to resume his MCing duties. "God told me," Brother Richie thundered to the crowd, "that if all of you open your hearts there could be an offering tonight of five thousand dollars." The crowd quieted and a collection among the crowd was taken by one of the assistant preachers. Then another young preacher passed a note to Brother Richie as he was counting the cash. Brother Richie furrowed his brow in dismay as he scrutinized the slip of paper;

the five-thousand-dollar goal had clearly not been reached. "The Lord is telling me that there are still people in the sanctuary who can give," Brother Richie continued, his voice becoming stern, "and that there are people out there"–he paused dramatically–"*who have hundred-dollar bills.*" My face went a pale, ghostly white. I was horrified. Immediately, a carnal side in me showed itself: *No, you're not getting it. You are not getting my hundred-dollar bill.* I'd been set up by Brother Richie. I was a preacher from a small town in Louisiana, but I knew right then that the plan was for me to turn over my hundred-dollar bill to Brother Richie so that I would be followed by congregants who'd do the same. But I refused to budge. The longer I sat in the pews, the more insistent Brother Richie's pleas became. Even though I feared that Brother Richie would hold my refusal to cooperate with his scheme against me forever, I still refused to stand before the camp meeting to fool them into thinking that God had inspired me to hand over a hundred-dollar bill. After several more urgent requests for cash passed, Brother Richie shot me a cold, hardened look. But I didn't blink. Then, to my relief, a pair of congregants strode to the stage and handed two hundred-dollar bills to Brother Richie.

Brother Richie's scheming aside, the profound faith of the young churchgoers at Pontotoc had moved me to tears. In their faith I saw a great future for myself as a young preacher. I'd travel the country with Kelli delivering God's word and hopefully one day I'd do so with the forcefulness and the connection to everyday folks that Brother Lloyd had displayed. But the Pontotoc revival brought unwelcome lessons about the business of ministering that caused small yet significant fault lines in my faith. Brother Richie's behavior demonstrated that preachers were all too human: they could manipulate the innocent and the sincere. This wasn't true of all preachers, of course, but the realization filled me with doubt and questions about my faith and my fellow preachers. I had to wonder, *Is Brother Lloyd aware of this side of Brother Richie?* I was also beginning to have doubts about my decision to get married so young. The

Pontotoc camp meeting was the first place where I'd truly been treated like a preacher and I saw the rock star–like status preachers could attain, particularly among young women.

On Sunday afternoon, I had the opportunity to preach a message along with several other young ministers. I was only granted a few moments in the spotlight–Brother Richie had us speak back to back–but I seized the opportunity. That afternoon, I was the fourth in line among the preachers asked to deliver a message. The ministers who came before me all slowly eased their way into their messages by wanly thanking God and the congregation. But I strode to the platform–which had wooden sides on it, so it was like stepping into a chariot–and dispatched with the ritual thank-yous and dove straight into my message, hitting it as fast and hard as I could. "If we're seeking God with all of our hearts," I cried, "then we will see the revival that will truly change the world." I'd outshined them all; I knew I didn't have any competition that day. There were, I realized after I delivered my message at Pontotoc that day, dozens of women who could be attracted to a charismatic young preacher like me. Perhaps the commitment I'd made to Kelli, and the financial woes we were already experiencing, were a hardship I needn't have borne in the first place. The next day, as Kelli, Brother Lloyd and I made the long trip back home to Louisiana, I grasped just how much money had been spent on the trip–on fuel, food and offering–and worried that the good fortune Kelli and I had been blessed with would not be with us for long.

The ministers, who preached at these revivals, were in earnest. They were zealous and sincere. They were not philosophers. To them science was the name of a vague dread–a dangerous enemy. They did not know much, but they believed a great deal.

–Robert Green Ingersoll, from *Why I Am an Agnostic* (1896)

After the camp meeting at Pontotoc, which was characterized by a disconcerting combination of Brother Richie's tricks and a direct hit to my finances, I feared for my future as a young Pentecostal preacher. I wondered if I could truly make a career out of my passion. I questioned my fellow Pentecostals like Brother Richie, who I believed did not possess intentions and faith as pure as my own. But my worries were tempered by the enthusiasm and ecstatic praise I'd witnessed from Pontotoc's packed crowds and my success in scheduling my first revival. Thanks to my incessant networking amongst the preachers at Pontotoc, I'd secured a revival at a church in Lucedale, Mississippi, for June of 1990, just weeks after the camp meeting at Pontotoc. The services at Lucedale were to be smaller in size than Pontotoc–it's a tiny town of about three thousand residents in southern Mississippi–but it was also going to be less expensive and more convenient, too. Lucedale is near Gulf Coast communities like Pascagoula and is only a six-hour trip from DeRidder, a vastly shorter trip than the nearly nine-hour trek to Pontotoc.

But even this trip presented significant financial hurdles for Kelli and me. We were still struggling to meet basic expenses and, to Kelli's chagrin, were still living at my grandmother's home. Our only mode of transportation was the Buick LeSabre that my mother had just donated to us. Even after my mom purchased a new set of tires for the LeSabre, I was still so worried about its creaky condition–its brakes felt soft–that I took it to a tire shop in DeRidder for a top-to-bottom inspection. At the shop, a tall, slender sixty-five-year-old African American mechanic raised up the LeSabre slowly on big, blue floor jacks. When the vehicle was finally suspended seven feet into the air, the mechanic stood under the floor jacks to scrutinize its undercarriage. "Your brakes are just plain wore out," he said as he slowly shook his head side to side in disgust. "Your tire rod ends, too." It was a disastrous diagnosis of the LeSabre with a cure that Kelli and I could ill afford. "Would you drive this car out of state?" I replied meekly. The mechanic looked at me over his wire-rim glasses and said, this time with a chuckle of disgust, "Son, I wouldn't even drive this car out of town."

But I had no choice *but* to make the trip to Lucedale in the LeSabre. So I mumbled a thank-you to the mechanic and then stood, silent and embarrassed, as he lowered the LeSabre down to the ground. Back at my grandmother's house early that afternoon, I reflected on the sad and inescapable fact that while the LeSabre was in rough shape, my finances were in even poorer condition. The six hundred dollars that I had believed to be a windfall from our wedding had, thanks to the trip to Pontotoc and my lack of a day job, left Kelli and me with about forty dollars to our name. So just before leaving for Lucedale, I made a painful decision: I'd put twenty dollars' worth of gas into the LeSabre's tank. The rest of our money–all twenty dollars' worth–would have to sustain Kelli and me throughout the revival, no matter how long it lasted. It was a perilous choice that could result in Kelli and me starving there: revivals could span weeks or even months if the energy amongst the churchgoers took off. At best, twenty dollars would get Kelli and me through a couple of days at Lucedale.

Kelli and I set out from Lucedale in the LeSabre on an unusually warm and humid Louisiana afternoon in June without so much as money for Cokes. The seven-hour trip was, unsurprisingly, torture. Because Kelli tended to get motion sickness, she took Dramamine and promptly passed out in the front passenger seat, leaving me without a companion to talk to pass the time. The air conditioning in the LeSabre wasn't working properly–it blew tepid, warm and musty air instead of the clear blast of cold that we so desperately needed during a Louisiana summer day. And I was so hungry and thirsty that as Kelli slept soundly beside me, I daydreamed about Cokes and steaks. It didn't help that as we made our way east along I-12 through Louisiana and then Mississippi, it seemed as though every billboard advertised hamburgers, steaks, boudin and barbeque. As we neared Lucedale, I was in a carnivorous haze.

When we finally made it to Lucedale just after three that afternoon, we pulled into the parking lot of Delchamps, a grocery store chain dating from the 1920s whose stores were a fixture in Gulf Coast cities in Alabama, Mississippi and Florida in the 1990s. By the side of the store, I slid a quarter into a rusty pay phone and made a call to Brother Page of Lucedale Pentecostal Church to inform him of our arrival. Just a few minutes later, Brother Page, a tall, lanky man in his late seventies who resembled Jed Clampett from *The Beverly Hillbillies*, pulled into Delchamps's parking lot with his wife, Sister Page. Sister Page was about half her husband's height and, with her gray hair pulled into a tight little bun and long skirt that draped around her feet, had the look of a classic Pentecostal granny. Because I was so starving, I looked at Sister Page rapaciously–I knew that she *had* to be a great Southern cook and that Kelli and I would be treated to dinner at the Page home in short order. But our hopes for a cozy night of down-home cooking in Lucedale were quickly dashed when we followed Brother and Sister Page out of the Delchamps parking lot to make the short trip to the church. Brother Page had poor eyesight and Kelli and I watched in horror as he made sudden turns into opposing lanes of traffic and took corners far too quickly. *Forget dinner,* I remember thinking, even though my stomach was churning with hunger. *I just want to survive this trip without watching Brother Page kill himself and Sister Page on the highway.*

Fortunately, we made it to Lucedale without incident. Yet there was more disappointment in store for Kelli and me when we arrived. The church was an ugly cinderblock building with a small, concrete front porch, just like Fullerton Church back home. Lucedale's run-down appearance was made uglier by the lack of even a single paved parking spot out front: congregants simply had to park on green grass or gravel. I felt all of the air leave me when we pulled up to the church. When Brother Page led Kelli and me to an auxiliary building behind the church, I remember thinking,

This is an old couple with an old church and this revival just isn't going to amount to anything. But as we approached the building, Brother Page told us that it was an evangelist's quarters. This would be our home for the revival and, because Kelli and I lived with my grandmother, it was to be our first home together. So when Brother Page unlocked the front door to the evangelist's quarters, it didn't matter that with its reddish-orange carpet, musty midcentury bedroom set and dark wood paneling, it looked as though it had been furnished from an estate sale from the home of an elderly person who literally hadn't opened their doors since the 1950s. An unpleasant reality soon set in again, though. Before leaving us to ourselves, Brother Page said that we'd sit down for dinner at the Page home *after* services that night. Because services were set to begin at seven o'clock, then Kelli and I wouldn't eat until at least ten that night.

As we got dressed for services that night, Kelli said she was overwhelmed with the moldiness of the evangelist's quarters while I complained bitterly about the depressingly ugly Victorian-style queen-size bed, pink painted walls and clunky vanity by the foot of the bed. It was far from what we imagined our first home as a young married couple would be. But we had to be honest with ourselves: neither was the back room in my grandmother's house. At the very least, we believed, the days, weeks or perhaps months spent in the evangelist's quarters would mark the first time that we were alone as husband and wife. *I hope,* I remember thinking then, *that this revival lasts a very, very long time.*

Just before seven, I strode into the sanctuary and quickly realized that it was as musty and outdated looking as the evangelist's quarters. Its carpet and pew cushions were a pale, unattractive brownish color. Though the pews were made of oak, the beauty of the wood had faded so badly that its natural amber hue had turned to a decayed-looking dark brown. There were no stained-glass windows–just old wood-frame windows–and even their slight charm was eclipsed by balky, perpetually rumbling window air-conditioning units. One of the sanctuary's few bright spots, the white tiled ceiling, was yet another reminder of its unkempt state. The tile was so filthy that it had lost its original color and had taken on a tan-colored sheen. While the stage on which the pulpit stood was wide and spacious, Brother Page had stuck a tacky, gold desk lamp there so he could read from the Bible better because of his poor eyesight. When I poked my head out the front door, I watched with dismay as congregants pulled their vehicles into the dirt-covered area out front. Because there were no parking places, the arriving pickup trucks, sedans and station wagons resembled a circling of wagons from the Old West.

Returning to the sanctuary, I began what would be a long tradition for me in the ministry: I knelt in the pews among the congregation and prayed with them. Then, just before seven o'clock, as the churchgoers found their way to their seats, I remained in the back of the sanctuary to continue to pray and watch it fill up. Fortunately, we had a packed house on that first night; there were over two hundred people in the church when services began. Congregants lined the walls and folding chairs were placed out into the aisles to accommodate the overflow. Brother Page, however, limply began with an exhortation offering encouragement to the church that was indistinguishable from a cheerleader leading a pep rally. "We're gonna have a great revival," Brother Page exclaimed, which was met with an uninspired silence from the crowd. "I *said,*" he continued, this time more forcefully, *"we're gonna have a great revival!"* *"Amen!"* the congregants shouted back. The crowd, it seemed to me, was simply playing its part; every line Brother Page said had been uttered a thousand times by other ministers before. As Brother Page preached, Kelli and I sat side by side in the sanctuary wincing at his constant references to me as Brother "DeMitt." We weren't the only ones embarrassed by Brother Page's faux pas: whenever he mispronounced my name as Brother "DeMitt," Sister Page put her head down and shook it sullenly from side to side.

At eight o'clock, I rose from the pews and took the pulpit. "All of the good things that we want to happen in our lives," I preached, "and to our families are all possible. But those things are *only* possible if we're able to devote our lives sincerely enough to God. That sincerity, that devotion, becomes a perfect channel for the Holy Ghost to come into our lives." As I preached, I struggled mightily with Lucedale's technical limitations. The church didn't have a cordless microphone so I pulled the microphone off the stand in order to move away from the pulpit and get closer to the crowd. But the wire on the microphone was so short that I couldn't take any more than two steps off the pulpit. I felt like a dog on a two-foot leash up there. Fortunately, the sanctuary at Lucedale was so tiny that the congregants in the back could still hear me.

After preaching for about an hour, I decided to mimic Brother Lloyd's style back home in DeRidder. I called out congregants from the audience one by one to minister to them individually. I began by asking the congregation to stand in worship of God. When they were on their feet, I prayed and worshipped to God myself and waited on guidance from the Holy Ghost. As I prayed, I slowly eyeballed the crowd in order to find a worshipper to connect to. Just then, I set my eyes upon a young woman in her twenties. "Sister," I said, "I know that you have been ill for some time. I am praying for you and I know that God is going to heal you. I believe that your illness resides in your gall bladder. And Sister, I know that while you are struggling and in pain now, God will begin to heal you and you will soon be on the mend." The young woman stood quietly and tearfully as I ministered to her. When I was through, she silently took her seat.

It was just after ten o'clock when Sunday-night services were concluded. I'd preached myself exhausted. Even though I was listless and hungry, I felt the same ecstatic, purposeful rush as when I'd received that six hundred dollars for our wedding. *My life as a preacher,* I thought to myself then, *was a done deal. I knew that I was right about my choice to become an evangelist. I knew that God had called me to preach.* The feeling that I was on the right spiritual path was confirmed when the young mother to whom I'd ministered approached me by the pulpit to tell me that she'd been suffering from gallstones.

After the congregants filed out of the sanctuary and piled into their cars, Brother and Sister Page approached Kelli and me and told us to follow them home for dinner. *Finally!* I thought. *After three hundred miles on the road and hours of preaching: food.* We were so hungry that we couldn't wait to get something–anything–into our empty stomachs. Just before services began, I'd seen a Coke machine just outside the sanctuary, so I took change out of the offering plate and bought Kelli and me two bottles of Coke. Feeling somewhat satiated by the Cokes, we jumped into the LeSabre and followed the Pages to their home, a white cinderblock structure that, when we arrived, made me think that Brother and Sister Page lived in a dairy barn. Because the house lights illuminated only tractors and rusty metal farm tools in the dark night, my suspicions about the home seemed justified. But when we went inside it was just a typical farm-style home and Kelli and I were so starving that we wouldn't have cared if we ate in a dairy barn or even an outhouse. We took seats around the round, oak dining room table and, sensing our hunger, Sister Page began moving plates of food from the kitchen counter to the dining room. First, Sister Page put out beautiful chicken fried steak patties accompanied by a hulking gravy boat. Next out was a steaming hot pumpkin pie for dessert. As we sat around the dining room table together, Brother Page said grace. But his prayer over the meal was said in a robotically rhythmical "now I lay me down to sleep" sort of way. *His prayer,* I thought disdainfully of Brother Page, *is not a prayer from the heart.* As hungry as I was at that moment, if Brother Page had asked Kelli and me to rise from the dining room table and go into the living room and pray until sunrise I would have been up for that. I wanted the Holy Ghost to use me, no matter what physical shape I was in. But a significant spiritual experience was not in the offing around the dining room table–Brother Page's pray over the meal was passionless and mechanical.

After Kelli and I took our plates, I hungrily eyed the chicken fried steak and slid a piece onto my plate. I then turned my attention to the gravy, which had the almost-gray color of homemade gravy. I picked up the ladle and began to languorously drizzle the gravy over the chicken fried steak. *This is it,* I rhapsodized to myself, *the down-home meal I've been waiting for.* Then, as I placed the ladle back into the gravy boat, I noticed a long hair draping over the ladle. *Are you serious?* I remember thinking. *We drove all this way, we haven't eaten in twelve hours, and I preached my heart out and now this.* But I was starving and I knew if I skipped the meal that night I would offend the Pages and worse, I'd set myself on a course for starvation. My sole sustenance in the last twenty-four hours, after all, was a can of Coke. So I put the hair-laden ladle back into the gravy and maneuvered the ladle so that I could scoop up some gravy *without* hair. It was a selfish move on my part–I'd just dunked the hair back into the gravy–but felt I had no choice. Sure enough, when I passed the ladle to Kelli *she* got the hair. Unfortunately for Kelli, she didn't notice the hair until it landed on her plate. Kelli was done. It didn't matter how hungry she was–she just wasn't going to feast on Sister Page's hair.

As much as I empathized with Kelli, I had chicken fried steak to eat. I cut into the meat and shoved a huge forkful into my mouth. There was something strangely gamey about its taste that reminded me of venison. But before I could contemplate what I'd just put in my mouth Brother Page turned to me and asked, "What do you think about the meat, Brother? You wouldn't suspect that had been in the freezer for three years, would ya?" I put down my fork and stopped eating. *We're gonna die,* I thought. *We're gonna die right here at the Pages'.* By the time dessert came around, I was so sickened by the food that I just nibbled at the pumpkin pie's crust. Brother Page, who had cleaned his plate of chicken fried steak and was obviously still ready for more, eyed my plate ravenously and then locked his eyes with mine. "Brother Jerry," he said, "you're not gonna eat your pie?" Before I could offer up an excuse, Brother

Page exclaimed, "Halleluiah!" and snatched the slice from my plate. When dinner finally ended just after midnight, Kelli and I left the Page home exhausted and still hungry. We stopped at Delchamps and bought a loaf of bread and a family-size can of beef stew that we hoped would last for the next few days. Surviving on just the barest of necessities was the life of a Pentecostal preacher delivering the word of God in small churches throughout the Deep South. I wasn't paid at Lucedale and even when large crowds came out for a revival, like they had at Pontotoc, they were always poor and could often muster no more than a few dollars for the collection plate. When an envelope of cash from the collection was handed over to me that first night at Lucedale, it had a total of eight dollars inside.

But when Kelli and I staggered back to the evangelist's quarters that night there was a huge surprise in store for us. When I opened the door to the 1950s-style icebox in the kitchen there were two of the most beautiful rib-eye steaks I'd ever seen, along with a twelve-pack of Coke. I'd been so hungry during the trip to Lucedale and I'd fantasized about a steak for much of the three-hundred-mile drive and now, standing in front of the bright light from the icebox, a pair of rib eyes laid there before me. *Thank you, Jesus,* I thought then, *thank you.* It was a spiritual hook that may seem trivial but in that moment of deep hunger, it rivaled my reunion with Ms. Blair that had led me to Swaggart's.

For the next two weeks, I preached every night at Lucedale Pentecostal. Two weeks was a good run for a revival though it wasn't unheard of for a great revival to last a full month. I preached at Lucedale Church but what I really was that spring–and at the dozens of revivals where I'd later preach–was not a preacher but a recruiter. A recruiter for Jesus. Just like the preachers at Swaggart's had promised, I was going to use these revivals to raise up an army for God. Though the revival at Lucedale was small, especially in comparison to the hundreds-strong camp meeting at Pontotoc, I felt the true spirit of revival grow over the two weeks I spent there preaching. I was also completely energized by a youth group that was brought to the revival every night by a pastor named Brother McKissick from a nearby church. Every night after services, the youth group decamped to the evangelist's quarters, filling up the living room and the kitchen. We'd sit for hours and they'd ask me for my opinion on doctrine, life issues and Pentecostal history. Because there were so many teenagers among them there were a lot of questions about lust. I counseled that God created us and that he knows how our bodies are made and the ways in which our bodies function. Therefore, I explained, God would understand lust because it is a part of our very humanity. I also told the youth group that the Pentecostal embrace of scripture like Matthew 5:28–"But I say unto you, That whosoever looketh on a woman to lust after her hath committed adultery with her already in his heart"–did not take into account the fact that even though it was found in the New Testament Jesus was still teaching under the Old Testament, the laws of Moses, at the time. What Jesus was actually doing through his teachings was demonstrating that humanity needed a savior because humanity could not please God on their own.

I wasn't much older than the teenagers in the youth group so we'd laugh and joke for hours. It was like a jam session for God each night, minus the music. Sometimes the youth group would stay in the evangelist's quarters well past three in the morning. I didn't mind the late nights because I fell in love with their passion for God and, I have to admit, the attention they lavished on me. I literally swam in the attention. I cherished every single second of my time with the youth group, every smile and every compliment they handed me. Kelli, meanwhile, grudgingly tolerated the services but would have been satisfied if each night I'd turned in early and said, "Let's just go back to the room tonight." She was uninterested in late-night discussions about theology, nor did she care for me counseling these kids on their life issues. Kelli had a self-reliant worldview: she always said that every tub sits on its own bottom. So when my "jam sessions" with the youth group stretched well into the early mornings, Kelli let me know in no uncertain terms that she was done playing host. She'd send me signals about her displeasure: she'd tap my hand or raise her eyebrows to let me know that it was time for everybody to leave. This was the beginning of the love triangle that would characterize my life with Kelli, which was between me, Kelli, my ministry and, to be honest, perhaps a fourth party: my own ego.

Kelli's unhappiness was made all the worse by my own insecurities about the harsh realities of my new career. After the enthusiastic but small crowds at Lucedale brought just a few dollars in the offering every night, I was scared to death. How on earth would Kelli and I survive on an eight-dollar-per-night offering? I began my career as a preacher with a conscious decision to focus on small churches. It was perhaps the most personal means of connecting to my fellow Pentecostals and I felt absolutely drawn to the work. But after Lucedale I knew that this was no way to make a living, a point of view shared by Kelli. To Kelli, we could not accumulate anything as a young married couple or even hope to move out of my grandmother's if I focused on small churches. I knew Kelli was right but I struggled to remain positive; I felt it was far too early to just give up on my mission. So I rationalized the failings at Lucedale: it was an old couple, an old church, I'd find newer churches, younger congregations elsewhere. My ignorance also prevented me from giving up. I had no idea if one, a hundred or a thousand dollars from the collection plate signified a successful night. So I figured that the best thing to do was get out there on the road again and find out for myself what a preacher's life was really like.

After arriving back home from Lucedale in late June, it was painfully obvious to Kelli and me that we were going to be living at my grandmother's home much longer than we'd anticipated. As promising as the revival at Lucedale was, particularly the adulation I received from the youth group there, the request to preach there was the sole invitation I'd received from my networking at Pontotoc. Despite our highest hopes, we knew that we weren't truly going to be on the road and preaching the word of God anytime soon. So, soon after our return from Lucedale, I scoured the names and phone numbers of pastors that I'd written down on notebook paper during the Pontotoc camp meeting. My motivation to get out on the road was twofold: I wanted to engage my mission to preach the word of God as much as possible and I sought to make Kelli feel like we had a home for ourselves outside of my grandmother's back room. But when I began to actually make the calls I felt like a Pentecostal prostitute. "Brother, this is Jerry Dewitt from Brother Lloyd's church," I'd begin the call. "We met at the Pontotoc camp meeting. I'm calling to see if you might be interested in holding some services?" It was extremely discouraging because ministering was exactly like being in sales. I had objections to overcome immediately–"This isn't a good time to talk" often came the reply, or "We just had this great revival with Brother Smith and it's too soon to do something else," or "We've already got Brother Jones scheduled for two months from now." The cold-calling made me realize just how naïve I was about the *business* of evangelism. I was horrified to learn just how many evangelists were out there. There seemed to be hundreds of young preachers all calling the same churches in the South. It was a highly competitive market that left little room for a young evangelist. I'll never forget that during one cold call I had a minister say to me in a voice that positively dripped with pity, "Brother DeWitt, I need to be honest with you. I get at least three calls like this per week. I'm very sorry."

The relentless cold-calling threw cold water on my notion of serving Christ. There, by the black rotary phone at my grandmother's house, I was painfully transitioning into an awareness that evangelism was actually an industry. It was essential that I hustle like a salesman to survive. I struggled mightily to accept these cold, inescapable facts. I thought that I simply could pray earnestly and live devoutly for God. God, in turn, would recognize my devotion and cut through the red tape of the church business so that I wouldn't have to compete with the evangelists who were just *busi-*

nessmen. But my life in the ministry would not be nearly so easy. And with that realization I succumbed to my deepest fears of rejection. Every time I picked up the phone to call a preacher, I felt a gut-wrenching agony that sickened me to my stomach. I think that anybody who has worked in cold calls or sales knows the feeling—the momentous mountain of rejection that you're likely to face as soon as you pick up the phone. When I finally gathered the courage to actually dial a number, I could not have been less respectful of myself if I'd walked the streets of DeRidder on a dog leash. It was a cataclysmic spiritual crisis and I needed to resolve it quickly. So I made a decision: *I'm gonna go the supernatural route.* I fasted for days on end and during the fasts did nothing but read my Bible. I hoped that through the fasts God would help me bypass the cruel business of Pentecostal preaching. I ended up feeling spiritually and emotionally lifted by the fasts but every day of devotion was just another day of disappointment for Kelli. To Kelli, a day that I spent fasting was no more than another day in which no money was brought home, a day that pushed the date we'd move out of my grandmother's back room and into our own home further and further into the future.

Fortunately, there was hope amidst the self-reflection and fasting. The dozens of cold calls yielded a revival at a church in Laurel, Mississippi. And during the Lucedale revival I had scheduled a revival with Brother McKissick's church, Lucedale Apostolic, which was just weeks away. It was Brother McKissick who'd brought the wonderful youth group to Lucedale; I just couldn't wait to connect with those kids again. With two revivals approaching, I quit my fasts and began working at my grandfather's mechanic shop behind the house. I was just a grunt, a grease monkey, but I appreciated the steady rhythms of a workday: every morning, I'd rise from bed, meet Grandma and Grandpa in the kitchen and then head to the backyard mechanic shop. As I worked, Kelli busied herself cross-stitching in the back room or cleaning my grandmother's house. When evening arrived, we'd have dinner together and then

Kelli and I would lock ourselves in the back room. We didn't have so much as a TV but the time alone gave us an opportunity to talk about our troubles. Our conversations on those quiet nights, however, consisted of Kelli rightfully complaining about life at my grandmother's. She'd express her hope that our lives would soon be better–and I, though I knew better, promised that it would be.

Brother McKissick's revival, held in the deep summer months of 1990, wasn't nearly as well attended as Brother Page's revival. But Kelli and I were grateful to be set up at an evangelist's quarters again and this time accommodations were far more comfortable than what we'd been accustomed to. We had free reign over a pleasant redbrick home with a large wooden deck. Kelli enjoyed having a home of our own again, even a temporary one, and I excitedly awaited the start of the revival at Lucedale Apostolic's sanctuary, which had new pews, bright-red carpeting and a soaring, cathedral ceiling. It didn't matter that when services began on a Friday night in early July, there were about one hundred congregants in attendance, about a third of the attendance at Brother Page's revival. It was a young crowd–most of the people in attendance were in their late teens or early twenties–and they were adherents of the supernatural side of Pentecostalism, which made the services thrilling. I tapped into that ecstatic feeling by prophesying to the congregants. I told Brother McKissick's son John that he would be a prophet equal to that of Isaiah in the last days.

A prophetic atmosphere permeated Brother McKissick's revival. One night, a member of Brother Page's church stopped by the revival to tell me that Brother Page's daughter-in-law was hospitalized in Mobile, Alabama, with a brain aneurism. After services that night, I prayed and asked God if I should travel to Mobile to pray for her. I believed that God would not only instruct me to go to Mobile, but he would also perform miracles for Brother Page's daughter-in-law. My confidence in God's abilities was buoyed by a belief I had at the time that Pentecostals were praying for too many miracles. What they needed to do instead was live devoutly enough in order for God to tell them which miracles he was going to perform. So I stayed up late that night in the evangelist's quarters at Lucedale and prayed in order to get assurance from God that he would heal this woman. Just before the sunrise, I laid out a fleece before God. In the Old Testament, Gideon lays a fleece, or a skin, on the ground and tells God that if he wants him to fight the battle against the heathen Midianites, then God should prevent the skin from becoming wet from the dew of the early morning. According to Judges 6:36–40:

> And Gideon said unto God, If thou wilt save Israel by mine hand, as thou hast said, Behold, I will put a fleece of wool in the floor; and if the dew be on the fleece only, and it be dry upon all the earth beside, then shall I know that thou wilt save Israel by mine hand, as thou hast said. And it was so: for he rose up early on the morrow, and thrust the fleece together, and wringed the dew out of the fleece, a bowl full of water. And Gideon said unto God, Let not thine anger be hot against me, and I will speak but this once: let me prove, I pray thee, but this once with the fleece; let it now be dry only upon the fleece, and upon all the ground let there be dew. And God did so that night: for it was dry upon the fleece only, and there was dew on all the ground.

In our Pentecostal world, then, asking God for a sign became known as putting a fleece before God. So I asked God to lead me to the hospital and then to the room of this ill woman, whose name I didn't even know. I told The Lord, "I will need you to have Brother Page there because if I open the door I won't know if it is her." That morning, Kelli and I took off on the forty-mile trip from Lucedale to Mobile; I believed that God was going to answer my prayer but at the same time I knew that the ball was in his court. As we neared Mobile, Kelli and I saw a hospital from the interstate. I immediately felt drawn to that hospital; not a physical attraction, but the sort of invisible pull between magnets. "This is where we're going," I told Kelli and pulled off the interstate and into the hospital's parking lot. Kelli and I rushed into the elevator and I pushed the button for a floor; I don't remember which floor we pushed because I simply pushed a button. When the elevator doors opened we walked slowly into the hallway. I felt that magnetic pull again, a pull that turned me left. I walked to the left and when I reached an intersection of hallways I prayed and waited to feel the pull again. Another pull came soon afterward but this time Kelli and I reached a dead end. As Kelli and I walked morosely to the end of the hallway, we noticed that there was a door to a patient's room. We opened the door, and standing next to the patient's bed was Brother Page. At that moment, I felt as if I was suddenly promoted to the level of the apostles of the New Testament. That moment carried with it the confirmation and weight of everything I had ever read in the Bible. *God is with me,* I thought then. *God is making these things happen.* I prayed for Brother Page's daughter-in-law but it was not a prayer of supplication. I was so convinced of my connection with God that I made a declaration. "In the name of Jesus Christ," I thundered by the hospital bed, "be healed." Though there were no physical signs that Brother Page's daughter-in-law was healed that day, I strode out of the hospital with complete confidence that she had been healed.

The long night of prayer that yielded that incredible trip to Mobile gave me an unprecedented spiritual high. My spirit was towering. I was in the clouds. But four days after the revival began it came to a horrible, screeching halt. What I didn't know then is that prior to Brother McKissick becoming pastor, the church was dominated by a much more conservative Pentecostal family. So late Monday night, two men from the older church family showed up for services accompanied by ten of their children. Their children, in turn, brought a youth group dominated by members of the old church family, resulting in Brother McKissick and *his* family being outnumbered. The older church family had a different interpretation of how the Holy Ghost interacted with Christians. They were not only suspicious of Brother McKissick and his belief in prophesies and mysticism, they were downright disdainful of him. I had no idea that bad blood existed between these families and Brother McKissick assured me after the arrival of the two men that, while there were tensions between the groups, I had nothing to worry about.

The next morning, at about nine o'clock, Kelli and I were asleep in the evangelist's quarters when we heard a strange sound by the front door. We were well into the revival, which brought late nights of prayer and fellowship, so Kelli and I were still in bed. At first, I didn't think anything of the noise because I figured that there were all sorts of noises that we might be unfamiliar with–the creak of a door, the throttle of an air conditioner coming on–because we were guests in the home. Then I heard a much louder, more forceful sound: someone was forcing their way into the evangelist's quarters. I quickly slipped on my dress clothes from the previous night and ran to the bedroom door. I had an uneasy feeling as I groggily stumbled to the front door because no one had hollered out to us. When I got to the bedroom door, I found the door slightly ajar and then, to my horror, I discovered two old men pushing it open further. "Brothers!" I shouted forcefully, trying not to sound angry. "My wife is still in the bed. Give me a second and I'll meet you in the sanctuary." The men backed off and I shut the door forcefully behind me. I quickly finished getting dressed and met the men in the sanctuary. They spent the next two hours lecturing me about just how wrong I was to be prophesying, which they condemned as the "wildfire" of the devil. By the end of our discussion we hadn't come to any resolution: I realized that it was all about them venting their frustrations with Brother McKissick's supernaturalism. I knew right then that Tuesday night would the last night of services. "I'd rather have wildfire than *no* fire," Brother McKissick preached from the pulpit that night defiantly, a clear jab at our unwelcome visitors. But that night when I told Brother McKissick about my decision to end the revival he reluctantly agreed that it was the right thing to do. I felt cowardly for caving to the pressure from the church elders but I also found it gratifying that I'd ministered a revival that had become so spiritual, and eventually so carnal, that it brought these men to fight.

> *We are going to die, and that makes us the lucky ones. Most people are never going to die because they are never going to be born. The potential people who could have been here in my place but who will in fact never see the light of day outnumber the sand grains of Arabia. Certainly those unborn ghosts include greater poets than Keats, scientists greater than Newton. We know this because the set of possible people allowed by our DNA so massively exceeds the set of actual people. In the teeth of these stupefying odds it is you and I, in our ordinariness, that are here.*
>
> **—Richard Dawkins**

After Brother McKissick's revival unexpectedly shut down that Tuesday night, Kelli and I drove back to my grandmother's home in Rosepine the next morning. After the spiritual high of the revival, which concluded with the astounding news that Brother Page's daughter-in-law had been healed from her aneurism, I was feeling depressed and enervated. It was mystifying to me that I could move the faithful at a revival and even be guided by the hand of God to heal a sick woman, yet I could not find steady work as an evangelist or even keep food on the table at home. I was beginning to resent my fellow evangelists: they were not demonstrating the signs and wonders that I felt like *I* was demonstrating, and their messages were extremely shallow. Yet they were all far more successful than me. Indeed, one particularly uninspired evangelist I knew, who preached *nothing* but simplistic messages, was booked two years in advance. I bitterly complained to Kelli that all he did behind the pulpit was say, "Jesus, Jesus, Jesus" hundreds of times. The messages he preached were nothing more than slightly different takes on Acts 2:38, scripture that was the bedrock of the Pentecostal faith: "Repent, and let every one of you be baptized in the name of Jesus Christ for the remission of sins; and you shall receive the gift of the Holy Spirit."

He was a preacher who, to use a tired cliché, simply preached to the choir. And he–nor any of the Evangelists I knew for that matter–never delivered a message that was meant to challenge the belief system of their congregation. But I quickly realized that their predictability was precisely why these ministers were so successful. What I was just beginning to understand then was that ministering isn't much different than retailing. When customers shop at Walmart, they know that they're gonna find a Sam's Club ham for a buck ninety-eight per pound or a fifty-dollar dirt bike for their kid. The same was true of the church: the appeal was knowing exactly what you were in for, which was spiritual comfort food. My messages that insisted on the deepest devotion possible among the congregation were well received but they certainly weren't sellable.

Back at home that July, with no revival work on the horizon, I was forced to return to preaching with Brother Lloyd back at the Church of the Lord Jesus Christ. It was a depressing backward step and, worse, at church I was very much in Brother Lloyd's shadow. The congregants even referred to me as "Little Lloyd." That Brother McMahon, the elderly Pentecostal preacher who was brought to the church by Brother Lloyd near the end of my high school years, was still preaching at the Church of the Lord Jesus Christ only intensified my suspicions that I was just a marginal figure there. I sought to build on the experience I'd gained at the revivals. But what little time was available to preach at our church was being divided between Brother McMahon and myself. Despair at my struggles at the Church of the Lord Jesus Christ quickly turned into anger and I found myself lashing out at everyone around me. I blamed Brother Lloyd's wife, Sister Lucille, for our church's low attendance. I was furious with Brother McMahon for stealing my opportunities to preach at the Church of the Lord Jesus Christ.

So I seized upon any mistake made by the church's leadership so I could rail against all of their flaws. I insisted that it was the Church of the Lord Jesus Christ's weaknesses, not my own, that were holding me back from my mission of delivering the word of God. One afternoon, Sister Kathy Walker, who taught Sunday school at the church, spent hours meticulously fixing up the Sunday-school room. She decorated the room with posters from a Pentecostal publishing company called Word Aflame Press that depicted scenes from the Old and New Testaments, from Jesus breaking the bread to Peter preaching to a crowd on the day of the Pentecost. The posters just made the room incredibly welcoming for the Sunday-school kids and I admired Sister Kathy's inspired handiwork. Soon afterward, Sister Lucille, who I didn't feel was engaged at all in the day-to-day life of the church, redecorated Sister Kathy's classroom without her permission, wiping out all of her hard work. When Sister Kathy saw what Sister Lucille had done she was devastated and rushed out of the classroom in tears. I was furious. To me, this was proof that the Church of the Lord Jesus Christ couldn't do *anything* right. *They couldn't build a congregation,* I remember thinking, *if they gave a million dollars to everyone who showed up for services on Sunday morning.*

The ill will that I felt toward the Church of the Lord Jesus Christ seemed all the more justified when Brother Lloyd began having tax problems. I wasn't aware of what the tax problems were–I was just an assistant pastor, after all–but I recall that the church's leadership was trying to prove to the IRS that much of the money they made was going right back into the offering plate. During one Sunday-morning service, Sister Lucille approached my grandmother, who was the church's treasurer, for help. My grandmother was sitting near the altar talking to several of her fellow congregants when Sister Lucille approached her, red faced and angry, and demanded that my grandmother state that Brother Lloyd had put a certain percentage of the church's profits into the offering plate. "There's no doubt that you gave that money," my grandmother calmly replied, "if not more. But you provided that money in cash. And I just can't say on paper what you gave without backup." Sister Lucille, who had an imposing Amazonian frame and sported a beehive that only magnified the towering figure that she cut in church, furiously turned away from the altar and stomped angrily out of the sanctuary. That afternoon, my grandmother resigned as treasurer from the Church of the Lord Jesus Christ. *All* of my anger at the church came to a head at that very moment. I wasn't getting anywhere professionally at the Church of the Lord Jesus Christ. I had lost trust in Brother Lloyd and Sister Lucille. And I was furious with myself–I actually hated myself–for not defending my grandmother right there in the sanctuary. The next day, I went back to the church one last time, placed my keys on the pulpit and turned around and left. I was finished with the Church of the Lord Jesus Christ. There was no going back.

Fortunately, just as I left the church, I began being courted by Brother and Sister Herrington of Fullerton Pentecostal. It was the church where Kelli and I were married and I'd never been enthusiastic about its leadership. But Brother Malcolm of Fullerton Pentecostal had just left the church, which opened up an opportunity for me to preach there. And my in-laws were attending services there, so at the very least I had family surrounding me, so I reluctantly took an assistant pastor position at the church. The job duties were the same as my work at the Church of the Lord Jesus Christ. I attended services on Wednesdays and Sundays and preached at services on Sunday evenings. Assistant pastors don't typically preach on Sunday mornings–easily the most popular service of the week–or Wednesday evenings, which are a second-string service reserved for the church's pastor. Sunday nights, which had vastly smaller crowds and a far less formal atmosphere, were left to assistant pastors like me. But I savored Sunday nights: there was less preaching and more teaching. Better still, Brother Herrington allowed me to preach at a revival there. I was so fired up during the revival that I set upon a well-meaning middle-aged older man sitting toward the front of the church who had the bad luck of falling asleep during my services. Looking back, I think that the man was probably just ill. But I was so single-minded in my mission to deliver the word God–and, to be honest, so in love with my own talents in doing so–that I woke him up by tapping on his forehead to the beat of my message. "GOD," I tapped. "COMMANDS." Another tap. "YOU." Tap again. "TO." Tap. "LIVE." Tap. "A DEDICATED LIFE."

My hubris masked a deep spiritual conflict raging inside me. I was frustrated that God was unwilling to help me start my own ministry. I didn't want a ministry of my own for purely selfish reasons. I believed that I had to encourage my congregation to live a life dedicated to God, which in turn would allow the spirit of God to access the real world. In my view, a life of devotion, which *everybody* on earth needed to lead, would open up a clear conduit to have the presence of God in our community. My beliefs were buttressed by the second chapter of the book of Joel, verse 28, in which God says that he will pour out his spirit upon all flesh. "And it shall come to pass afterward," God said, "that I will pour out my spirit upon all flesh; and your sons and your daughters shall prophesy, your old men shall dream dreams, your young men shall see visions." I insisted that if God poured out his spirit upon us then that would bring about a *universal* revival. But God would not simply perform this act upon unfaithful people, so the question for me as a young preacher was, How can we can get enough people to live right enough to have the Holy Ghost poured upon all flesh? I thought once again about my experience at Swaggart's and the congregant's prophesy of raising up an army of God. We needed that army of God in order for God to pour his spirit upon all of humanity.

The path to a universal revival seemed simple. But I began to question God–if God really does love everyone, why is it so difficult for God to pour out his spirit? Why doesn't he just do it, make it come to pass? Ironically, it was my unyielding belief in the promise of a revival–which would bring Christ into our world and yield prosperity, healing, peace and righteousness among all people–that led me to question God. Why, again, doesn't God pour out his spirit and save everyone and bring about a universal revival? And if God loves everyone, doesn't he want everyone to be saved?

I began to see a dilemma in the message that I was preaching. I preached that everyone should lead a life devoted to God but I also believed that God loves *everyone* even if they are not devoted to God. Yet just because I loved people as much as I loved God didn't mean that I could spare everyone from hell. So I wanted God to quickly pour his spirit upon us and bring about a universal revival so that as few people as possible were lost. Indeed, I didn't want *anyone* to be lost. I knew that I loved everyone. *But if God really loves everyone,* I thought, *why do we have all these hurdles to jump through?* I sought a faster and more humane way to bring people to Christ. I believed in the truth–that all people needed to live a life devoted to God–but my love for people kept me from saying, "The truth is the truth. I'm sorry that some people have to go to hell. But that's just the way it is." Truth be told, I hated that anybody had to go to hell. And my love for these people–my love for *all* people–made me step outside the truth and say, "Why does this suffering have to happen in the first place?"

As I wrestled with the very character of God, back at home I was struggling with a wife fed up with our lives at my grandmother's home and a dire financial outlook that was showing no sign of improvement. My sole source of income was my assistant pastor job at Fullerton Pentecostal, which didn't bring in a salary but merely an honorarium ranging from fifty to a hundred fifty dollars per week. The income from preaching was supplemented by occasional work at my grandfather's mechanic shop. But I wasn't even a mechanic–I'd simply perform menial tasks like scraping gunk out of an oil pan for Grandpa for fifty dollars.

In my grandfather, whom I loved very dearly, I saw a potentially dark future for myself. He had lost not one but two opportunities for retirement and had been on financially shaky ground ever since. As a young man, he worked for a local lumber company, Long-Bell, which has a huge, historic significance to DeRidder. The current site of city hall, 200 South Jefferson Street in downtown DeRidder, is the very place where the Long-Bell sawmill once stood. In the early 1900s, at the moment when the town of DeRidder was incorporated, Long-Bell established a sawmill that for decades was the town's largest employer. But when my grandfather got within eyesight of retirement, Long-Bell folded. Undeterred, he went to work as a truck driver for West Brothers Department Store, another company that meant a lot to DeRidder. West Brothers was founded by DeRidder natives H. O. West and his brothers W. D. and J. A. West. It would later be seen as a predecessor to Walmart. But once again, just as my grandfather had retirement within his grasp, the company for which he worked so hard for so long–he worked at West Brothers for two decades–shut down. In May of 1988, West Brothers unexpectedly closed its doors, citing "circumstances beyond its control." The closure of West Brothers not only devastated my grandfather; coming after the collapse of his career at Long-Bell, it left him completely hopeless.

My grandfather gave up on looking for a job ever again. He spent much of his time at home in Rosepine eating–he had an addiction to Vienna sausages and mayonnaise–watching TV or attending dirt track races. Though he was raised in the church and he and my grandmother met and courted in church, by the time his unexpected and unwelcome retirement arrived, he had become profoundly disenchanted with the church. He hated the fact that Brother Lloyd came down so hard on TV because he savored watching television in his old recliner in the living room. Grandpa loved TV so much that he placed his recliner near a window in the living room so that when the signal became weak, he could send me outside and then shout to me through the window about the direction in which I should turn the antennae. My grandfather's conflict with Brother Lloyd over TV may sound trivial but to my grandfather it was a real symbol of the too restrictive and excessive conservatism of Pentecostal doctrine. I remember that one morning when I was getting dressed for Brother Lloyd's church in my traditional preacher's outfit of black slacks and a white dress shirt, my grandfather, who was dressed in his usual white T-shirt and dark-blue work pants, eyed me with disdain from his recliner. "Jerry," my grandfather scolded, "you're gonna go to church this morning and all of you Pentecostals are gonna preach the Baptists into hell because they don't speak in tongues. And at the same time the Baptists are gonna preach *you* into hell because you *do* speak in tongues. After preaching each other into hell, ya'll gonna go to Master Chef and eat fried chicken together." Master Chef was a hugely popular restaurant in DeRidder that served great fried chicken beloved by everybody in town, Pentecostals and Baptists alike. What Grandpa was saying that day was that Christians were spending so much time exacerbating–and damning each other for–our differences when deep down we were all very much alike. His words lodged deep within my heart. I couldn't deny my grandfather's logic; he formed an argument that I found undeniable.

Though I was a deeply devoted Pentecostal, I admired my grandfather's free-thinking ways as well as his savvy fixing of old cars. He'd get contracts with local auto dealerships to rebuild engines and then the dealers would resell the vehicles at auction. My grandfather was a whiz with engine mechanics and he did these contract jobs for next to nothing. His goal was simply to pay for his medicine–heart trouble started for him at the age of forty, the result, I think, of his towering, twin career disappointments with Long-Bell and West Brothers. So I was happy to help my grandfather out in his shop in the back of the house, even if it was grunt work that only brought in a few dollars.

By the end of the summer of 1990, my grandfather's health took a significant turn for the worse. He lived with nitroglycerin capsules in his pants pockets and had a fated attitude toward his doctor's instructions on diet. One night, a Popeye's commercial came on the TV and he said angrily, "If I can't eat, what's the point?" Later, on a sultry, humid Louisiana night that August, my mother took Grandpa, or "Paw-Paw" as I usually called him, to the dirt track races in Silsbee, Texas. On the long, nearly 80-mile ride back to Rosepine they stopped at a convenience store and had a honey bun, one of my grandfather's favorite snacks.

Just before sunrise the next morning, I was awakened by hysterical banging on my bedroom door. It was my grandmother and I jumped up from the bed to see what was wrong. Through a veil of tears, my grandmother told me that she had awakened to the sound of my grandfather gurgling. He was in cardiac arrest and we didn't have much time to save him. I ran into their bedroom and straight to my grandfather, who was lying in a hospital-style bed, and attempted to do compressions on his chest and check his airway. I say "attempted" because I didn't know what to do. I had not paid attention to CPR class. It has haunted me my entire life that I couldn't remember what to do to help my grandfather that day. And I am still haunted by the fact that even in that most desperate of moments, I struggled to give my grandfather mouth to mouth because I just found it hard to put my mouth on his mouth. This was, after all, a person I would have given my life for–*What was I doing and why did I hesitate to do what was necessary to save his life?* As I attempted to revive my grandfather, my grandmother dialed 911. It was so dark and foggy outside when the call was made that we had to flag down the ambulance because they couldn't find our house. I'll never forget feeling the relief at the sight of the ambulance headlights cutting through the soupy mist toward our house and then, moments afterward, the sheer horror of watching the lights fade into the distance.

When the EMTs finally arrived, they tried to lift my grandfather off of the hospital bed. But the EMTs were so slight physically—one of them appeared to be in his teens—that they dropped him to the bedroom floor with a sickening thud, leaving us to pull Grandpa to the kitchen. Inside the kitchen, we set him on the floor, a hard surface on which the EMTs could perform CPR. After inserting an IV into my grandfather's right arm, the EMTs applied the shock paddles to his chest. Even though Grandpa didn't respond to the resuscitation attempts, the EMTs tried to soothe us, to tell us that things were going to get better. Out of sheer desperation, we chose to believe what we knew not to be true. After a final attempt with the shock paddles, the EMTs lifted my grandfather from the kitchen floor and pulled him toward the ambulance. We followed close behind as the ambulance sped toward Beauregard Memorial Hospital. When the doctors met us in the emergency room, they said that they had done all they could but could not revive him. In shock, my mother stumbled backward and bumped against a wall in the ER and then slowly slid down it, wrapped her arms around her knees and assumed a fetal position. My grandmother had been praying continuously since the moment I entered their bedroom and she was still praying in the ER. But her prayer was no longer a plea for help from God: it had shifted into something more despondent and more desperate to confirm that she still loved God in spite of what was going on at the moment.

The doctors allowed us to briefly see my grandfather's lifeless body, a sorrowful sight, as he seemed to be almost bound to the hospital bed by breathing tubes. *It's my fault that he died,* I remember thinking, *because I didn't know what to do. It's my fault that I knew within myself that I couldn't bring him back.* I was particularly angry with myself because I believed that I had not reached the spiritual level where I could literally bring him back to life. *I blew it,* I told myself, *and this is the result.*

It was nearly midday when we drove back to my grandmother's home in a long, slow, sad caravan of cars. Friends and family were trickling into the house when we arrived. As I made my way inside I was distracted by my grandfather's beloved willow chair on the front porch. A willow chair is made from willow limbs, which are long and gangly and lend the chair a gnarled, rustic and snaky appearance. For my grandfather, who was raised in rural Kentucky, willow chairs were just about the only furniture he'd ever known. So when I was a little boy, Grandpa would take me out on humid summer afternoons to gather willow branches by creeks in the DeRidder area. The memories of those afternoons came rushing back to me when I stared at his willow chair. Overwhelmed with emotion, I fell forward onto the front porch with my elbows on the willow chair and began to cry, pray and speak in tongues.

In the days after my grandfather's death, I experienced yet another turbulent spiritual crisis, one that touched upon my then-longstanding questions about God's character. I worried that my grandfather had gone to hell because he had left the church. It didn't seem right to me that my grandfather, a good, decent, hardworking man who loved his family, would not be loved by God, a god who was supposed to love everyone. With the fate of my grandfather's soul unknown, I felt acutely responsible for not bringing him back from the dead. A remark that one of my uncles made the day he passed resonated with me and wracked me with guilt. "There's no way to do CPR properly on that hospital bed," he said. "You have to have a hard surface." With questions about God's love and my own role in my grandfather's death haunting me, I got down on my knees in my bedroom one night in hopes of talking with God directly. "God," I asked, as Kelli slept soundly in our bed, "how did you let this happen? Why was this all dependent on me?" I then heard God, in my voice, reply, "Have I ever failed you?' I could only stammer a quiet, "No." "Nor have I this time," God said, again speaking in my voice.

My exchange with God that night restored my faith and I enthusiastically returned to preaching at Fullerton Pentecostal, which yielded even more profound spiritual revelations. One Sunday night that fall, I stood at the pulpit leading services at Fullerton Pentecostal. Aunt Donnie was playing the piano and I was feeling spiritually lifted by being back at church, even though the notion that my grandfather may have been sent to hell simply because he didn't attend church services weighed heavily on my heart. At one point in the service, I raised my hands into the air in ecstatic praise to the Lord when all of a sudden my vision became foggy. I rubbed my eyes but my eyesight only grew increasingly blurred. Then the fog started to clear and I found myself standing in a beautiful green meadow. There was a huge gray rock nearby; it was the sort of dark gray that appears to be wet but is actually dry. Sitting on that rock was my grandfather, but he was in his thirties. On the ground next to him was another young man, who also appeared to be in his thirties, who I did not recognize. My grandfather and his companion were thin, strong and radiating with contentment, a beautiful sight to behold after standing over his lifeless body at Beauregard Memorial Hospital. But just when I started to move toward them, the fog began slowly rolling back. I was losing them. It was as though I was trying to catch an elevator door as it closed. When the vision ended, I opened my eyes and just began squalling. I cried so incessantly it seemed as though I would never stop. *He is saved,* I thought. *God does love everybody.* The vision of a healthful and happy Paw-Paw confirmed this idea in my heart. But my spiritual conflict was not vanquished by the vision; indeed, the clash between my heart and church doctrine only grew that much more intense afterward. Church doctrine, after all, taught that it was simply not possible for my grandfather to be saved.

As I struggled to resolve my feelings about God and theology, my home life lay in tatters. Kelli was miserable because we were still stuck at my grandmother's house. That it was the late fall of

1990 and a slight chill had finally arrived in Southwest Louisiana only heightened her feelings of hopelessness. The seasons were changing yet our life together as a young married couple had literally gone nowhere. One night, during a particularly cool spell of weather, Kelli was in bed and asleep and I lay awake. Our bedroom was lit only by moonlight coming through our window, so the room was bathed in a gorgeous mix of blue and black hues. I had long been praying every night before bed but when I knelt down that night I hadn't realized how despondent I had become. I tried to pray but I couldn't make a coherent prayer. "God help me," I said, words that were stammered through tears, snot and bated breath. Out of pure exhaustion from that desperate prayer, I crawled into bed with Kelli, lay down and immediately fell asleep. And then another vision presented itself to me. I was facing a wall, on my knees, kneeling on a thin carpet. The vision was exactly where I was at that point in my life: facing a huge, seemingly impenetrable wall. As I became aware of myself, I had the sort of sensation that you get when someone is staring at you and you're compelled to look over your shoulder. So I turned to look over my left shoulder and, about one foot away, there was a man standing near me. I could immediately tell that it was Christ. The features on his face were hard to distinguish but he was dressed in the type of material that is used to make an old feed sack, like a rough-hewn, thick yarn. The clothing was draped over him and it reached all the way to the floor, to his feet.

When I saw Christ and realized that it truly was him, I pivoted my body to get a better look. His hands were by his side and he turned his palms out and lifted his hands toward me, at about the height of my head. Instinctively, I reached out to him and the palms of my hands touched the back of his hands. Touching the back of his hands, I felt callous skin. I then looked at the palms of his hands and saw scars. "It's true, it's true, it's true," I cried. I was so overcome with the encounter with the son of God that I slumped forward and let go of his huge, calloused hands, the very hands of a carpenter. As I lay down, his hands touched my feet and I said, "It's true" again.

The vision then shifted perspective again. This time, I was against the window looking at myself with my hands on Christ's feet. And then, suddenly, the words and emotions that I had not been able to say when I was in prayer just moments earlier were coming out of my back. It was a stream of words–a vision of numerous, incoherent syllables and letters, none of which formed actual words–flowing into the chest of Christ, which was like a black hole drawing in material. Then I heard a voice behind me–I didn't know if it was my voice, Christ's or an angel's–say, quoting Hebrews 4:15, "For we have not a high priest that cannot be touched with the feelings our infirmities."

The vision shifted once more. I was standing in the wings of a large stage in a sprawling tent. As the vision became more clear, I realized that I was at a massive tent revival, held at nighttime. Thousands of faithful were in attendance though in my vision all of their faces were blurred. I stood at the pulpit with thousands of people in front of me. It was a makeshift stage constructed of plywood, the pulpit was made from rough-cut lumber and everybody in the audience was seated in old, rickety folding chairs. But the crowd was thousands strong; it was the revival of my very hopes and dreams. When I realized what was happening, Christ spoke to me over my left shoulder. "Tell them," he said, "that you have seen me." The vision shifted one last time. I was sitting in my grandfather's recliner and I had my face in my hands. I was just crying to the point where my whole body was shaking and I heard an angel's voice say, "By this you shall know that all of these things have surely come to pass."

When I awoke from the vision it was already morning. Kelli was in the kitchen fixing breakfast in her terry-cloth robe. Still in my pajamas, I rose from the bed and wandered down the narrow hallway to the kitchen, grateful for the warmth emanating from our gas heater on a cold Louisiana morning. I hadn't given a thought to my vision when I sat down in Grandfather's recliner. "How did you sleep last night?" Kelli called from the kitchen. With those words, I relived the vision in its entirety. It hit me like a thunderbolt. I took a huge breath and immediately began to squall. At first, I merely remembered the very end of the vision—"By this you shall know that all of these things have surely come to pass"—but then the rest of the vision came to me, which I breathlessly recounted to Kelli and my grandmother. They thought I had gone insane and I couldn't blame them. But I could not rid myself of the vision. The moment when I stood before the thronging crowd at the tent revival was, for a young preacher who only felt spiritually fulfilled during the weeks-long, praise-filled revivals, told me everything I needed to know about my path in life. *This is my calling,* I thought. *I need to find the people I preached to in my vision.* By preaching God's word to those people, all of my questions—about God, about faith, about myself—would soon be answered.

> *No man hath seen God at any time, the only begotten Son, which is in the bosom of the Father, he hath declared him.*
>
> **—John 1:18**

It was the early spring of 1991 and the great revival that I had so clearly glimpsed in my vision that winter was far from being realized. Indeed, I was no further along in my career as a young evangelist than when I started out one year earlier. I was still preaching at Fullerton Pentecostal Church and picking up revivals wherever I could in small towns like DeQuincy, about thirty miles from DeRidder in nearby Calcasieu Parish. The revivals brought in pitiful pay, sometimes as little as fifty dollars. While money was never a central part of my mission, I had to admit to myself that making it as an evangelist had become all the more challenging after my grandfather's passing. With Grandpa gone and with his mechanic shop shuttered, my work there vanished and I had to scramble furiously to find other part-time work to pick up the slack. I cleaned vinyl siding on homes and the outside of propane tanks. I cut the grass at Fort Polk, Louisiana, a US Army installation near DeRidder. I worked in the yards at Stine's Lumber, a Sulphur-based supplier to residential building contractors. My lack of a full-time job made me feel as though my career as an evangelist was not dead; with part-time work crammed in between revivals I could still claim that I was a preacher. But while I possessed all of the trappings of the life of an aspiring evangelist—an assistant pastor position at Fullerton and the occasional revival, which served as a platform for my message about bringing God into everyday life—my career was as lifeless as a set of lungs without air.

Kelli felt the disappointments of our lives all the more acutely. Her primary goal in life had always been to have her own home and, as our first anniversary quietly passed, we were still stuck at my grandmother's. No matter how successful I was in my part-time work or how spiritually rewarding the revivals could be, Kelli felt a keen sense of failure with every hour of every day that we did not have a home of our own. I shared in Kelli's disappointment but it didn't bother me that we were living at my grandmother's home because for me, it was all about the mission. If I was uncaring about my physical surroundings it was because I believed that I existed on a higher spiritual plane. Kelli, conversely, was very much grounded in the trials of everyday life at my grandmother's, from the noise emanating from the nearby train tracks and highway to the stampede of relatives who took advantage of Grandma's graciousness by visiting on a daily basis. My family believed that my grandmother's home was a communal space and Kelli, naturally, felt that there was no part of the home that was truly her own. Our bedroom was our only private space, yet Kelli had come to feel that she was a prisoner to it.

That spring, however, a tent revival in Sugartown beckoned, which I felt sure would raise our dampened spirits. A tent revival is a traveling, almost circuslike event, in which a preacher is led by the spirit to go into communities that seem to him to be ripe for revival. The preacher negotiates with a private landowner about setting up a tent on his or her property and must also deal with permitting from local governments in order to adhere to their regulations about large-scale outdoor events. Perhaps most dauntingly, a tent revival preacher manages the mechanics of everything from raising the tent to renting electrical generators or, in the case of highly ambitious revivals, installing temporary electrical poles. Mounting a tent revival is laborious and expensive, yet the preachers who work this circuit almost always come from the humblest backgrounds. They're in the business of tent revivals primarily because they cannot afford the prime real estate in a city or town in order to put their roots down permanently. It's a real estate–driven brand of preaching; indeed, the guiding principle behind tent revivals is very much the mantra of the buying and selling of property: *location, location, location.*

The Sugartown revival had such great promise because its preacher, Brother Brown of Gillis, Louisiana, was the quintessential Pentecostal entrepreneur. To Brother Brown, *everything* was a business opportunity; if he could have sold fishing lures from behind the pulpit he would have done it. Brother Brown's sharklike business savvy was complemented by his mobster looks: he was olive complexioned, had jet-black hair that was balding on top and he had a short, wide, barrel-like frame that made all of his suits seem ill fitting. There simply was no way for a suit jacket to encompass his incredible girth, so the shirt sleeves of his white dress shirt struggled to cover his stubby arms.

Brother Brown seemed born to the world of tent revivals. In his spiritual arsenal he boasted a sprawling trailer, and an enormous white tent and an upright piano. His expertise was evident as soon as Kelli and I arrived at his tent revival on a cool, clear Wednesday night in the spring of 1991. There were stringed lights underneath the huge white tent that made the darkness outside seem almost blinding. Underneath the tent, however, the stringed lights gave off a warm, welcoming glow. Brother Brown's truck's flatbed trailer served as the stage, which was raised about three feet high. On each side of the stage were plywood ramps that sloped to the ground. An upright organ sat to the left of the stage, where Brother Brown's music minister played deeply soulful renditions of old Pentecostal favorites like "I'll Fly Away." As Kelli and I took our seats that night with about one hundred of our fellow worshippers, I bathed in the music minister's virtuoso organ playing. *If I had this guy traveling with me,* I said to myself, *I'd really be in business.* At the very center of the stage were two folding chairs reserved for Brother Brown and Brother McManus of Sugartown United Pentecostal, the church sponsoring the revival. Just before the revival began, I thought about how after being raised attending church in a claustrophobic building, it just seemed unnatural to be sitting and waiting for services to begin on a folding chair with my feet in the grass. Brother Brown's tent revival was certainly nothing like the church I knew–it was like attending a carnival or a fair. But its unfamiliarity masked a spiritual core that I could very much relate to. With the music radiating out of the tent into the night and the PA cranked up so loud that the messages of its speakers could reach not just attendees but passersby, I felt as though the Holy Ghost would literally penetrate the cars as they drove by. When Brother Brown finally took his seat on the stage just after eight o'clock, the music reached a crescendo with the attendees singing the chorus of "I'll Fly Away"–"I'll fly away, Oh Glory / I'll fly away / When I die, Hallelujah, by and by / I'll fly away (I'll fly away)"–over and over until they just totally lost their inhibitions and rose from their folding chairs to jump, dance and sing. The music then quieted and Brother Brown rose from his folding chair, stood at the pulpit and delivered a thunderous message in his deep baritone voice about overcoming the adversary. In Brother Brown's telling we were all like the heroes of war stories from the Old Testament like David and Joshua. Our enemies in life, Brother Brown said, were the Canaanites and we, like Joshua's conquering of the Canaanites in the battle of Jericho–"And it came to pass at the seventh time, when the priests blew with the trumpets, Joshua said unto the people, Shout; for the Lord hath given you the city"(Joshua 6:16)–would vanquish our enemies. Brother Brown's message was the very essence of Pentecostalism, a message of deliverance after struggle. In the Pentecostal worldview the enemy was poverty, unpaid bills, the bank calling in the note on your house or your car, your boss giving you a hard time or even your child's illness. So the promise of deliverance over the enemy was profoundly appealing to the Pentecostal faithful who are almost always poor, from-across-the-tracks people.

With Brother Brown's message complete, he moved toward the crowd to minister to them individually. As he stood waiting on the stage, a prayer line of dozens of Pentecostals formed in hopes that Brother Brown would anoint them with oil. As the line moved, Brother Brown put his hands on the heads of the congregants and shook and moved them physically as he bellowed, "Bring that sick child forward! Bring that empty wallet to me!" When Brother Brown wasn't ministering he offered piercingly direct prophesies to the faithful. "Thus Sayeth the Lord," he said, "my child, I the Lord speak to thee this evening and I say to thee that the way thus far has been hard and the journey has been long. But through my mouthpiece I say to thee, my child, that the change you have sought is at hand. I have heard your cries! My heart has been moved and my spirit of power and deliverance is about to move into your life like a wave crashing against the shore." I just stood in awe of Brother Brown and his ability to channel the Holy Ghost and to so deeply tap into the hopes, fears and struggles of his impoverished congregants.

I also savored the feeling of being so connected to the history of my home state through the tent revival. *Out here in the tent,* I thought, *we're not only connecting to God, we're also connecting to political giants.* This very medium–speaking to the poor outside of traditional venues like a church or a statehouse–has been present throughout Louisiana history, most notably in Huey P. Long's second and successful gubernatorial campaign in Louisiana in 1928 in which he famously made six hundred speeches across the state, mostly to poor people and from the most unvarnished of places, like standing atop a car.

When Kelli and I arrived back at my grandmother's home that night, I felt spiritually nourished in a way that I'd not experienced in my own career as a preacher. The schizophrenic dichotomy of sky-high anticipation followed by brutal disappointment that I'd felt while struggling to make my way in the revival circuit had left me exhausted and feeling less connected to God. How could I make God a reality in my everyday life, much less in the everyday lives of others, if I was unable to preach God's message? It seemed that God had put one hurdle after another in front of me–the deaths of my father and grandfather, failure in the business of preaching, grinding poverty–and that deliverance was far out of reach. During the fall of 1991, my anguish over my life's many failures became so profound that when Kelli delivered the greatest of news–she was pregnant with our first child–I could only stammer a response that conveyed little in the way of love and much about my anxiety over our future. "Really?" I said as Kelli walked into the bedroom from the bathroom where she had taken the pregnancy test. *"Are you sure?"* From the perplexed frown on Kelli's face I could tell that I hadn't displayed the exuberance she expected, craved and *needed*–and for a young wife who endured my single-mindedness about my mission to the detriment of our marriage, deserved.

As winter approached, Kelli insisted that we find a place of our own before the baby arrived. So we turned to family for help and, within weeks, we had an offer of housing. Kelli's brother Mark had asked his in-laws if we could have their old trailer and they happily acquiesced to the request. It was a well-worn, early 1970s model mobile home with an ugly combination of tan and dark-brown accents on the exterior and a rusty orange carpet and bright-green fixtures on the interior. Worse, its plumbing in the master bath was broken so we'd have to use a guest bathroom. But its price tag—two thousand dollars—was well within our reach. And for once, fortune smiled upon us: just as we were offered the trailer, my father-in-law donated an acre of land in Pitkin to Kelli and me. The only real hurdle in making the trailer our first home together as a married couple was its location: Cravens, Louisiana, just seven miles away from Pitkin, but a distance that required that we hire a tractor driver to move the trailer for us. So I turned to Brother Brown, who had an infinite fleet of trucks and trailers at his disposal, for help and he offered to pull the mobile home for us from his hulking Bobcat tractor. Even more blessedly, when Brother Brown arrived in Cravens for the job he found that the mobile home's tires were flat—the unit had been left lying in a watermelon patch—and he donated a set of new tires to us. Once the mobile home was back in Pitkin, I bought the biggest window air-conditioning unit that I could and slid a huge couch under it. From that moment on, it was the only place in the trailer that was cool.

Life at the mobile home provided Kelli not only a desperately needed sense of independence, it literally saved our marriage. I had no doubt that Kelli wouldn't have made it through yet another winter at my grandmother's house. But the trailer's state of deep disrepair made it far from a comfortable first home. Soon after we moved in in the late winter of 1991, we discovered that there was no septic tank on the property and, unable to afford to purchase one, we ran the plumbing into the woods. Finding work, whether secular or spiritual, was still ferociously difficult. Revival work remained spotty and the string of menial part-time jobs I'd found provided little in the way of income. With the imminent arrival of my firstborn, I sought to become more serious in my pursuit of a day job. Because of my experience making cold calls to book revivals, I decided to pursue a job in sales and quickly found a job at

Magnolia Life Insurance selling whole life insurance. It was the key product for Magnolia yet I wasn't an enthusiastic salesman. I believed that whole life–so named because it is a policy that remains in force for the insured's whole life and requires premiums to be paid every year into the policy–was inferior to term life, which provides the insured coverage at a fixed rate of payments for a limited period of time. After the expiration of the term, coverage is no longer guaranteed and the insured either loses coverage entirely or obtains new coverage with different payments or conditions. Term life is deemed a riskier product because of the set term it provides for the insured–and the lack of insurance when that term expires. But I thought that the lower monthly payments of term life made financial sense for most folks in our area. I subscribed to the philosophy of the late billionaire insurance guru Arthur L. Williams who said, "Buy term and invest the difference."

To most salesmen, whether they're selling cars, life insurance or Amway, preference for one product over another is immaterial. A sale is a sale, after all. But to me, of course, I had to *believe* in the product. I was a strong and passionate advocate of term life insurance because of the early deaths of my father and grandfather, who, when they passed, hadn't left nearly enough for the loved ones they had left behind. It was an oversight that had huge, life-altering ramifications for our families because a term-life payout could have relieved all of their financial burdens.

I feared that I could never believe in the whole-life product enough to truly be successful selling it. So day-to-day life at Magnolia Life unfolded in a manner that mirrored my days and nights spent on the phone trying to book revivals. It was the same, sad cycle that I'd grown accustomed to of cold-calling, constant rejection and then the inevitable, desperate follow-up calls. As I relentlessly worked the phones pitching whole-life insurance to skeptical customers on the other end of the line, I fretted constantly about what a rejected sales pitch meant to my finances or, conversely, what a sale or two might do to help Kelli and me pay our bills. By the late spring of 1992, I was making about fifteen hundred dollars a month at Magnolia Life, which at first just seemed like a whole world of wealth. But even with the steady salary, somehow Kelli and I were always at the end of our grace period on the light bill or on the note on the mobile home. We'd lived with nothing for so long and had dug such a huge, almost insurmountable financial hole for ourselves that when my biweekly paycheck came it was like a storm in a drought-stricken land. The rainfall is sustaining at first but because it has been so long without rain, the water is immediately absorbed and the land is quickly bone dry once again.

Just before dawn on June 24, 1992, a new and better day seemed to have arrived. Our son was overdue and that morning, Kelli's doctor called to tell her to come down to the hospital to get induced. After packing an extra set of clothes, Kelli and I made the forty-five-mile trip from Pitkin to the Women's and Children's Hospital in Alexandria, Louisiana. It was just after five o'clock when we checked in and, about an hour later, the doctors began to induce labor. But as the hours ground on there was no progress with Kelli's labor. A check of the baby then revealed that the umbilical cord was wrapped around his neck not once but twice. The doctor said that the baby had gotten so wrapped up because Kelli's water had broken three days earlier; we were so young and naïve we hadn't even been aware of that birthing milestone. To help Kelli along, a heavyset African American nurse literally got on top of Kelli and began pushing on her stomach as I stood by Kelli's head to support her. Kelli's obstetrician, meanwhile, stood in front of the stirrups near Kelli's open legs. Then, just moments after the nurse began her heavy pushing, Kelli's doctor turned to me and said, "Mr. DeWitt, would you like to come and witness your son's birth?" I was clamoring to be the first person to welcome my son into the world so I eagerly joined the obstetrician by the stirrups. As my son was slowly pushed out of the womb, however, I was wracked with fear at the near-oceanic amount of blood pouring from Kelli. *Kelli is going to die,* I thought. *She is not going to survive this experience.* But as my anxieties hit a near unbearable peak, my son was born. In order to unravel the umbilical cord that had wound so tightly around his neck, the obstetrician turned him in his hands like a punter rotating a football. And then the doctor turned my son toward me. "Welcome, Paul!" I cried. The arrival of my son, who was named after Paw-Paw, had huge, life-affirming significance coming so soon after the loss of my grandfather. I was simply overcome with joy to have him in my world.

That Kelli and the baby were healthy–so healthy in fact that she was discharged from the hospital the next day–brought me an immeasurable sense of joy, pride and a hope for a future that might be far brighter than our past. But as I brought Kelli out of the Women's and Children's Hospital in a wheelchair that morning, she told me that she had arranged with her brother Mark to take her home in *his* car. The air conditioning in the old Buick LeSabre that my mom donated to us had given out and Kelli wanted Mark to drive her and the baby home. Kelli's decision felt like a huge betrayal–how could I not be the one to drive my wife and baby home?–but my sadness was mixed with a burning anger at my dismal financial condition. *How long will this fucking poverty continue?* I cried to myself as Kelli sat next to me in the wheelchair rocking Paul. At that moment it seemed that all of my problems in life stemmed from money. I wasn't bringing home enough money to even have proper plumbing in our mobile home; my inability to get the air conditioning in our beat-up LeSabre meant that I'd have to miss out on a huge life milestone, bringing my firstborn home for the first time.

After solemnly following Kelli and Mark home, Kelli and I settled into our mobile home with Paul and, for the moment at least, I felt a sense of bliss and satisfaction that I'd never experienced before in my entire life. When Paul slept between us in bed it was absolute heaven. But with the responsibility of taking care of Paul came even more reminders of just how unsuccessful I was in my career. We were feeding Paul off WIC, the federal government's

Special Supplemental Nutrition Program for Women, Infants and Children. We had a home health care nurse funded by a state-run program that assisted low-income parents. There was no doubt about it: Kelli and I were lying at the very bottom of the social safety net. Where we couldn't get assistance from the state or federal government, we turned to our families: Paul's clothes were provided by my parents and my in-laws. I felt like it was WIC and our families, not me, raising Paul. I seethed at myself. I just couldn't get my crap together, I couldn't catch a break, I couldn't find a niche. And, as young parents, Kelli I were overwhelmed by every episode of teething, stomachache and colic from Paul. We lived in fear that something terrible was going to happen to Paul and that we'd have no idea how to help when that terrible something happened.

Late at night, long after Kelli went to bed, I'd pace the floor of the mobile home with Paul in my arms, praying for him and his health, and praying to God to have mercy on us all. Just before dawn one morning, I prayed quietly as I cradled Paul. My thoughts drifted to the death of my father and then my grandfather and our life of quiet desperation in the trailer. I felt as though I was living out the saddest country music song ever. I was just waiting for the next horrific thing to happen and, worse, that my suffering stemmed from my inability to dedicate myself fully enough to God. My insufficient level of devotion, I believed, was going to lead to God fully withdrawing his protection from me, thus causing further tragedies to occur. I viewed the notion of God's withdrawal from my life with absolute terror–it seemed much like my grandfather dying from my inability to perform CPR properly on him. The cruel cycle at work seemed apparent: if God was not real in my life twenty-four hours a day, seven days per week, than I was not devoted enough. And if I was not devoted enough to God then God would not protect Kelli, Paul and me and we would *all* suffer as a result. The realization that my insufficient devotion was wreaking such havoc on all of our lives led me to an intense moment of prayer. *God,* I prayed, *guide me, lead me, forgive me for not figuring out how to be completely devoted to you.* As I prayed in the mobile home early that morning, a vision arrived. It did not come with the clarity of the earlier visions about Jesus or my grandfather but I did see Paul, as a healthy teenager, running through a yard of almost ebulliently green, fresh-cut grass. It was God telling me that Paul was going to survive. Through the vision, God was saying that the struggles of childrearing would soon pass and Paul, despite our inexperience as parents, would be okay in the end. That was enough for me. I finally had hope that everything was going to work out with Paul.

The predawn prayer that led to a vision of health for my son momentarily calmed my fears. But it also forced me to redouble my efforts to demonstrate my absolute, unsparing devotion to God. So I quickly transformed the broken master bathroom in the mobile home—which I viewed as yet another symbol of my financial failure—into a prayer closet, a private space for worship inspired by Matthew 6:6: "But thou, when thou prayest, enter into thy closet, and when thou hast shut thy door, pray to thy Father which is in secret; and thy Father which seeth in secret shall reward thee openly." Because Kelli and I had been using the bathroom as a storage closet, I moved our balky, brown-cardboard moving boxes to the opposite side of the bathroom in order to make an open space in the middle for myself. Building the prayer closet was so critical for me because I felt besieged with everyday problems that were pulling and chipping away at my devotion. These troubles were so significant—revivals were scarce and I was consumed with both the responsibility of caring for my son and for the crushing disappointment that I could not properly support him or my wife—that I considered taking a full-time job and abandoning the ministry altogether. But the more I wrestled with my worldly struggles, the deeper my devotion went, a devotion that I believed would reveal the secret formula of experiencing God in the most personal way possible.

Redemption, however, didn't arrive in the prayer closet in our mobile home. During the early fall of 1992, Brother Herrington of Fullerton Pentecostal loaned me cassettes of a Pentecostal preaching series called *The Fourth Dimension*. The central theme of these sermons–the importance of walking more devoutly with God–completely hit home with me. In *The Fourth Dimension*, preachers urged Pentecostals to adopt a fanatical devotion; they instructed, for instance, that when you're in the midst of a fast you should refrain from brushing your teeth because most toothpaste has flavoring and thus flesh is reenergized by the flavor from the toothpaste. Brush your teeth with baking soda, they urged, and you will screw your devotion to God tighter and tighter like a screwdriver to a screw. If being a Pentecostal is like setting your spiritual oven at 400 degrees–the preachers of *The Fourth Dimension* series sought to ratchet up the temperature to 425.

At the same time, I began to drift back toward Brother Lloyd's teachings to me as a teenager about William M. Branham, a Kentucky-bred preacher who gained enormous popularity among Pentecostals in the 1950s and 1960s because of his healing-driven revivals. Back then, Branham insisted he was the Elijah promised in Malachi 4:5–6–"Behold, I will send you Elijah the prophet before the coming of the great and dreadful day of the Lord: And he shall turn the heart of the fathers to the children, and the heart of the children to their fathers, lest I come and smite the earth with a curse"–and many Pentecostals believed him. When I was preaching at Brother Lloyd's church in my late teens, he told me a story about a Branham's healing revival that certainly supported the notion that Branham was prophetic. Brother Lloyd explained that in the early 1960s he and his wife, Sister Lucille, struggled to have children. Believing that they would forever be childless, they set off from Evans to Shreveport to attend one of Brother Branham's tent meetings. Just before the service began, Brother Branham's staff handed out numbered cards to all of the participants. When the service ended, Brother Branham called out the numbers. "Let me have numbers fifty through seventy-five," Brother Branham proclaimed. The attendees who had the corresponding cards in their hands formed in line in front of the stage and Brother Branham, operating in the gifts of the spirit, diagnosed their problems. "Don't take a card," Brother Lloyd told Sister Lucille. "Leave it for those who are sick." The staff member who handed out the cards, however, scolded Brother Lloyd. "You let her have that card," she said angrily, wagging her finger at Brother Lloyd. "You just don't know if Brother Branham is going to call her number." Sure enough, when Brother Branham called out the numbers fifty through seventy-five Sister Lucille was fortunate enough to be in that number. Sister Lucille then lined up by the stage and when her number was finally called, she stood at the pulpit facing Brother Branham. "This is a matter between a man and a woman," Brother Branham said as he eyed Sister Lucille in the midst of a sort of spiritual diagnosis. "You shall conceive the child you desire in one year's time." Just as Brother Branham prophesied, Brother Lloyd and Sister Lucille soon had Donald Lloyd, their firstborn, months later.

The story of Brother Branham's revival floored me and sent me on a frantic search for tapes of his messages. Fortunately, in 1981 Brother Branham's son Joseph started a company called Voice of God Recordings that distributed Brother Branham's recordings of his father's sermons, much of it free of charge. The tapes were eagerly passed among the faithful and soon after Brother Lloyd had told me about Branham, Jerry Craft, the father of my then-girlfriend Kristi Craft, gave me a Branham tape. I'll never forget listening to a Branham tape for the first time: I was seventeen and was on a riding mower at my grandfather's, mowing his lawn. I had the Branham tape in my Walkman and I listened, totally engrossed, as Brother Branham preached about the doctrine of annihilation, which asserted that there is no eternal hell. People who are not saved, Brother Branham preached, were just *winked* out of existence. Because I had such a strong dilemma at the time about those who were not saved going to hell–I couldn't reconcile the idea that a God who loves everybody also sent people to hell—Brother Branham's doctrine of annihilation completely resonated with me.

So as I prayed in my makeshift prayer closet in a broken-down bathroom in our mobile home in Pitkin, I suddenly realized that there was no greater example of a man becoming closer to God than Brother Branham. Perhaps, I thought then, by following in Brother Branham's footsteps I could get out from under the weight of my worldly troubles and move closer to my goal of bringing God into everyday life.

> *But in the days of the voice of the seventh angel, when he shall begin to sound, the mystery of God should be finished, as he hath declared to his servants the prophets.*
>
> **—Revelation 10:7**

In the months after I made my desperate pleas to God from my prayer closet in Pitkin, I plunged into my study of Brother Branham's messages with the ferocious passion that approached my earliest and most enthusiastic revivals. I read dozens of transcripts of Brother Branham's sermons in so-called message books, which were published by Voice of God Recordings; transcripts that didn't just capture his words but every pause, every "uh" and "ah," every stutter in his speech. Like the Branhamites, I had come to believe that Brother Branham walked so closely with God that God was speaking directly *through* him. So every word and utterance from Brother Branham mattered and his messages were not just oratory—because of Brother Branham's closeness with God whatever he preached would actually come to pass.

One message—"The Spoken Word Is the Original Seed" preached by Brother Branham on March 18, 1962, in Jeffersonville, Indiana—made a sledgehammerlike impact on my faith with its emphasis on the importance of revival and the eternal truth of God's word. "Now, this Word of God," Branham said, "is eternal. God, being infinite, cannot speak one thing and then later on change it to something else, to a better decision, because *every* decision of God is perfect. Once His Word is once spoken, It can never die. It lives on, on, on, and can never die, because It is God. His Word can no more die than He can die." Brother Branham then paused and quoted John 1:1 and John 1:14: "In the beginning was the Word, and the Word was with God, and the Word was God . . . And the Word was made flesh, and dwelt among us (and we beheld his glory, the glory as of the only begotten of the Father), full of grace and truth."

That very same word, Brother Branham preached, "that was spoken in the beginning with His eternal purpose came on over and was made flesh and dwelt among us: God's Word." Of revivals, Brother Branham proclaimed that "each revival has its own revival—each generation has its revival. God raises Him up a man, sets him with His Word, and starts him out for the message for that age." I loved the way in which Brother Branham detailed a sort of spiritual chain of command. God delivers his word to man and then man, though the medium of the revival, delivers a message to the faithful, a message specific to the age in which he lived. This is exactly what I had been trying to do in my small, sputtering career as an evangelist: walk closely with God and deliver his word through revival.

Through Brother Branham's messages I believed that he had a relationship with God in which he was not just God's mouthpiece but godlike; the very words of God and Brother Branham were interchangeable. Brother Branham's words were his words and his words were Brother Branham's. I also insisted that the powers of healing demonstrated in Brother Branham's healing-driven revivals were so profound that if I ever attained his level of devotion to God, I could minister to amputees, pray to God to restore their limbs and God would heed my prayers because I was living so closely with Him. My embrace of Brother Branham's teachings seemed to me to be the next logical step in my quest to realize the deepest of possible to devotion to God and I sought to find a way for God to use me in the same way he used Brother Branham.

During the late fall of 1992, as I tried to reach a Branham-like devotion to God in my prayer closet through listening to cassette tapes of his messages and poring over sermon transcripts, I realized that Brother Branham had mentioned a pastor named Pearry Green in several of his messages. Curious about the name, I then found a cassette of one of Brother Green's messages, which was delivered at the dedication of his church, Tucson Tabernacle. *If Brother Green is still living and if he's accessible to an outsider like me,* I thought, *then he could teach me how to walk with God in the way that Brother Branham did.* So this time I turned not to God but to a more worldly place: 411. I called information and asked for the number to Tucson Tabernacle. When the telephone operator connected me to the church, I asked if Brother Green was in. My call was transferred to his office and, to my amazement, Brother Green himself picked up the phone. After introducing myself as Brother DeWitt, a young Pentecostal preacher from Louisiana, I gushed enthusiastically to Brother Green that I had been fanatically listening to the cassette tapes of Brother Branham's messages, seeking to understand their doctrine and his devotion. Brother Green seemed taken aback by the devotion to Branhamite doctrine by a complete stranger. "It's amazing," Brother Green told me, "that you've never even attended any of our services yet you're engaged in such deep study of our messages." To Brother Green, however, my outsider's embrace of Brother Branham wasn't less worthy than that of his followers; in fact, quite the opposite. Brother Green told me that I possessed a more pure interpretation of Branhamite doctrine because I had not been influenced by the factions of Branhamites that had emerged since Brother Branham's death in a car accident near Friona, Texas, in 1965. "A Christmas convention hosted by our church is coming up," Brother Green said, "and there will be believers flying in from all over the world to attend. Would you be willing to fly out here to preach?" Without any hesitation, I said that I would.

In the early morning hours of Thursday, December 24, 1992, I flew out of Lake Charles, Louisiana, on a Continental Airlines flight bound for Houston, Texas. There I'd pick up a connecting flight to Tucson. It was to be my first flight on a commercial airline–I'd never been able to afford an airline ticket, and this trip was paid for by Brother Green–so I was clueless about air travel. The flight from Houston to Tucson is a little over two hours but I thought that it was less than one hour because my ticket had me landing in Tucson one hour after the Houston departure. I didn't realize that the arrival time reflected the two-hour time difference between Louisiana and Arizona. When I arrived in Houston after the first leg of the flight, the scene at the airport was so crowded and chaotic that I was sure I was going to end up being stranded or miss the connection. To me, the frenzied atmosphere at this huge international airport appeared to be what the UN must look like when delegates from all over the world clamored over a vote. I felt like I needed a translator for the reality surrounding me. It seemed so otherworldly, I don't think I could have felt more out of place if I'd been on an adventure to Mars. Fortunately, I made the connecting flight and, during the two-and-a-half-hour trip, marveled from my window seat at the vastness of the orange-and-brown desert below, a landscape that I'd never seen. But as we made the descent into Tucson I was terrified: it felt as though the plane was slowing to the point where we would simply stall out and drop from the sky.

After deplaning and picking up my luggage at Tucson International Airport, Brother Green met me outside the baggage claim in an old Cadillac. Brother Green was tall, dark haired and broad shouldered like a football player, and with his thick glasses he had the look of a sort of swollen Clark Kent. As we drove off from the airport, Brother Green told me that he had some pastoral business to attend to before heading over to Tucson Tabernacle. That afternoon, as we scooted around town in his Cadillac, I was just a tagalong. But I savored the dry southwestern air, which came as a huge relief after the wet and humid atmosphere in Louisiana, which often wreaked havoc on my allergies. Just before sundown, we stopped at a house in a busy, cramped Tucson subdivision. The home's corrugated metal walls resembled a shack in a Mexican village, an odd and completely new sight to me. When Brother Green and I walked into a back room in the home, things just got stranger. Brother Green spoke in a hush-hush, almost indecipherable manner with the resident of the home, a short, balding, middle-aged man. I felt like the two men were purposefully being unspecific and I was further confused by their constant references to a globe, which had pins sticking out of it, sitting on a workbench. As the conversation progressed, it seemed as though every so often Brother Green would throw me a bone as to what he was talking about. Then I realized that the two men were discussing the documentation of UFO visitations; the resident of the home was tracking UFOs and had marked such visits on the globe with the stick of a pin. He told Brother Green that he was trying to make a correlation between UFO sightings and angels; perhaps, he said, UFO sightings *were* angels. He then insisted to Brother Green that the increasing number of sightings meant that we were nearing the end times. I was stunned into silence by the exchange; the mountainous terra firma of Tucson was alien to me but this conversation was truly otherworldly.

As the sun set, Brother Green and I piled back into his Cadillac and headed back into the center of the city. After the bizarre exchange in the subdivision, I was made more at ease with Brother Green thanks to the stream of personal stories he told about Brother Branham. Brother Green told me that Brother Branham had affixed a crucifix to the rearview mirror of his vehicle, which he said was meant to refocus his attention on Christ whenever he spied attractive women on the sidewalk. With dinnertime approaching, Brother Green suggested that we eat at a local barbeque restaurant and when we entered the place, I was thrilled by its quintessentially southwestern-looking wood walls and booths. "Brother DeWitt," Brother Green said between mouthfuls of pulled pork, "what are some of the things that we do in our following of Brother Branham that trouble you?" I was forthright in my answer. "Well," I began, "in your songs you sing about Brother Branham." What I meant by this criticism was that I thought it was inappropriate to sing of Brother Branham and not of Jesus. "In your Pentecostal songs," Brother Green retorted, "don't you sing about the apostle Paul and the apostle Peter?" "Yes, we do," I shot back. "Well, Brother DeWitt," Brother Green continued sternly, "we feel that Branham is on the same level as Paul and Peter." I allowed the debate to end there—I was Brother Green's guest, after all—and after we cleaned our plates, Brother Green rose from the table and told me that he'd get the bill. "I need to use the bathroom before we head out of here," Brother Green said as he took a toothpick from beside the cash register. "Let's just meet by the long bench out front." I thanked Brother Green for his generosity and took a seat on the bench. After waiting for what seemed like hours, I worriedly wondered if he'd simply left and I'd have to make it to Tucson Tabernacle on my own. But then Brother Green emerged from the bathroom. After acknowledging his absence with a smirk, he turned to me and said, "Brother Jerry, there's gonna come a time when a good bowel movement is better than the best sex of your life."

From the restaurant we made our way to Brother Green's Tucson home, which had all the grandiosity of an estate because there were several homes along its long, winding driveway occupied by his immediate family. Brother Green's home itself was a 1970s-style ranch home that appeared dated at first—a disco ball hanging from the ceiling wouldn't have been out of place—but because it was so well maintained it seemed as though it could have been built yesterday. There was an enormous stone fireplace in the living room, a massive structure complemented by a long, rectangular 1970s-style couch. Despite the imposing layout of the living room, there was a warmth to the house that immediately made me feel at home. I was further put at ease when Brother Green told me about his wife who was from Ferriday, Louisiana, the same community where Swaggart was raised. Brother Green then reeled off a great story about Brother Branham's belief that Swaggart, Jerry Lee Lewis and Mickey Gilley (Swaggart's country music–star cousin) were all born under the same musical sign and that their incredible gifts were the result of that sign. Sister Green, he explained, was also born under that same musical sign, a celestial alignment that meant that she, too, could play a mean piano. As we laughed and talked about Swaggart and Sister Green, Brother Green warily eyed my worn, rumpled suit jacket and pulled a loose thread sticking out the suit's shoulder. "Don't pull it loose," I nervously stammered, only half joking. "It may come apart." Brother Green looked at me empathetically. "If it does," he said soothingly, "I'll give you my jacket." "If you do," I shot back, "I'll make two suits out of it." Then he looked down at my feet and joked about my small size, "What size shoe do you wear?" I meekly replied, "Seven and a half." "Out of all the missionaries," Brother Green continued, "no one has feet as small as yours. But that's okay. Help is on the way."

Because it was getting late, Brother Green decided that it was time to bring me to the evangelist's quarters at Tucson Tabernacle. The church, located at 2555 North Stone Avenue in downtown Tucson, was an imposing, modern brown-brick structure with tall, swaying palm trees out front. As we passed through the church, I breathlessly took in its high ceilings and dozens of rows of pews, which could accommodate hundreds of worshippers. It was a world of worship unto itself; the church even had its very own bookstore. I was, however, a little disconcerted by the sheer number of photographs and portraits of Brother Branham that adorned the church's walls. *These people,* I said to myself, *have given themselves over completely to idolatry.* After we reached the second floor of the church, Brother Green led me to a closet–the back wall of the closet was a door that opened up to the evangelist's quarters. It was almost like a safe room. The evangelist's quarters were just as strange as the entryway. In the bedroom were mounts of animals that Brother Branham had slain; on the ceiling above the bed was the head of a wild boar. Its tusks protruded so far downward that it looked like they could spear a guest sleeping on the bed. I had difficulty sleeping that night because the light of the moon illuminated the boar tusks, which seemed to bear straight down upon me.

I rose early the next day and was greeted by a tour bus outside the church filled with eager Branhamites. Brother Green ushered me to the bus and explained that the day would be spent touring Brother Branham's home and the nearby mountains. As I climbed aboard the bus, I even thought, *These people are a little delusional.* I didn't have any doubt that the miracles attributed to Brother Branham were true. But I was in Tucson to learn *how* to repeat those miracles and not to worship Brother Branham. I just couldn't accept the Branhamites' devotion to Branham, which I believed was far better directed toward God. And I couldn't swallow the notion that Branham was the last prophet or the seventh angel.

Our first stop, Branham's house, only bolstered my skepticism about the Branhamites. The home, on Ina Road and First Avenue in Tucson, was a modest, modern ranch home made of tan brick with large windows out front. It was an unremarkable home yet on the front door Brother Branham had carved wildly elaborate symbols that were expressive of his ministry. At the door's center was a pyramid–Brother Branham believed that the pyramid represented the multifaceted nature of the Godhead. To Branham, the Godhead–Father, Son, Holy Ghost–were all different sides but were still one, just like the pyramid. Above the pyramid was an eagle clutching a long, swooping sword in its claws. The sword represented the word of God and the eagle was God's servant who flew so high that he could see the world from God's point of view. On the inside of the front door Brother Branham had carved out the continents he'd visited. After entering the home, we were led into the den and its walls were covered with hunting mounts–a deer head from a deer Branham nicknamed "Big Jim," rams, wild boar, goats, rainbow trout–as well as Brother Branham's collection of long hunting rifles. In one corner of the den there was a wall of cassette tapes featuring his messages while in another corner, on the floor, was a waterfall and miniature pond. To me, the den wasn't inspiring–it reminded me of the Jungle Room at Graceland. The tour felt like a Brother Branham theme park and the devotion to a *man* displayed there was wildly inappropriate.

As we toured Brother Branham's home, I was made even more uneasy when I talked with Brother Green about the divisions between the Branhamites that had arisen since Branham's passing in the mid-1960s. Brother Green considered himself to be a moderate in his views about Brother Branham–he felt as if his unfulfilled prophesies would come about naturally; so naturally in fact, that one might not even realize they were being fulfilled. A prophecy, Brother Green explained, could be realized through what seemed like a normal chain of events. Brother Green, like me, had faith that the ministry could bring about a worldwide revival. A separate, opposing faction of the Branhamites was far more radical in its beliefs: they insisted that Brother Branham would rise from the dead and then evangelize throughout the world, thus creating a worldwide revival. So fervent were these Branhamites in their worldview that they believed Brother Branham's resurrection was the *sole* path to a worldwide revival. Indeed, Brother Green told me that a wealthy Branhamite in Tucson purchased a private plane and stored it in a secret location so that it could be utilized by Brother Branham to preach around the globe after he rose from the dead.

When the tour of the Branham home wound down, we all climbed back onto the tour bus and traveled to Sabino Canyon in the Santa Catalina Mountains just north of Tucson. The Santa

Catalina Mountains, formed millions of years ago, dramatically rise to over nine thousand feet and Sabino Canyon sits between gorgeous, sloping mountains that are dotted by mesquite brush and tall cactus trees. The tour bus came to a stop at a campsite near a dramatic rock face where Brother Branham said that he had been visited by God. According to Brother Branham, these visits from the "Angel of the Lord," another phrase for Holy Ghost, came in a whirlwind, like a tornado. The friction from the great wind propelled by the Angel of the Lord caused the tops of trees to be sliced off and triangle-shaped pieces of rock to be torn out from the rock face, which were thrown across the nearby desert landscape. As we stood at the campsite, Brother Green told us that our mission was to find these triangle-shaped rocks; if we discovered these special rocks, Brother Green explained, it would serve as confirmation that the Angel of the Lord had visited Brother Branham there. Listening to Brother Green's story about Brother Branham and the Angel of the Lord, I didn't doubt that Branham had experienced these very things at this very place. Instead, I doubted myself: Was I called to the level of ministry that Brother Branham had achieved during his lifetime? Then, standing on the rocky, sandy terra firma, I prayed to God. *If Brother Branham had been visited by the Angel of the Lord,* I prayed, *then let me find one of these rocks.* My prayer, in turn, sent a stark, sharp feeling of guilt through me. Was it a form of idolatry to value a piece of rock with such intensity? Unable to answer that question, I decided that if I found a rock I wouldn't hold on to it in an idolatrous manner–I'd just give it away to a fellow Branhamite.

That afternoon, I set off in search of a triangle-shaped rock. At first, I scoured the area surrounding the campsite and then moved several hundred yards away to a nearby creek bed. As I searched for the rock, I saw Branhamites from the bus milling around the campsite searching for the rocks, also seemingly without any success. So I refocused my energies on the creek bed, which was sprawling and dry; it seemed that there was nothing but millions of rocks below me. *How in the world is anyone supposed to find these rocks?*

I thought to myself. Coming from Louisiana, where the creeks had soft, muddy bottoms, the rocks of Sabino Canyon seemed as numerous and limitless as stars in the sky. But I pushed forward and crawled slowly up the creek bed, which was about four feet high and had a forty-five-degree slope. Near the top of the creek bed I felt drawn to stop and look to my right, the same magnetic feeling I felt when I encountered Brother Page's daughter-in-law at the hospital in Mobile, Alabama. There were mesquite bushes everywhere but I noticed an opening that seemed large enough to crawl through. As I neared the opening I realized just how wide the opening was–it had the width of two men–and I enthusiastically crawled through it. When I reached the opening on the other side, I got goose bumps from the top of my head to the bottom of my feet. It was the presence of the Holy Ghost, or maybe the Angel of the Lord, as the Branhamites referred to it. I looked down and next to my right foot was a black rock with a near-perfect triangle shape. I knew then that God had led me up the creek embankment and through the mesquite bushes and, despite my discomfort with the tackier aspects of the tour, everything I had come to know about Brother Branham was right and real.

I quickly hurried back through the thick cluster of mesquite bushes, stumbled down the embankment and joined the Branhamites back at the campsite. The group was stunned to see the sharp, triangular rock in my hand and I soaked in their adulation and envy. But remembering my promise to God, I ambled over to a Branhamite pastor from New York and placed the rock in his hand. I somewhat reluctantly gave up the rock but the experience was too real in my mind. There was no doubt that God had led me to that rock and I had to honor my promise to God to give up the rock. Minutes later, a young Branhamite rushed up to me holding a rock about one half-inch thick, which was triangle shaped but had rounded points, in his hands. "Brother DeWitt," he enthused, "I feel moved to give you a rock that I have found." It was yet further evidence of Brother Branham's experience in this land and of my connection with God. God had given me a rock and because I had stayed true to my word to God, I received a rock in return.

The bus ride back from Sabino Canyon to Tucson Tabernacle that afternoon was filled with excited chatter among Branhamites about our discoveries. Back at church that night, as I settled back into the evangelist's quarters I heard a knock at the door. It was Brother Green, holding a pair of black dress shoes in his hands. "Remember," Brother Green said, "when I asked you about your shoe size back at my house?" The dramatic day at Sabino Canyon eclipsed my other memories from the trip, so I had to pause for a moment to recall what he was referring to. Then I remembered: he'd joked about my small shoe size. "These shoes," Brother Green intoned dramatically, "were Brother Branham's dress shoes. I want you to wear them." I didn't know what to say; all I could do was take the shoes. As I slid them onto my feet I realized that they were far too tight a fit and when I tied the shoes I feared that I was going to snap the laces. *What do you do,* I thought, *if you break a prophet's shoestrings?* And where, I wondered, did Brother Green get the shoes anyway? As if hearing my innermost thoughts Brother Green explained that he had prepared Brother Branham's body for his funeral. He'd dressed Brother Branham in the suit retrieved from the trunk of the car involved in the Texas wreck that took Brother Branham's life. But when Brother Green brought the suit and the dress shoes to the funeral home, its director told Brother Green that he didn't dress the dead with shoes. So, Brother Green explained, he had held on to the shoes ever since. "You're the first person to come visit us with feet small enough to wear these shoes," Brother Green told me. "I want you to preach tomorrow with Brother Branham's shoes on." I was rendered speechless by Brother Green's extraordinary generosity to me, an outsider. But my encounter with relics from the Brother Branham era did not end there. After handing the dress shoes to me, Brother Green strode toward a cabinet in the evangelist's quarters and pulled out a cardboard box. He carefully opened the box and pulled out a piece of shattered windshield. The shard of glass was larger than a serving plate and it had red drops of blood spattered all over it: the very blood of Brother Branham. Brother Green explained that he had scooped the windshield from the car wreck, cleaned it up and taken possession of it and hidden it away, lest people worship it. *If you didn't want it worshipped,* I remember thinking, *why didn't you just throw it away?* The familiar feeling of discomfort that haunted me throughout the trip, that there was something idolatrous about the Branhamites, washed over me like a tide again. But I didn't betray my doubts to Brother Green. I, after all, had to preach the next day in the prophet's shoes.

The next morning I rose early, put on my suit and carefully slid on and tied Brother Branham's dress shoes so as to keep them looking as unworn as possible. When services began at Tucson Tabernacle that afternoon, its sanctuary was packed and overflowing with Branhamites from all around the world. Feeling nervous and jittery about the size of the crowd and my inexperience in the world of the Branhamites, I met with Brother Green in his office just before I took the pulpit. He whispered to me that I should not let anyone know that I was wearing Brother Branham's dress shoes. I was happy to keep the secret: the ill-fitting shoes were causing enormous pain in my feet and I was literally terrified that I was going to break the shoelaces with every step. When I returned to the sanctuary and waited to take my turn at the pulpit, I watched the surprisingly dull and lifeless services with dismay. The services didn't have the *umph,* flair or the ecstatic music of a Pentecostal revival or even a Pentecostal Sunday service. And I felt that the Branhamites were straining so hard to mimic Brother Branham's style that they ended up being just a silhouette of the man. It seemed apparent to me that my big, outsized personality behind the pulpit wasn't going to work in this setting. I'd have to restrain myself. The Branhamite church was just not going to blossom into what I wanted it to be. My fears were realized when I finally took the pulpit that afternoon and preached a message in which I scolded the congregation for being more concerned with emulating Brother Branham instead of Jesus Christ. "Instead of focusing on Brother Branham," I said, "you need to focus on Jesus. The only way to bring about a revival is to live right for God–and right now you're all living right, *but for Brother Branham.*" From the confused and angry-looking faces in the crowd, I knew that my message wasn't received well but I dug in deeper in my insistence that devotion should be directed toward God and not Brother Branham, until eventually a pall of silence was cast over the sanctuary.

Fortunately, the conclusion of my message was greeted by a smattering of polite applause. When Brother Green took me out for dinner that night he wasn't angry with me for confronting the congregants. Instead, he gently counseled me that every congregation is accustomed to the style of their pastor and that I could find success in my budding career as a preacher, even with an uncomfortable or unfamiliar message, if I observed the style of the pastor and then emulated his style on the pulpit. It was a profound, long-lasting lesson for me to learn. From then on I would watch the manner in which a pastor made an announcement, led services or got his first laugh before I took the pulpit myself. I was also encouraged that night by the presence of a youth group at dinner. As I feasted on a perfectly grilled teriyaki hamburger topped with pineapple, a radically new dish for me, I talked with the teens about their love for the messages of Brother Branham. It felt good to end the trip this way after feeling so many doubts about the Branhamites.

Early the next morning, I got on a plane heading back home to Pitkin. During the nearly three-hour trip from Tucson to Houston, I mulled over my future. It seemed to me that I had two possible paths to choose from. One was to go home, devote myself to whatever part-time job I managed to find and be content with family life. Embracing a nine-to-five life would relieve me of my agony about my evangelist career and my mission to bring God into my everyday life and the everyday lives of those to whom I preached.

I'd regain the mindset I had before I felt called to preach. I chuckled to myself as I remembered telling my high school girlfriend Joetta Foshee that all I needed from life was a singlewide mobile home and a wife and son who would meet me at my truck when I arrived back at home from work. The second path was far more difficult: I could view the pain that was inextricably attached to my mission as the price I'd have to pay in order to bring about a revival. I kicked these opposing futures for myself back and forth in my mind during both legs of the trip back home. Just before we landed in Lake Charles, I decided to take the rocky and much rougher second path. I would devote myself to seeking an even deeper level of devotion than I'd already given to God. If that meant more spiritual pain and less time and energy to my wife and family, then that was a sacrifice I was be willing to make. I had made the pilgrimage to Tucson Tabernacle in hopes that I could study with the Branhamites and return home with a clear sense of how to attain Brother Branham's profound level of devotion. To me, the trip was like heading out to Graceland to hang out with Elvis and the Memphis mafia with the idea that you didn't just want to fraternize with them at the king's mansion in Memphis—you hoped to soak up their lives and lessons so that *you* could be the next Elvis. But the Tucson trip had taught me that no one in the Branhamite movement knew how to do what Brother Branham had done in his lifetime. If I wanted to realize a profound level of devotion, I'd have to turn even further inward spiritually. I was truly on my own.

When I arrived back at our mobile home in Pitkin, however, I could not yet engage in my spiritual mission. Just before I'd left for Tucson, Kelli had come down with a nasty ear infection and while I was traveling she'd hid just how dire the infection had become. I felt like a monster for leaving Kelli in such great pain—and for leaving our son Paul for the first time—and my feelings of guilt were magnified by returning home to see her in such terrible physical shape. I rushed Kelli to the hospital and the doctors had her stay there for an entire week, a stay that failed to heal the infection.

When Kelli returned home from the hospital, my mom saw the infection and urged us to go to an ear, nose and throat specialist in Lake Charles. It was well after office hours when Kelli and I set off for Lake Charles and when we arrived at the doctor's office, an after-hours specialist saw Kelli. He told us that Kelli's condition had worsened so dramatically that she needed to undergo emergency surgery. We were sent to a doctor at Lafayette Charity Hospital who did work for low-income patients. In Lafayette, Kelli underwent two days' worth of surgery and as I waited for her to emerge from the operating room, I feared that her dangerously poor health was entirely my fault. It was my fault that I didn't know biblical doctrine the way it should be known; it was my fault that I wasn't devoted enough to God in order for God to prevent Kelli from falling ill. And I was wracked with guilt for not giving my full attention to my family. I had always felt the siren call to be somewhere else, to be more devoted to God, yet there in the waiting room at Lafayette Charity Hospital, I understood just how turbulent and traumatic the path that I'd settled on during the trip home from Tucson truly was. Yet I was not deterred. What I needed to do, I concluded, was get my doctrine straight. Any day now, I was going to stumble across that missing doctrinal piece that would help me reach that sky-high level of devotion I had sought and ached for for so long. The Holy Ghost would then fully operate through me and then the multitude of problems in my life, from health to money, would no longer afflict my family because I would have a worldwide ministry. *Any day now,* I thought, humming Elvis's beautiful, inspirational song of the same name, *the breakthrough is coming.* My sense that I'd reach the truest sense of devotion–any day now!–pacified my anguish about the responsibilities I evaded and the relationships that I had frayed. All I had to do now was wait for the next phase of my mission to begin.

For some people Hell is simply the consequences of their actions here on earth.

A person who spends every day getting drunk, will ruin their health, marriage, family and career; they will make their lives a living Hell. But that still falls far short of the chronic alcoholic being condemned by a just God to literally burn in Hell forever and ever.

For others it may very well be that the punishment merited by their sins is greater than what they receive in this life. For those people perhaps there will be some kind of punishment after death, but we believe that it will be remedial and corrective rather than just punishment for punishment's sake. Exactly what that will be and how long it will last we don't know. Will Hell for some people last 10 minutes or 10 million years . . . we don't know. But this we do know; Hell will not last for eternity; it will not be endless.

—Bishop Carlton Pearson

As 1993 dawned, I hoped that the new year would bring better health for Kelli and a greater, more pure devotion to God from me. But I wasn't engaged in the church the way I hoped to be. I was preaching only sporadically at Fullerton Pentecostal Church and my mentor there, Brother Herrington, was distracted by troubles of his own. Brother Herrington was new to the congregation and was never fully embraced by the congregants, even after he moved to Pitkin and, as a show of commitment to the area, bought a doublewide mobile home trailer on a ten-acre lot that he purchased from my in-laws. The uneasiness with Brother Herrington felt by Fullerton Pentecostal was worsened by his conflicting views with his congregants on social issues. Brother Herrington was socially stricter than the congregation was accustomed to; he was even opposed to the church youth engaging in high school sports, which he believed to be far too worldly. His extreme social conservatism seemed odd to the members of Fullerton because, personality-wise, he seemed like a mushy, wishy-washy people pleaser. Brother Herrington would have fit in a lot better with this tiny, in the woods, country church if he'd come across like a swaggering cowboy; a projection of toughness would have made his social stridency easier to swallow. Brother Herrington wasn't providing the church with the confidence it needed, and it seemed he either pushed too hard or was a pushover.

I deeply felt the growing discomfort with Brother Herrington. Yet as rumors swirled among the congregation about his departure, I, ever the faithful right-hand man, began to deliver messages with an unmistakable emphasis on the importance of supporting a man of God. "Supporting your pastor," I preached, "is a critical part of your devotion to God. And do not even *think* about talking bad about your pastor at home." With these messages I was hoping to put forward a unified front to the community in order to *save* the community; I wasn't simply looking to save Brother Herrington's job. Yet there was no backlash from the congregation to my messages, which were clear words of support for Brother Herrington. I think the lack of outcry from the congregation, who were united in their dislike of Brother Herrington, came from my insider status within the church and within the community. If the folks at Fullerton were comfortable with you, then you could say whatever you wanted to say with little fear of the consequences. Just the same, these were rugged country folks and they were going to do whatever they wanted to do regardless of what you said. So it wasn't a tolerance for dissent that made my disagreeable messages possible at Fullerton but instead a tendency to just wall out what they didn't want to hear. If the congregants viewed you with disfavor, however, it was a completely different ball game. You became like the sick chicken in the coop who gets pecked to death. That's what was happening to Brother Herrington in the early spring of 1993: he was in the process of getting slowly pecked to death by his flock at Fullerton. Soon, he would leave not just his own church but Pitkin itself–he even sold his ten-acre lot back too my brother-in-law, Mark.

As Brother Herrington was pushed out of Fullerton, Kelli and I were forced to find a new church for our family. We settled on Six Mile United Pentecostal Church on the outskirts of Pitkin. It was a typical country church for the area: a rectangular redbrick building sitting on an uncomfortably empty lot that resembled a cow pasture. During my first visit to the church, I warily eyed the dozens of tree stumps in the field adjacent to the property and thought that the entire area had fallen victim to clear-cutting. At one time, I thought, standing there alone on the ugly parcel, Six Mile was a bucolic, shaded setting. But the clear-cutting made the church appear as though it was raised in an abandoned lot. Six Mile's appearance was made even rougher and rustic by the cracked slab on which it sat. It seemed as though the entire building was about to be split in two thanks to its severely damaged foundation. And like so many of the small, country churches where I'd preached, there was no parking lot, just a cleared-away, dirt-covered area for cars. Inside Six Mile, things were just a little bit prettier: it had hazelnut wood paneling that was not nearly as brown, faded and dated looking as the paneling back at Brother Lloyd's church.

My quibbles with Six Mile's aesthetic were trivial next to my absolute love and devotion to its pastor, Brother Robertson, a tall, exceedingly slender man with an almost linear physical form, an elegance only slightly dissipated by a thin, slight comb-over on his bald head. Brother Robertson was by far the most intelligent pastor I had ever met. He was a trivia buff knowledgeable about subjects ranging from science to literature. It seemed as though there was nothing he didn't know *something* about. Brother Robertson's savvy and intelligence, however, never came off as pretentious: he was approachable and he shared information with the passion and enthusiasm of a great college professor. Brother Robertson was also a fantastic storyteller. He was marvelous at taking an Old Testament story and using it as an allegory about life and while telling his stories, he'd get out from behind the pulpit and walk out into the sanctuary in order to give his services a highly personal, intimate feel. When he preached, he displayed a commanding authority–he was *the* pastor. I called him the "prince of preachers."

But I most truly and deeply admired Brother Robertson for his devotion. Before becoming a pastor, he had worked with his father in a local logging company, a job that instilled in him an ironclad working-class work ethic that translated into a disciplelike devotion once he entered the ministry. Each and every morning, Brother Robertson would pray for three to four hours in Six Mile's sanctuary before most people even got out of bed. I made a few attempts to join him in early morning prayer but because I'm naturally a night owl, I couldn't make it through more than a handful of prayer sessions. When it came to prayer, Brother Robertson was a marathon runner and I–though I was still seeking the deepest devotion possible–was just a sprinter.

In Brother Robertson's theatrical style at the pulpit, however, I sensed the soul of an evangelist and not a pastor. He was an evangelist trapped in a pastor's career. Pastors deliver messages that exhort or strengthen the congregation or simply educate them. A pastor teaches doctrine from the Bible in order to make the congregation stronger. It's a fatherly relationship to the church. An evangelist, by contrast, is consumed with saving that next person and bringing new blood into the church community. I often compare the work of an evangelist to an addiction because one derives such ecstatic pleasure from seeing a new Christian born again that nothing else compares to that feeling. I saw the soul of an evangelist in a cousin of mine, James Edward Williamson, who pastored at an Assembly of God church, and I saw it in Brother Robertson, too.

Though Six Mile was often packed with hundreds of congregants, Brother Robertson confided in me that he had a vision of going out on the road evangelizing. In conversation it was obvious to me that Brother Robertson was waiting for his children to be old enough–he had two elementary school–age kids at the time–to evangelize again. Yet Brother Robertson knew, as I had come to understand while trying to support Kelli and Paul with occasional revivals, that the trap is always responsibility. Responsibility immobilizes. Familial responsibility brings nest building and nest tending and very few evangelists are able to raise their children on the road. I don't believe that Brother Robertson ever intended on pastoring. Indeed, I learned that before taking the pastor position at Six Mile, Brother Robertson had been evangelizing. The Six Mile congregation approached him and asked him to try out for the pastor position; out of respect for a church, an evangelist will often engage in a tryout and that's just what Brother Robertson did. Somewhat to his chagrin, I think, he got the job. By the time I began attending Six Mile, Brother Robertson had been pastoring there for about five years and, even with the passage of time, had come to feel that he was simply a steward of the church and not the owner of it. Evangelizing, after all, always called.

Soon after attending Sunday services at Six Mile, Brother Robertson allowed me to preach there. I preached a message of maturing in our relationship to Christ–that should be the goal of our devotion. But during one such message, instead of "mature" I said "manure," which just sucked all of the oxygen out of the sanctuary. I nervously looked out into the congregation and, in a sophomoric effort to save face joked, "I guess that's what I get for doing all my praying out by the pigpen." I thought that I was particularly clever for making the praying-pigpen alliteration but the church members just chuckled politely. I had the good sense to move on. As I grew more confident at Six Mile, however, I began to treat the services like a revival and would even operate in the gifts of the spirit in which I would call congregants out, divinely diagnose their illnesses or struggles and then pray for–or prophesize–to them about the how the Lord might intervene in their lives to help them solve their problems. I remember ministering to a middle-aged woman who I suspected of having an extramarital affair. I didn't address the affair directly with her but I did allude to it as I ministered to her. I told her, in front of her fellow congregants no less, that she was engaged in an inappropriate relationship. My directness–and frankly my cold-heartedness–chilled the atmosphere in the sanctuary that day. No one at Six Mile was accustomed to such a harsh, unforgiving rebuke from a minister, so I couldn't blame them for being uncomfortable with me. When services ended, I overheard Brother Robertson tell a cluster of church elders gathered around him, "I don't know what it is about these young preachers who are always operating in the gifts of the spirit." Brother Robertson didn't minister that way and, naturally, I felt like I wasn't supposed to have heard the criticism. So I slid over to Brother Robertson and joked with a nervous smile, "Well, maybe it's because our mothers microwaved our bottles."

Brother Robertson didn't mind my lame attempts at humor nor did he overtly criticize me about my style of ministry that was very much at odds with his own. He also empathized with Kelli and me about our disastrous financial condition. We were so poor and, frankly, so broke that, in the late spring of 1993, he offered to pay me two hundred dollars per month to join Six Mile as an assistant pastor. Because Brother Robertson knew that what I really wanted to do was be out on the road evangelizing, the job was essentially just a title with few responsibilities attached. All it required was traveling with him every once in a while to pray for a sick church member or deliver a message whenever I felt inspired to do so. Brother Robertson and I did end up traveling together to pray for congregants in ill health but because I had such a deep well of respect for him, it was a true privilege. We often ministered to the sick at hospitals in Alexandria, Louisiana, and on one occasion we had to pray for a middle-aged man who was stricken with a severe autoimmune disease. Brother Robertson and I had to completely suit up in hospital scrubs, masks and booties on our shoes to pray with the man. I was petrified that, even with the protection, I might catch his disease and become deathly ill. Brother Robertson must have noticed my nervousness because just before we strode into the sick man's hospital room he turned to me and said, "Brother Jerry, don't worry about it. He'll either get better or die, but either way we got services this Sunday." It may sound like a somewhat insensitive joke but it didn't feel inappropriate to me because I knew that Brother Robertson had such a great heart for people. All he was saying was, life goes on, as does our work to become as devoted to God as possible. Inside the hospital room, Brother Robertson and I stood over the sick man, who lay silent because he was connected to a maze of breathing tubes, and delivered a forceful prayer for healing. "Heavenly Father," we prayed, "we come to you in the beautiful and majestic and powerful name of Jesus. Father, you see our dear brother–your son–who has been afflicted by this illness. Father, in the mighty name of Jesus we ask you to rebuke the powers of the enemy that have taken over this earthly body. We pray that you drive out every bit of sickness and illness. Lord we ask this of you because we know that you have the ability, and the power, to make this body whole. Lord we know that you love him even more than we love him, so let your healing powers flow so that this body can be made whole in Jesus's name." The intensity of our prayers drained me. Though we visited at the hospital for about ten minutes that day, it felt like ten hours. My heart just went out to the man and my emotional, empathic pull toward him made me feel as though I had been grieving for one of my own.

As I confronted illness and death with Brother Robertson, I began to truly resolve in my mind the concept of hell. It was always back there and something I was wrestling with, but ministering to the sick brought it right back to the fore of my conscience. The idea of hell had become increasingly important to me because when I started my mission to achieve a pure devotion it was not just about acts–the act of praying for the sick, for example–but about the purity of doctrine. I sought to interpret the Bible so precisely so that I understood the teachings of the New Testament with the sophistication of the early Christian church. The revival at the beginning of the New Testament–that's the watermark I believed we needed to bring the spiritual tide back to. We had to live like an apostle and believe like an apostle. So the highest level of understanding of doctrine was key to the life of devotion I hoped to lead. And I sought to find an interpretation of doctrine that rejected the notion of eternal punishment. Because Brother Robertson and I were growing closer, thanks to my assistant pastor position at Six Mile, I thought that if I just got close enough to him then I could broach a taboo subject like eternal punishment.

But a great tragedy disrupted my plans. In the fall of 1993, Darren Holloway, a teenage member of Six Mile, was killed in a horrific car accident. Darren had been riding in a small pickup truck and his vehicle was hit by another car. His neck was broken in the impact of the accident and he died immediately. Darren was just a gorgeous child–he had a big smile and was loved and adored by everyone–and I taught him in a Sunday-school class I occasionally took over at Six Mile. For Darren it seemed that the sky truly was the limit. The night Darren died, Brother Robertson asked me to travel with him to his parents' home to deliver the bad news. We showed up at the Holloway house, a small cottage near Pitkin, very late, well past dark. Darren's parents, who were older folks who seemed almost like grandparents, answered the door. Brother Robertson gave them the news and they both just collapsed, falling to the floor. They worshipped Darren, just like we all did. Brother Robertson went back and forth between Brother and Sister Holloway, praying for them. Then, several minutes into the visit–the most heart-wrenching visit I'd ever participated in; I'd truly never seen anything more tragic–Brother Robertson began speaking in other tongues. As he spoke, we all sensed that he was going to provide interpretation. I quieted my prayer and then Brother Robertson explained, on behalf of God, that he allowed this accident to happen. Because Darren was so smart, so attractive, and loved people so much, Brother Robertson said, Darren would go to college and be led astray and face eternal punishment. The tragic car accident, Brother Robertson told a stunned Brother and Sister Holloway, prevented Darren from meeting this fate. In essence, God had killed Darren to save him. Brother Robertson's words didn't soothe the Holloways because they were in shock and so emotionally gone, but they had an earth-shattering impact on me. At first, I silently asked myself a self-centered question: *Why do I have to live with the chance of being lost?* My next response was far from a question; it was a firm judgment. *This is bullshit.* There was no denying that Brother Robertson did the best he could to provide a spiritual salve to the grief of the Holloways but he was simply pulling out the last tool in his toolbox to help these folks. I also didn't believe that God was speaking through Brother Robertson or that God had provided a ludicrous rationale for an accident that stole a young man's life. *God saved Darren by breaking his neck?* That just stretched things too far. The tragic encounter with Darren's grieving parents forced me to lift the curtain and look behind the stage of Pentecostalism. From then on, I felt that I could no longer fully participate in the Pentecostal play I felt that we were all actors in.

When I drove back home to our mobile home in Pitkin that night, I realized that Brother Robertson and I were not going to have the conversation about eternal punishment I had sought for so long. We were just not at the same place spiritually to do so. With no relief in sight, all I could do was agonize over the dilemma that had dogged me for years: I was torn between my desire to be a family man and to achieve the pure devotion possessed by the apostles. I believed that I could square the circle by becoming a perfect Christian, which would lead to a revival and a successful ministry for me. With success in hand, I could then properly care for Kelli and Paul. But I was nowhere near achieving my goals. I felt uneasy about doctrine, particularly when it came to concepts like eternal punishment, my revival work was sparse and Kelli and I were still mired in deep poverty in Pitkin. I desperately needed a breakthrough. *Take me off of this shelf,* I prayed to God that night in my prayer closet, *and use me.*

With the arrival of a new year, 1994, it seemed as though change was coming. Early that year Brother Thibodeaux, a pastor at a church in Duson, Louisiana, a small town about eighty miles from Pitkin, called Brother Robertson and asked him to preach at a revival. When Brother Robertson told Brother Thibodeaux that he couldn't make it, he recommended me to take his place. I was thrilled to get the opportunity and also happy to see Brother Thibodeaux again. He had deeply impressed me when he preached–in French, no less–at Brother Brown's tent revival back in Sugartown, and I laughed to myself when the attendees thought that the French was actually Brother Thibodeaux speaking in tongues. When I pulled up to Brother Thibodeaux's church on a chilly, early spring evening, to my disappointment it was yet another a small, rinky-dink building. I wouldn't have been surprised if it was no more than twenty feet wide and fifty feet long. I'm not sure why I always expected a grand structure whenever I arrived at revivals across the deep South. I suppose that I was hoping to find a church that matched my messiah complex. Inside, there was barely enough room for a single column of pews–it was like holding services in a Sunday-school room–and there was no stage, which intimidated me because I'm small enough physically where even a boost of a couple of feet provided a lift to my confidence.

But while the church was small and uninspiring I found Brother Thibodeaux to be smart, tough and engaging. He told me that he felt called to start a church in his own neighborhood, so he purchased this lot and quickly built the church. In the beginning, Brother Thibodeaux assumed that his congregants would be white and French speaking. But to his great surprise he soon attracted a significant following of African American Pentecostal folks from Duson. As an increasing number of African American folks began attending his services, the whites became uncomfortable and stopped attending church altogether. The white flight from church left Brother Thibodeaux, a very white guy himself who resembles Professor Farnsworth from *Futurama,* in the surreal position of pastoring a black church. It was a totally unexpected outcome but Brother Thibodeaux said he had no regrets because his congregation was so warm, loving and enthusiastic. I admired Brother Thibodeaux for his open heart and a true love of humanity all too rare in the fire-and-brimstone world of Pentecostalism. Even just moments after arriving at Brother Thibodeaux's church, it was obvious why he was so pleased with his congregation. The churchgoers treated us as if we were family. One deacon, a huge black man named Brother Chavis, even took Kelli and me under his wing.

One night after services, Brother Thibodeaux and I had a late dinner at a local Godfather's Pizza franchise. As we talked, I realized that he and I were on the very same quest of trying to find the right style of devotion while delving into the deepest doctrinal truths. In essence, we were both trying to get our doctrine straight. Brother Thibodeaux's critiques of the church also hit home with me. He felt that pastors were businessmen trying to grow their "retail stores" (their church) while evangelists were often no better than car salesmen. At one point in the conversation, which was more like venting, Brother Thibodeaux turned to me and said, "Why do I need to I go to all these revivals? What does a twenty-year-old evangelist have to tell me?" It seemed at first like a jab at me–I was a young preacher in my twenties after all–but then I stepped back a bit from my feeling of having my ego bruised and realized that it wasn't really about me. Brother Thibodeaux was asking the very questions that I asked: *What are we really doing here? What do I have to say to the faithful as a preacher?* My connection to Brother Thibodeaux seemed all the stronger when I remembered that during one of the services I had prophesized to Sister Thibodeaux that, while I knew she was enduring the difficulties of being a pastor's wife, she should not be discouraged. "Your energies," I told Sister Thibodeaux that day, "will not be in vain. One day there will be a payoff for you and your husband." I thought about how that prophecy had made me cognizant of something I unfortunately had not given enough thought to: the sacrifices Kelli made to be with me.

That night I felt a kinship to Brother Thibodeaux that I had never experienced with another preacher. He shared in the struggles I faced, asked the questions I posed to myself all the time and was discomforted by the commercial aspects of Christianity that for so long had disquieted my conscience. I know that Brother Thibodeaux felt the same way about me because the next morning he enthusiastically shared with me a cassette tape of a message delivered by Brother Lloyd Goodwin of the Gospel Assembly Church of Des Moines, Iowa. Brother Goodwin's message on the tape finally provided the guidance I sought on the question of eternal punishment. In Brother Goodwin's message, he offered a stark departure from both the Pentecostal and Trinitarian beliefs about the concept of God. Pentecostals believed in the "oneness" of God, that essentially the Father, the Son and the Holy Ghost were all a singular spirit. In the Trinitarian view, represented in mainstream Christianity, the Godhead was three distinct, divine persons: the Father, the Ghost and the Holy Spirit. In Brother Goodwin's reckoning, however, there were actually two gods: God the father, and Jesus the son. To Brother Goodwin, God birthed Jesus and there was no third Holy Spirit distinct from the Father–the Father is the spirit. Brother Goodwin said that whenever the Father does something on earth, you could call it the Holy Spirit but it is just the Father at work. To me, Brother Goodwin's interpretation of the Godhead fit the wording of the apostles' letters much more precisely than the Trinitarian or Pentecostal interpretations. Indeed, Brother Goodwin's idea of a dual Godhead is mirrored in the words of Paul in Philippians 1:2: "Grace be unto you, and peace, from God our Father, and from the Lord Jesus Christ."

Brother Goodwin's view on the Godhead, of course, had nothing to do with the concept of eternal punishment that I had obsessed over for so long. But what Brother Goodwin's message did for me was cast doubt on the *entire* Pentecostal worldview, including the concept of eternal punishment. If Pentecostals were wrong about something so important–the Godhead–then maybe they were wrong about *everything*. Circling back to my quest to bring about a revival, I wondered if the wrongness of Pentecostalism on the concept of God was standing in the way of the great revival I longed for. After all, the critical building blocks in the creation of a worldwide revival were pure devotion and a correct understanding of doctrine. For years, I'd been trying to get my doctrine straight and suddenly it seemed that Brother Goodwin had an unassailable take on doctrine. The obscurity of Brother Goodwin only made his message more appealing. I surmised that he was part of a secret, uniquely wise denomination and that if many more us adopted his interpretation of the Godhead, then the revival I sought would be close at hand.

Brother Goodwin, I would soon discover, was also a strong believer in the concepts of both predestination and annihilation, which held that those who were not saved would just cease to exist instead of suffering eternal punishment. These were the ideas that magnetically pulled me to the Branhamites. I loved the *humaneness* of the ideas of predestination combined with annihilation. For me, the concept of eternal punishment–and more importantly the plan of salvation–was like boating out to a shipwreck, throwing a life raft out and saying, "Whoever can make it to the life raft and has the strength to hold on to it can be saved." It's essentially up to the victim instead of the rescuer to be saved. With predestination, by contrast, a God of inexhaustibly vast resources chooses who will be saved; those who are not saved face a gentle fate, simply ceasing to exist instead of suffering in eternal punishment. Of course, not everyone is saved in the concepts of no eternal punishment or predestination, which was difficult for me to swallow because I truly believed that God loves everyone. Still, I embraced predestination *combined* with annihilation because of its humaneness. Just as important, there was clear support for predestination in doctrine, specifically in Romans 9:19–21:

> Thou wilt say then unto me, Why doth he yet find fault? For who hath resisted his will?
>
> Nay but, O man, who art thou that repliest against God? Shall the thing formed say to him that formed it, Why hast thou made me thus? Hath not the potter power over the clay, of the same lump to make one vessel unto honour, and another unto dishonour?

Here, Paul said that a person doesn't have the right to complain to, or question, God because God is the potter and we are simply clay. God has created out of that lump of clay vessels of honor (the saved) and vessels of dishonor (those who are not saved). So what Brother Goodwin offered in his messages was a humane version of Christianity–predestination with annihilation–supported by, best of all, doctrine.

With the teachings of Brother Goodwin and Brother Branham seemingly in spiritual lockstep, I felt that all of the pieces of the theological worldview I needed to bring about a revival were coming together. It was like a tumbler on a lock spinning to the correct combination of numbers. It seemed that there was a group of faithful people in another state–Brother Goodwin and his followers in Iowa–with a purer and more correct interpretation of the Godhead and eternal punishment. Perhaps, I thought then, Brother Goodwin's church were the very people of my vision of a great revival.

Brother Thibodeaux was just as taken with Brother Goodwin's message. So in late May of 1995, he made the nearly thousand-mile trek from Duson to Des Moines for a Memorial Day convention–"convention" is just another word for a camp meeting–held by Goodwin's Gospel Assembly Church. I couldn't make the trip because of work at Six Mile but felt that I could instinctively trust Brother Thibodeaux's take on the convention as if it were my own. When Brother Thibodeaux returned from Des Moines, he excitedly told me that he had fallen in love with the Gospel Assembly Church, with both its doctrine and people. Brother Thibodeaux stood in awe at the way in which the Gospel Assembly Church elevated the ministry to a position of worship. He said that when he pulled up to the church parking lot, he was greeted by a swarm of young, male attendants dressed in expensive black and dark-gray suits who toted walkie-talkies. As he made his way into a parking space, there were four attendants, one assigned to each door of his four-door vehicle. When his car came to a stop, the attendants opened each of the doors in unison. After being helped out of his car, Brother Thibodeaux was escorted to the sanctuary by a group of attendants who took hold of his effects: a Bible, a notebook and church commentaries. As Brother Thibodeaux strode toward the sanctuary he walked alongside several other ministers, all accompanied by Gospel Assembly Church attendants tightly clutching their briefcases. To Brother Thibodeaux, the scene looked less like a camp meeting and more like a business convention.

Inside the sanctuary, Brother Thibodeaux breathlessly told me, there was a standing-room-only crowd of hundreds of congregants that included worshippers from Africa, India, Russia and across the United States. The speakers delivered messages about the Goodwinite worldview that were entirely familiar to Brother Thibodeaux–the dual nature of the Godhead, the concept of predestination–but with a sense of supreme self-confidence that he had never witnessed before. Members of the Gospel Assembly Church insisted that it was *their* fellowship–a fellowship is essentially a loose-knit denomination–and their fellowship alone that were God's messengers on earth. Furthermore, in the Goodwinite weltanschauung, their church was the faultless church "without blemish," the bride of Christ of Ephesians 5:25–27:

> Husbands, love your wives, even as Christ also loved the church, and gave himself for it; That he might sanctify and cleanse it with the washing of water by the word, That he might present it to himself a glorious church, not having spot, or wrinkle, or any such thing; but that it should be holy and without blemish.

The Goodwinites also insisted that they would produce the "hundred forty and four thousand" unique to God, the anointed faithful of Revelation 14:1: "And I looked, and, lo, a Lamb stood on the mount Sion, and with him an hundred forty and four thousand, having his Father's name written in their foreheads." It was *they* who were more perfect than everyone else and it was they who would be saved. So deeply believing were the Goodwinites in their relationship to God that they kept a pair of vacant apartments on the Gospel Assembly Church's Des Moines campus reserved for the two witnesses seen by John in Revelation 11:1–14. These two witnesses were given the authority by God to prophesy–"And I will give power unto my two witnesses, and they shall prophesy a thousand two hundred and threescore days, clothed in sackcloth"–and imbued by God with frightening power to vanquish their enemies: "And if any man will hurt them, fire proceedeth out of their mouth, and devoureth their enemies: and if any man will hurt them, he must in this manner be killed." After being slain by the beast, the two witnesses were resurrected by God and rose to heaven where their exaltation caused a great earthquake below, which killed seven thousand people, and then "the remnant were affrighted, and gave glory to the God of heaven." When the two witnesses of Revelation returned, they would have a place to rest their weary heads: the Gospel Assembly Church apartments in Des Moines.

But it wasn't just the church's confidence in its connection to God or its love of the ministry that most impressed Brother Thibodeaux. What completely captivated Brother Thibodeaux was

Brother Goodwin's attempt to restore apostolic order to the church. Restoring apostolic order meant a return to early Christianity when churches were led by apostles, not pastors. The inspiration for a church governed by the apostolic order was inspired by the church structure outlined in 1 Corinthians 12:28: "And God hath set some in the church, first apostles, secondarily prophets, thirdly teachers, after that miracles, then gifts of healings, helps, governments, diversities of tongues." At the Gospel Assembly Church, Brother Goodwin was the "first apostle" of Corinthians and he demanded a level of obedience from his members deserving of a modern-day apostle. What Brother Thibodeaux found so inspiring about the apostolic order of the Gospel Assembly Church was not its exalting of Brother Goodwin, but his belief that the restoration of the *right* order implemented by Brother Goodwin would bring about the revival that Brother Thibodeaux and I had so longed to see come to fruition.

After hearing Brother Thibodeaux's ecstatic praise for the Goodwinites, I knew that I had to make the trip to their next convention. Fortunately, a Gospel Assembly Church convention was just months away, on Labor Day of 1995, in Kingsport, Tennessee, an eight-hundred-mile trip from Pitkin, but well worth the drive. Just before Labor Day, Kelli and I piled into a van with Brother and Sister Thibodeaux heading out to Kingsport. We had a wonderful journey to Tennessee in which we discussed doctrine but also talked and laughed about Brother Thibodeaux, who was of Cajun descent, and his odd phraseology for any number of mundane, everyday things like getting out of the car (Brother Thibodeaux would say that we needed to "get down from the car"). It was little things like that that kept the fourteen-hour drive from becoming unbearable.

We arrived in Kingsport late in the afternoon on Friday that Labor Day weekend. An early welcome dinner that night meant that we barely had time to change or unpack our belongings at our hotel. The dinner was hosted at a grand, colonial-style home in

Kingsport. We took seats by a long, wooden dining room table that was set with fine silver cutlery. It appeared as though there were fourteen different forks and ten different spoons for each seating, all to be used during what was sure to be a multiple-course dinner. At the head of the table sat Brother Goodwin–a severely stern and serious-looking middle-aged man with pale, ghostly white skin who was dressed in a black suit and navy tie–accompanied by his closest advisers, Brother Voorhees and the Reverend Lee Ray, who affected a similar elder church statesman look. Further down the table were deacons and trustees, who were considered third-tier members of the church. Near the end of the table was a fourth tier who were merely church members. Lastly, there was us, the fifth tier–Brother Thibodeaux and me–who were simply being courted by the Gospel Assembly Church. The strict hierarchy represented at the dining room table lent an almost electric sense of tension to the room; there wasn't even small talk to break the silence. No one wanted to speak up lest they say something that would displease Brother Goodwin, a spiritual leader who not only expected perfection of his followers but would not hesitate to call out his flock if they dared to utter a remark that he considered inappropriate or stupid. I was so intimidated by the nervous atmosphere that I didn't have more than a bite of dinner; all I could do was nervously pass a silver gravy boat down the table.

I had never seen a fellowship that carried itself with such profound seriousness. Though the mood at the dinner was grim and unsmiling, I found that solemnity to be appealing. The Goodwinites were uniquely serious in their faith; even the Branhamites, with their worship of Brother Branham and their belief in an unrelenting devotion to God, cracked jokes every now and then. *Perhaps,* I thought at dinner that night, *these were the people of my vision.* After the dinner plates were cleared, Brother Goodwin retreated from the dining room and, after an uncomfortable few minutes marked by his absence, returned bearing an armful of hard-bound books bundled together in plastic wrap. As Brother Goodwin broke the plastic wrap, I felt honored to be receiving one of the church's new publications. When I opened the book I recognized that it was about the Calvinist TULIP doctrine, an acronym that stands for total depravity (T), unconditional election (U), limited atonement (L), irresistible grace (I) and perseverance of the saints (P). The TULIP doctrine is about predestination–the concept of unconditional election, for example, means that God chooses who he saves based upon *his* will and not the merit of the individual. Having Brother Goodwin place a book on the TULIP doctrine in my hand that night redeemed all the long nights and early mornings in my prayer closet in Pitkin obsessing over the idea of predestination.

After distributing the TULIP books, Brother Goodwin and Brother Voorhees retreated to a screened porch where they took seats on long, tall-backed rockers, furniture that seemed positively made for these most upright of men. Brother Thibodeaux and I then slowly approached the pair. When it appeared that we would be granted an audience with these great men, we drew even closer. "How are you coming along with the messages?" Brother Goodwin asked Brother Thibodeaux. "I understand them," Brother Thibodeaux replied. "I get them. I am coming along fine." Brother Goodwin said nothing in response; he merely acknowledged Brother Thibodeaux's progress in understanding the doctrine with a closed-mouth smile. Brother Goodwin then rose slightly from his rocker to remove his suit jacket, revealing he wore a gorgeous, expensively tailored, crisp, freshly pressed white dress shirt. As I fixed my eyes on Brother Goodwin–he was so charismatic that I felt I could never avert my gaze from him–I noticed that the dress shirt had purple stripes. There was a blandness to the dress of Brother Goodwin and the Gospel Assembly Church leadership, so the splash of purple had a searing, majestic quality about it. Easing back into the rocker, Brother Goodwin turned to me and said, "The only way you're going to grow in God is to be part of my ministry." I nodded my head in silent agreement; I had no idea what to say. "I want you to move to Des Moines to be under my ministry,"

Brother Goodwin continued, furrowing his brow as he spoke. "This is the only way you are going to grow your ministry in order to make it into what you are looking for. And when your ministry has reached its potential, Brother DeWitt, I will set you up in a church of your own. I'm asking you now—*right now*, Brother DeWitt—for a commitment. What is your answer?" I had always resolved decisions large and small through prayer, so I meekly asked Brother Goodwin, "Can I pray about it?" Brother Goodwin said that I could. But it was obvious to me that Brother Goodwin suspected I was stalling. He had asked for a commitment and I had refused to give it to him.

Knowing that Brother Goodwin would not wait long for an answer, I moved toward Kelli—who was standing on the opposite side of the screened-in porch because she and Sister Thibodeaux weren't allowed to participate in what was considered men's conversation—and asked for her advice. "Do whatever you think is best," Kelli replied. This may sound like a cold or lifeless response to a life-altering proposal but Kelli meant what she said. My career was going nowhere and our lives in Pitkin were rudderless and completely without direction. Kelli simply felt that if joining Brother Goodwin in Des Moines was the right thing to do, then I should not hesitate to do it. I knew that moving to Des Moines to start a ministry under the tutelage of Brother Goodwin was my best option, not just because I believed that Brother Goodwin had the right doctrine but also because it was the *only* way out of Pitkin and a sputtering career of preaching at revivals. The rightness of the choice, however, unsettled me. I didn't want to leave home. I couldn't imagine being so far away from my family, particularly my grandmother, who was still mourning my grandfather's death.

The convention at Gospel Assembly Church, which stretched over two days that Labor Day weekend, made my fear and frustration over the move to Des Moines seem foolish. The Goodwinites had a full orchestra—with seemingly every instrument known to man, from French horns to a thundering timpani—that sounded unlike any Christian worship music that I'd been exposed to. I was accustomed to the theatrical showiness of Swaggart and ecstatic singing of small Pentecostal churches. But the orchestra at the Gospel Assembly Church, whose members had been trained at the Goodwinites' own school where music was a central part of the curriculum, had a huge orchestral sound merged with the rhythm and soul of Pentecostal music. They took that barn-raising music of the South and put music sheets in front of them while playing music they shouldn't have been playing in the first place. When the music reached an awe-inspiring crescendo, the young men of the Gospel Assembly Church made their way down to the open space between the stage and first pew and danced together. In most Pentecostal churches, churchgoers danced only when they were in such ecstasy that they were *moved* to dance; dancing was done with eyes closed and with the dancers completely oblivious to the world around them. Worshippers danced until they were almost in a trance. Achieving that trancelike state assured dancers that they were in the spirit and *not* in the flesh. True believers didn't dance for dancing's sake: they danced only if the Holy Ghost possessed them. The emphasis on ecstatic dancing meant that young Pentecostals didn't have confidence to dance unless they were being filled to overflowing by the Holy Ghost. So it touched my heart deeply that the young men of the Gospel Assembly Church felt that they had, to use a Pentecostal phrase, "the liberty" to get up and dance wide-eyed with no pretense that they were in the spirit. They danced for the joy of dancing.

Brother Goodwin's messages couldn't have been more starkly different from the reassuring "God loves everybody" or "our church loves you and takes care of you" messages that were so often preached at Pentecostal services down South. Instead, Brother Goodwin's message was tougher, scarier and far from comforting. "If you don't honor this ministry," he warned, "then the judgment of God will come into your life." And where most Pentecostal preachers beat up on smokers, drinkers and gamblers–fire and brimstone directed solely toward the lost or the blatantly disobedient–Brother Goodwin judged *everybody* and judgment began right there in the Gospel Assembly Church sanctuary. Indeed, Brother Goodwin's messages embodied 1 Peter 4:17: "For the time is come that judgment must begin at the house of God: and if it first begin at us, what shall the end be of them that obey not the gospel of God?"

No one was safe in Brother Goodwin's messages. He lashed out at wives who did not have meals ready for their husbands when they arrived home from work. He angrily denounced anyone who believed in the idea, widely accepted in mainstream Christianity, of accepting Christ as your personal savior. In Brother Goodwin's worldview, this was false doctrine because it's not your choice to accept Christ–Christ has to accept *you* as one of the saved. He blasted homosexuality as symptomatic of society's decline. "History has taught us," Brother Goodwin preached, that "every society that has embraced homosexuality has fallen." Taxation–specifically property taxes–were yet another target of Brother Goodwin's ire. To Brother Goodwin, property taxes usurped God's authority because the earth belongs to God, not man.

These were uncompromisingly angry messages delivered in a take-it-or-leave-it style that was completely at odds with the salesmanlike style of most Christian ministers who wanted to save as many souls and bring as many souls into their church as possible. Brother Goodwin wasn't selling anything because he didn't have to; under the doctrine of predestination you can't be part of the church unless God asks you to join. Freed from mainstream Christianity's emphasis on salesmanship, driving up church membership and the pressure to put on a fresh new show for every service, Brother Goodwin focused on doctrine, hammering the same biblical verses over and over again. It was such a relentless doctrinal approach that the speakers at the Gospel Assembly Church convention knew better than to stray from Brother Goodwin's subject matter. This doctrine-driven approach gave the convention the feel of a biblical boot camp: Brother Goodwin was the drill sergeant who could make you feel small and unworthy but by the time the convention was over you truly felt like a solider in God's army.

Back at home after the convention, however, I still could not manage to make a decision on the move to Des Moines. I found it extremely difficult to work out the positives and negatives in my mind. Normally, if I faced a difficult decision I'd just rip out a piece of notebook paper and draw a line down the middle and tally the pros and cons. This time, however, I struggled with Brother Goodwin's offer even though the path to Des Moines had been substantially smoothed by Kelli, who was willing to make the move, and my family, who, though not thrilled with the idea of us leaving Louisiana, felt that I had to do what God wanted. Grappling with what I knew should be an easy decision, I realized that the problem was not the decision. The problem was with me.

So I took to my prayer closet and obsessively prayed during not just the nights and early mornings but the afternoons as well. One afternoon, as I lay on my bed in prayer I heard a voice–it was audible, like someone speaking to me–speak directly into my ear. "If you don't do it," the voice said, "it's over." The voice was so real that it nearly scared me to death; it panicked me as though I'd heard a gunshot in the next room. I believed that the voice was that of God speaking to me and the very realness of the voice just immediately broke my heart. What I interpreted the message to mean was that God was not only urging me to go to Des Moines, indeed, what God was saying was that if I did not move, the quest that I had been on for so many years would be over. I'd wanted to get my doctrine straight and find the right people to preach to in order to bring about a revival and there was little doubt that the Gospel Assembly Church was where my dream could be realized.

God was telling me to man up or he would simply drop me from his favor, thus ending my spiritual search. Right there and then on the bed I squalled like a baby. When the crying finally subsided, I told Kelli and my family, "We're going."

Within weeks, Kelli and I sold nearly everything we owned at a garage sale. What we couldn't sell we gave away and we kept only what we absolutely needed. We knew that it was going to be cold in Des Moines so we held on to every sheet, every blanket, our towels and all of our clothes. Kelli and I purchased a huge, blue duffel bag for our clothes and linens, which we hoisted atop the roof of our '92 white Ford Aerostar van. I'll never forget thinking as I tied the bag down with thick nylon straps to the van's roof, *What in the hell am I doing?* I knew that moving to Des Moines was the right thing to do, but indecision and fear plagued me as we began the nearly nine-hundred-mile drive from Louisiana to Des Moines that October. It didn't help that before we made the trip I had made a mixtape by recording my favorite Southern gospel songs from bands like Gold City and the Hinsons off Christian radio. But on the road to Des Moines, I was so wracked with stress that I forgot that I was listening to the tape, so when a news report came on about a horrific flood in a small town in southern Iowa I panicked. "We're headed straight toward the flood!" I shouted to Kelli, which set off a frantic search through the pile of maps stacked high on the backseat of the Aerostar to determine if we could somehow reroute our trip around the flooded town. But then the cassette ended and I realized that we'd just been listening to an old news report. After the embarrassing false alarm, I redoubled my efforts to focus on the new life that lay ahead in Des Moines. I hoped I'd quickly rise up through the order of the Gospel Assembly Church and then have a church of my own. But I couldn't stop myself from worrying–and crying. I think I cried all the way through the state of Arkansas. As we neared the Missouri-Iowa border, I finally made peace with my decision. I surrendered everything back in Louisiana because this was the final stage in my search for the right doctrine and the right people to preach that doctrine *to*. And I had to be completely real with myself. I was out of options in the ministry. For me, the Gospel Assembly Church was the only show in town.

Wherefore, brethren, covet to prophesy, and forbid not to speak with tongues. Let all things be done decently and in order.

—1 Corinthians 14:39–40

Kelli, Paul and I were exhausted when we finally arrived at the Gospel Assembly Church just before sundown on a chilly mid-October night in Des Moines. We were relieved that it had not yet begun to snow—Des Moines would see its first snow just two weeks later, on October 30—but the temperatures hovering in the upper forties felt freezing to us thin-blooded Southerners. The excitement I felt taking in the sprawling, ten-acre Gospel Assembly Church property—which had a soaring sanctuary, a complex of three residential apartment buildings and a school all interspersed with lush islands of greenery, even in its imposingly huge parking lot—eased my fears about leaving Louisiana and my family so far behind. I wasn't even bothered by the cold modernism of the Gospel Assembly structures, which resembled an office park or the headquarters of a Fortune 500 company. *This is the headquarters for God's truth*, I thought to myself. *I wouldn't be here if it were anything else.* Because nightfall was coming, Kelli and I quickly drove the Aerostar to the cluster of three residential apartment buildings at the rear of the property. What we were told by Brother Goodwin—indeed, what we were *promised* by Brother Goodwin—was that we would be housed in one of the Gospel Assembly Church apartments. I was also assured that I had a job with the church, though because I was so intimidated by Brother Goodwin back in Kingsport I hadn't even asked about a job title or a salary. I assumed I'd just work at the church library or in its school.

When we arrived at the apartments, we were greeted by one of the church elders, a woman in her sixties who was an organist with the church. As Kelli and Paul stayed back with our belongings in the Aerostar, the organist took me on a tour of the spacious two-bedroom apartment that she shared with her daughter. It was so neat and spotless that it resembled a resort. I couldn't wait to move my family in. As we completed the tour, we were met by Brother Vernon Goodwin, Brother Goodwin's brother. Brother Vernon bore an eerie resemblance to the apostle himself–he had dark, slicked-back hair, heavy glasses and wore a dark-blue suit, a style of dress made all the more dour by his pale white skin. Without even a hint of emotion, Brother Goodwin informed me that there weren't any available apartments on the church property. Instead, we'd be living at the home of a prominent Gospel Assembly Church couple, Brother David and Sister Kay. I was so taken aback by what Brother Vernon told me that I just stood in front of him in total silence. *Paul is still in his baby seat,* I thought to myself, *and a Gospel Assembly Church promise has already been broken.* Crestfallen, I walked slowly back to the parking lot, where the Aerostar was parked with its motor still running, to break the news to Kelli. Kelli was not angry with the shattered promise by the Goodwinites but instead seriously troubled by it. "We're off to a bad start," she said with a sigh. It was hard to disagree with her. But Kelli and I were so exhausted–and, more importantly, so very aware of just how helpless we were so far from home–that we acclimated ourselves quickly to the idea that we would not have an apartment of our own. There was nothing we could do about it. We didn't have the money for a hotel and we couldn't turn around and drive back to Louisiana. There was, after all, nothing to drive back *to.*

With Brother Vernon's directions in hand, we navigated the Aerostar to Brother David and Sister Kay's home in Urbandale, a sleepy middle-class Des Moines suburb dominated by sprawling subdivisions. Just after eight that night, Brother David and Sister Kay greeted us at the front door of their home, a split-level contemporary built in the 1980s that sat perched upon a small hill. To anyone else, it would have been an unremarkable suburban home, but to Kelli and me, who had spent nearly our entire adult lives evangelizing in small towns in the rural South, the modern home made us truly feel like we had moved to a foreign country. Sensing our discomfort, Brother David and Sister Kay made a big effort to make us feel at home. Brother David, a big, strapping, middle-aged man with a thick head of gray hair swept back like a polished TV news anchor's, gave me a warm, empathetic handshake at the door. As we greeted each other, I noticed that his hands were bigger than my feet–I'd soon learn that he spent his life engaged in harsh physical labor, from plowing snow in his hulking '85-model Dodge Ram, which had a huge plow on its front, to performing mechanical work on school buses. Sister Kay was his exact opposite physically: she was about half her husband's height, and with graying brown hair, gold-colored glasses, long sleeves that covered her small, thin arms and a dress that reached to her feet, she resembled a pioneer schoolteacher. Her somewhat rugged look was offset by an absolutely beautiful demeanor: she had a constant smile and was extremely accommodating. Yet the warm welcome could not mask the fact that the move to their home instead of our own apartment was one of the most awkward and humiliating moments in our lives, in which we'd already seen more than our fair share of humbling times. I'd uprooted Kelli and Paul from our home with the purpose of finding that right doctrine that I'd sought for so long. But the move was only truly justifiable from a family perspective by the freedom of the apartment that we were promised by Brother Goodwin. With the offer of an apartment withdrawn, that justification was gone. Worse, at Brother David and Sister Kay's we didn't even have the independence of separate living quarters. All of us–me, Kelli and Paul–were put up in a guest bedroom with a small adjoining bathroom. Our little family were essentially Brother David and Sister Kay's roommates.

As Brother David and Sister Kay led us on a tour of their residence, it was quickly obvious that we were not the first Gospel Assembly Church members to share their home. Indeed, it seemed that their ministry was housing faithful folks like us and, in turn, they displayed a deep interest in my story and in my ministry. I told them about getting saved at Swaggart's church in Baton Rouge, which at the time was something like a claim to fame for me. But before I could say much else, Kelli nudged me slightly on my right side, a sign that she was ready to turn in for the night. So we thanked Brother David and Sister Kay for their hospitality, pulled out a change of clothes from the Aerostar and prepared for bed. As we slipped into our pajamas, Kelli's crushing disappointment at our first night in Iowa was obvious. "The Lord has better plans for us than just living in somebody else's home," I said soothingly. "God did not bring us all the way up here to Des Moines to live in someone else's home." Kelli shot me an icy stare. "You need to know," she said, "that we're getting out of here as quickly as possible."

That night, we slept with the windows open because it was so cool and dry outside; a new experience for us Louisiana residents who were so accustomed to wet and humid weather. The next morning, I awoke just before sunrise to what sounded like a riot. But when I focused my groggy eyes on the street outside, I realized that what I was hearing was a recycling truck lumbering down the block with its workers throwing glass bottles into its recycling bin. After getting dressed, I skipped breakfast and instead headed straight for the Gospel Assembly Church to meet with Brother Goodwin in order to get my job assignment. Because of the broken promise on housing, the job took on monumental importance during that first meeting. It was at once a promise that *had* to be kept and a salary–any salary at all, really–was the only way out of Brother David and Sister Kay's home. So I strode into Brother

Goodwin's office with such a strong sense of purpose that I wasn't intimidated by the office's majestic décor, gorgeous brown-leather couch, beautiful dark-wood desk and a hulking, hearthlike fireplace. Everything about office said to me that this was the center of God's work on earth–but that day its heavenly feel didn't humble me. I just needed a job.

Brother Goodwin, who was as always dressed in a dark-blue suit, greeted me with a strong handshake at the door of the office. Though he gave me a gracious welcome there was something foreboding and distant about him. I had his undivided attention, true, but it was like he wasn't there in the room with me. There wasn't even an ounce of empathy in his spirit–not for a moment did he feel my pain, which was diametrically opposed to the many ministers I'd encountered in my life who were country, touchy-feely good ol' boys. Brother Goodwin strove to be above all that; it was as if emotion wasn't worthy of the apostle. "You will not be going to work for the church," Brother Goodwin told me coldly. "You'll be working for a church member named Rhonda Abshire. Rhonda manages one of our interests, an insurance company called Preferred Risk. There are jobs waiting for you and Kelli there. While you're working, Brother DeWitt, one of our church's sisters will be Paul's babysitter." Hit with yet another unexpected dose of bad news, I stammered, "Yes, sir." It never crossed my mind to disagree or challenge Brother Goodwin but not because I was frightened of him. I was more worried about how I was going to tell Kelli about our jobs and convince her that staying in Des Moines was the right thing to do.

I hurried out of Brother Goodwin's office and sped back to Brother David and Sister Kay's to break the news to Kelli. As I told her about my new job–about *our* new jobs–she displayed a quiet strength and a tolerance for all of the disappointments and life-altering changes that came with my life's mission that she would display at dozens of points in our lives. Kelli said that the news about the jobs was disappointing but that she was most concerned about being forced into a job where she had to hand over childcare duties to a babysitter. Kelli had always planned on being a stay-at-home mom and we had come from a Pentecostal world in which being a stay-at-home-mom was a given. The moms who didn't stay at home with their kids were the exception, not the rule, yet here at Brother Goodwin's the exception *was* the rule. But Kelli, mindful that generating income from employment was the sole path out of Brother David and Sister Kay's home, said that she was fine with the arrangement and urged me to get us into our jobs as quickly as possible. But when I called Sister Abshire from the phone in Brother David and Sister Kay's kitchen, she didn't offer a start date but a demand: Kelli and I had to submit our résumés, fill out applications and even take drug tests. As I put the phone back on the receiver, I had to wonder, *Do we really have the jobs*? Undeterred, I piled back into the Aerostar and drove to Preferred Risk's headquarters in West Des Moines even though I had no idea what jobs Kelli and I were applying for. As I pulled into the parking lot at Preferred Risk, I was encouraged by the building's futuristic, almost *Logan's Run* look–a long, rectangular structure fronted by a seemingly unending stretch of windows–a modernist architectural style it shared with the Gospel Assembly Church center. I snatched the applications out of a secretary's hands and then headed back to Kelli in order to start filling them out immediately. When I arrived at Brother David and Sister Kay's I couldn't help but think, *Is our life at the Gospel Assembly Church a done deal or not a done deal? We have already been lied to about the apartment and the job, so who can you trust around here? What is actually true here*?

We waited exactly one week to hear back from Preferred Risk but for Kelli and me each day might as well have been seven years. If we didn't get the jobs we'd be jobless and homeless. When we finally received the congratulatory call, a wave of relief was followed by an intense, claustrophobic feeling of pressure. No matter how gracious Brother David and Sister Kay were, we were trapped in their home. It was humiliating for us to realize just how dependent we were on the care of strangers. And the week without any income had brought Kelli and me to the brink financially. If the wait had lasted any longer, we would have been broke. On our first day of work that fall, we arrived at Preferred Risk just before nine o'clock for orientation. Management informed us that I was going to be working in the mail and file distribution center, which distributed incoming mail and case files to the three hundred underwriters on the second floor, while Kelli would be performing clerical work. To our chagrin we were told that we'd be working about thirty feet from one another. The news made us feel uncomfortable–we worried that our coworkers would suspect that we'd arranged to sit together and would resent us for it.

Such worries, however, turned out to be unfounded because I spent my days at Preferred Risk pushing six-foot-tall, wide wooden bookshelves bearing thick files for the underwriters across the building's second floor. When I wasn't distributing files, I worked with a scanning machine used to digitize Polaroid pictures that agents in the field had taken of insured properties. In a decision that was cutting edge at the time, Preferred Risk sought to have a paperless office and I fed hundreds of Polaroids into a hulking scanner resembling a conveyor belt at a grocery store. It was magical machinery that seemed to work at warp speed and both Kelli and I were just awed by the futurism of the office. The sprawling second floor was wide open–there were few cubicles, a striking departure from the layout of most offices–and in the center of the space was an opening where one could view the first floor, where the computer mainframe sat protected by thick glass. Upstairs, there was a staff cafeteria serving a free breakfast and lunch selection consisting of a slew of breads, bagels, cereals, juices and pasta, soups, and chicken breast. Best of all, soft drinks were all-you-can-drink so I kept energized by a steady stream of Cokes while Kelli's coffee cup remained full all day. We felt fortunate to have our jobs at Preferred Risk because we looked at everything through the prism of our poverty back home. I remember driving home after one of my first days of work and rhapsodizing about my salary—*eight dollars per hour!*—and then passing a help wanted sign at a local McDonalds franchise offering jobs starting at seven dollars per hour. I thought I was making great money but in Iowa I wasn't much better off than a burger flipper.

But I didn't leave my life behind in Louisiana to work in the insurance industry in Des Moines. It didn't matter that I thrilled at the futurism of Preferred Risk or felt cared for by the extremely generous company benefits. Work was secondary to my mission. I was in Des Moines to get my doctrine straight and then, with Brother Goodwin's help, start my own ministry, which would bring about the revival I had sought for so long. Brother Goodwin, however, displayed no interest in helping me realize my goals; not only was I getting nowhere in getting my own ministry off the ground, I wasn't even preaching at the Gospel Assembly Church. My role there consisted of standing up on stage in the sanctuary to utter a few words to reaffirm Brother Goodwin's messages during Sunday services. Week after week, his messages were centered almost entirely around chapter 4 of the book of Ephesians in which Paul speaks about the oneness of God—"There is one body, and one Spirit, even as ye are called in one hope of your calling; One Lord, one faith, one baptism, One God and Father of all, who is above all, and through all, and in you all"—and how God spoke to *one* group of faithful comprised of prophets, apostles, evangelists, pastors and teachers. It's a chapter and verse that is typically regarded by most Christians as an inclusionary message about how so many of us, from apostles to teachers, grow and mature into Christ inside of one body (Christianity) through the baptism of the spirit that one receives when they are saved. But in Goodwin's messages, Paul's messages in Ephesians were considered to be *exclusionary.* Goodwin taught that it was his ministry alone that could perform the task of "perfecting of the saints" (Ephesians 4:12), that *he* is the apostle spoken of by Paul and that the pastors, teachers and evangelists who were called to do the work of God could only be found in his ministry. To Goodwin, if you belonged to a church that didn't have one of his ministers then you simply were not part of the "one body" of Ephesians 4:4. The unity of those serving the Lord described in Ephesians, then, was not a unity of Christians but instead a unity within Brother Goodwin's small fellowship.

So steadfast was Brother Goodwin in his belief of the supremacy of his church that there would be awkward, almost stunned silences when he concluded his message during Sunday services. The young ministers like me seated on the stage behind Brother Goodwin hesitated to stand up and speak because one had to feel that *he* was the one that the Holy Spirit had chosen to speak through. So it took a huge amount of courage just to simply stand and reaffirm Brother Goodwin's message; I was particularly worried about rising from my seat when another minister rose. Only one of us, after all, could be led by the Holy Ghost; when two stood up simultaneously then one of us had to be wrong. At the same time, I wanted to prove to Brother Goodwin that I was a capable young minister because that was the only path to get a church of my own. But I struggled to even provide the equivalent of an "Amen" to Brother Goodwin's messages. Instead, because I was accustomed to the empathetic style of Pentecostal preaching in the South, I would stand up and offer an interpretation of Brother Goodwin's messages meant to encourage and strengthen the congregants to make their way through their day: positive messages delivered with a friendly, affable wink and a smile. Brother Goodwin, naturally, was far from enamored with the substance or style of my messages. After one Sunday-afternoon service, Brother Goodwin took me aside by the stage and growled, "Don't you wink again! Are you a preacher or a playboy?"

As 1996 began and months of life in Des Moines were behind us, it was painfully obvious to Kelli that the ministry at the Gospel Assembly Church was built on a cult of personality centered around Brother Goodwin. "What's gonna happen when this guy dies?" Kelli would whisper when Sunday services concluded. I told

Kelli that the Gospel Assembly Church would live on because it truly was God's ministry on earth. It was an answer I wasn't entirely convinced of, especially after witnessing Brother Goodwin preach on Ephesians week after week that it was his church and his church alone that was the "one body" spoken of by Paul. Fortunately my shaky, tentative faith in the fanatical, me-first teachings of Brother Goodwin was shored up by more practical, earthly concerns. Within weeks after starting our jobs at Preferred Risk, Kelli and I had saved up enough money to move out of Brother David and Sister Kay's spare bedroom. We found an apartment in Urbandale, a spacious, third-floor, one-bedroom unit with a playground on the premises for Paul that, while owned by church people, seemed incredibly cosmopolitan to us. We also thrilled at, for the very first time, buzzing up guests to our home. It was country come to town for sure. The church also purchased a full set of furniture for our household including a long, sectional turquoise couch, a small brown kitchen table and four straight-back chairs and held a "pounding" for us–a food offering–which yielded four tables filled with groceries. At last, Kelli, Paul and I would not have to scrimp and save for food or fret that the balance on our bank account might hit zero just when the pantry was empty.

But as much as the Goodwinite doctrine appealed to me in a number of critical ways–particularly the concept of eternal punishment, which had brought me to Des Moines in the first place–I was still finding it extremely difficult as a humanist to just write off my fellow Christians as the Goodwinite doctrine demanded. Even though a part of me was on a search for the one group of people that I was supposed to preach to–the congregation that possessed the doctrine that would bring about revival–I was now confronted by a part of myself that I had not entertained: the ecumenical side of my heart. I believed in a sense of unity among the faithful that was the opposite of Brother Goodwin's supremacist worldview. While I could accept that Brother Goodwin knew more about doctrine than any of the ministers I'd studied under, I could not accept that a man of God who was sincere, intelligent and devoted to God, like Brother Robertson of Six Mile Pentecostal back in Louisiana, was simply going to be written off by God.

With doubts about the Goodwinite doctrine growing, I made a silent pact with myself. I would stay with the Gospel Assembly Church to receive just a few more pieces of the doctrine that I was destined to learn and then move on. Brother Goodwin's ministry, then, became for me a stepping stone in my journey to bring about a revival; it was not, as I had previously believed, the final stage in the process. As I came to grips with my lessened expectations for the Gospel Assembly Church, Brother Goodwin traveled back and forth from Des Moines, Iowa, to Kingsport, Tennessee, in order to help grow his church there. When Brother Goodwin was gone, the Gospel Assembly Church transformed into a completely different, jubilant place. It was like watching flowers bloom before your eyes. Church members and ministers alike had a far greater sense of liberty and seemed to be more comfortable in their own skin. During weekly Wednesday, Saturday and Sunday services, there was just volumes and volumes of joy emanating from the sanctuary. Where once the congregation had only stood and worshipped after Brother Goodwin did the same, suddenly they stood whenever inspiration struck and clapped their hands and vocalized their approval with ecstatic "Amens." With Brother Goodwin in Kingsport, his sidekick, Brother Lee Ray, led services with a style that was ecstatic, exciting and empathetic and just thrillingly Pentecostal. "Yes, we're all special," Brother Ray preached, "yes, we're unique, yes, we're the 'one body.' But that just means that we have more resources. So we're all gonna make it–because God loves us."

During one Wednesday-night service in the early spring of 1996, Brother Goodwin was once again out of town and I took to the pulpit. Brother Goodwin had recently corrected me about what he perceived to be my showboating and showmanship so at first I was tentative and nervous. Looking out onto the crowd, I silently scolded myself for the fact that my presentation was far too unlike

Brother Goodwin's. But then I began to preach and suddenly felt moved to prophesy. It was like the part of my brain that simulated repercussions from Brother Goodwin had been turned off. *Brother Goodwin is not going to find out about this,* I said to myself, *even though he'll be back from Kingsport next week.* Feeling the Holy Spirit was moving me, I addressed the crowd with a boldness that I hadn't displayed since Kelli and I had left Louisiana. "Revival is going to break out very soon," I thundered, "and it will start with the young people."

The next morning, church school began as usual but during prayer service revival broke out. The kids fell into a moment of worship reminiscent of the frenzied Pontotoc camp meeting: they strode through the classrooms in spiritual ecstasy, offering a stream of prayers to and praises of God. School was shut down and, incredibly, the revival overflowed into the Saturday-night services. That night, the congregation, one by one, testified about the revival that had just broken out. "The revival has come just as Brother DeWitt had prophesied!" one man shouted. Seizing on the ecstatic mood, Brother Ray took the pulpit. "We're gonna have an old-fashioned prayer service," he cried. Brother Ray then instructed members of the congregation to form two lines, one on each side of the stage. The ministers divided themselves up and Brother Ray invited me to stand in his line, a great and until then unimaginable honor because I knew I was just a third-string preacher at the Gospel Assembly Church. On stage, I didn't take individual requests for prayer from the congregants but instead spoke directly to God. "God, I want you to fill your children," I cried, "move upon your children. God bless your servants, let your anointing heal your children." Nearly overcome in the moment, I stopped my prayer and steadied myself on the stage. "Yes, yes," I cried, "yes, brother, that's the Holy Ghost!" My prayer was met with absolute pandemonium. The church members danced, ran and clapped thunderously–the entire room was as joyous as though all of their loved ones had risen from the dead. Several church members were even slain in the spirit and collapsed to the floor like a sack of potatoes. *It is happening,* I thought, observing the frenzied scene before me. *The revival is breaking loose. But this is just the beginning. What's happening here is going to spread. My vision is coming to pass.*

But just as the revival was about to spread out from Saturday-evening services, Brother Goodwin arrived unexpectedly back from Kingsport. It was Sunday morning and he made it back in time for one o'clock services. Immediately, it was back to grim business as usual, which forced me to wonder, *Why did the revival happen—why did we feel God's presence—when Brother Goodwin was gone?* Brother Goodwin, naturally, could sense the dampened mood in the sanctuary and during his message he directed off-handed, derogatory comments at Brother Ray. "You all acted so different while I was gone," Brother Goodwin sneered, glaring at Brother Ray. I had always been sensitive to the jealously of older ministers so I often made extra effort to give my elders as much credit and honor in order to blunt just such a response. So I felt terrible when Brother Goodwin directed his ire at Brother Ray and guilty somehow for participating in the revival.

After Sunday services ended, I ran back to the apartment to see Kelli and Paul. I had to confess my doubts about Brother Goodwin to Kelli because I knew that I wasn't going to weather them much longer, especially with Kelli already so skeptical of the Gospel Assembly Church. My confession of doubt, however, merely provided fuel to her fiery anger at the church. Kelli said that she was unhappy with our lives in Des Moines: the babysitter assigned to Paul, the cultlike style in which Brother Goodwin ran the church, the cold Iowa weather, even our apartment that, because it was owned by the Gospel Assembly Church, made her feel even more like a prisoner. "I'm going home," Kelli warned when she finally stopped ranting, *"with or without you."* At first I thought it was just an idle threat made in a moment of despair but then Kelli said that she'd already talked to her brother Mark and arranged for him to come pick her and Paul up. I was devastated that Kelli had already made plans to leave Des Moines. It felt like the greatest betrayal I'd ever faced because even though I was filled with doubts about Brother Goodwin, I still hung on to the belief that his church was the place where I'd get my doctrine straight. I felt broken but the feeling that I'd been crushed, spiritually split in two, gave way to a miserable confusion. *Why would God have audibly spoken to me,* I wondered, *and told me to come to Des Moines to realize my vision of a revival only for it to all end with Kelli simply packing up and leaving*? With my plan for a revival and my marriage in tatters, I realized that I had to act quickly to save them both. We'd saved up enough money from our jobs at Preferred Risk for a trip to Louisiana, so I told Kelli that we could make a visit home and then decide what to do about our lives here. Kelli, naturally, jumped at the offer and as we packed our bags for what was to be a weeklong trip, I realized that every part of the Gospel Assembly Church experience–six months so far–had truly been a nightmare for her. As I folded a white dress shirt into my suitcase, I remembered a particularly horrible, freezing night that winter when our Aerostar had become stuck in several feet of snow in a mall parking lot in Urbandale. I'd asked Kelli to climb into the back of the van in hopes that the extra weight would somehow nudge the vehicle out of the snow. When that plan failed to work, I asked Kelli to jump up and down in the Aerostar, which miraculously freed us from our snowy trap. It was a small moment in an immensely troubled time for us but the desperate image of Kelli hopping in a beat-up old van stuck with me.

Back at home in Louisiana, my homesickness overtook me. Everything from reconnecting with my grandmother to feasting on Popeye's chicken and biscuits every day made me realize that Louisiana was my true home. But that feeling of knowing where I truly belonged only served to make me more miserable about Des Moines. I was still at a loss as to why it would work out this way–how could such a critical juncture in my mission to bring about a revival fall completely flat? As we packed our bags to return to Des Moines, the stress and the anxiety reached a breaking point for me physically. My heartbeat began racing so frantically that I worried that I was having a heart attack. I didn't betray my fears to Kelli because her parents were about to arrive to drive us to the Lake Charles Regional Airport for our flight back to Des Moines. I simply couldn't break down in front of my in-laws. In the waiting area at the airport, however, I told Kelli that I couldn't breathe. Before she could respond, our flight was called and we walked out onto the tarmac and boarded the airplane, a small regional jet with one row on each side. The jet's cramped cabin only increased my anxiety and when the stewardess announced over the PA that we'd all have to go back to the waiting area because the flying conditions were too windy, I interpreted the announcement as God telling me not to board the plane. We boarded and then deplaned two more times because of wind warnings.

As Kelli and I waited to be called to board for what we hoped would be the final time, I stared at my sweaty palms and remembered how my very first flight had not only thrilled me but had instilled in me a sense of God's beauty and greatness. In high school, a local pilot named Bonnie Lee Smith took me along for a flight in a replica of a vintage Boeing-Stearman, a biwing, vintage military trainer aircraft built during the 1930s. As we rolled slowly down the sod-covered runway, Bonnie Lee, who was seated behind me in an open cockpit, looked at me and said, "Do you get airsick?" I smiled at Bonnie Lee and replied, "I don't know, sir, I ain't never been up in the air before." Bonnie Lee shot me an exasperated look. "Son, you see that rearview mirror?" he continued, pointing to the mirror to the left of the cockpit. "From there I can see you. If you start to get sick I'll have you down on the ground before you throw up." The idea that Bonnie Lee could pull off a near-instantaneous landing of the Stearman was no exaggeration: the plane is used for air shows and crop dusting and is able to perform gut-busting dives. As we continued down the bumpy runway, however, the engine died. But just as quickly as the engine sputtered out, Bonnie Lee got it going again and we were aloft. As the Stearman climbed into the air, I saw the horizon for the first time from the air. I began to tear up and I shouted, "God, how big you must be!" It was an awe-inspiring sight and then Bonnie Lee rolled the plane and took it straight up. Just when it felt as though we were going to shoot straight into the atmosphere, he killed the engine and the Stearman went into free fall. The wind just howled over the wings as we made our dizzying descent and I fearfully remembered the engine dying on the runway. And as I looked earthward I realized that we were not spinning–the earth was spinning under us. But then Bonnie Lee kicked the engine back in, stopping the free fall. "Are you sick?" Bonnie Lee shouted over the hum of the engine. I was fine and gave him a thumbs-up. With the free fall behind us, it was time for one final trick: Bonnie Lee aimed the Stearman at the hangar below and we buzzed it, upside down no less. Best of all, as we passed the hangar I saw my preacher cousin, Gary Wayne Walley, clasping his hands together, his head held down in prayer.

Back in the waiting area at the Lake Charles Regional Airport, the fearlessness I felt on the Stearman was replaced with an overpowering sense of impending doom. I visualized the jet crashing–I believed that the wind was going to knock us to the ground. God, I believed, was clearly signaling to me that Kelli and I should not board the plane. So I knelt down in the waiting area, placed my elbows on the seat and began praying. I asked God what I should do and, this time, I didn't hear anything back. "We can't get on that plane," I frantically told Kelli. "Jerry, that's ridiculous," Kelli shot back. "Everything we own is in Des Moines. What are you thinking?" I refused to back down. "We can have someone in our family drive up and get the car," I sputtered. Before the argument went any further, an announcement came over the PA: our flight was boarding. Kelli grabbed my arm and we began walking to the tarmac. As we approached the plane, I stared at its tiny door and it seemed that with every step the door became smaller and smaller until it appeared to be the size of a pinhole. Terrified, I stopped walking, causing the passengers lined up behind us to crash into our backs. "What are you doing?" Kelli said, scolding me. "I'm not going!" I replied. "Yes you *are,*" Kelli insisted between clenched teeth. She grabbed my right arm and pulled me into the plane. When we took our seats and buckled in I turned to Kelli and said, "If we get killed I'm gonna hate you forever." She just rolled her eyes. I couldn't blame Kelli for being exhausted with me, particularly because as the jet clambered down the runway my panic inexplicably lifted.

Arriving back in Des Moines that spring only intensified my fears. Kelli and I had agreed that it was time to abandon the Gospel Assembly Church but I still held out the slimmest of hopes that somehow I'd rediscover the purpose that brought me there in the first place. So I confessed to Brother Vernon Goodwin that Kelli and I were considering leaving the church. Brother Vernon was surprisingly understanding of my plight and he soothingly told me, "Brother DeWitt, things will get better." He said that he'd pray for me but what I truly needed was not Brother Goodwin's advice but the word of God. So during every service–Wednesday, Saturday, Sunday–I prayed with a ferocious intensity to God and asked him to intervene on my behalf. "This is the most important decision of my life," I told God. "You know that I was called to preach. You know that my aspirations have always been humble. You know that before being called to preach all I asked for was a nine-to-five job with a wife and son to meet me at end of the workday. You know that I have lost both my father and my grandfather. And now you are asking me to give up my son?" By then, the Gospel Assembly Church had assumed such monumental importance in my spiritual quest that it was almost as cherished to me as my son, Paul. It was an Abrahamic moment; it was that type of test. Brother Vernon had told me that the Lord was telling me to remain in Des Moines and that it was all going to work out in the end. But the decision to stay or go was of such importance that I needed the Lord–not any of the Goodwinites or even Brother Goodwin himself–to instruct me not to give up on my life in Des Moines. "You know that

I'm not going to give up my son," I told God, "without you speaking to me directly just like you did with Abraham."

But the Lord did not speak to me, just as he had not spoken to me in the waiting area at the Lake Charles Regional Airport. I feared that God's silence meant that I was not meant to stay in Des Moines. It was a realization freighted with all the pain and grief and mourning of a death in the family. That I made the decision alone–Kelli had stopped attending services entirely–only deepened the hurt. I felt that Kelli had abandoned me in a moment of spiritual crisis and that changed the dynamics of our marriage forever. I knew then that I loved Paul more than I loved Kelli. I could live without Kelli but I could not live without Paul. I also began to understand that my spiritual quest was indelibly shaped by having lost my father at such a young age. Perhaps what I was looking for was a father figure and the more larger than life that father figure was, like the towering Brother Goodwin, the more appealing he was to me. God's refusal to answer my prayers forced me to question everything I had counted on until now. I truly believed that God had spoken to me and had urged me to join the Goodwinites to bring a revival. But when I asked for his guidance about whether or not I should remain in the place that would usher in a revival, God had nothing to say.

As I wrestled with the meaning of my unanswered prayers, Brother Vernon bore down on me and urged me to confess to Brother Goodwin that I was contemplating leaving the church. So I made an appointment to see Brother Goodwin on a Monday afternoon in the spring of 1996, when I had a day off from Preferred Risk. A Gospel Assembly Church convention was planned for that May, which only ratcheted up my fears about the meeting with Brother Goodwin; it would seem remarkably faithless to break from the church just before such an important event. When I walked into Brother Goodwin's office, I knew that he was already aware that Kelli and I were considering leaving the church. The gossip mill churned relentlessly in Des Moines and news of our decision making had spread far and wide among the ministry. There was also a sense that *any* news about the ministers needed to be reported immediately back to the apostle. After taking a seat on a brown-leather loveseat in the office, I laid out Kelli's and my plight anyway because I wanted Brother Goodwin to feel that I was being fully honest with him. "Kelli wants to go home and she's going to take Paul with her," I said, staring at him from the loveseat where I had my elbows on my knees. Brother Goodwin sat silently behind his desk, straightened his back and looked back at me and said, "Let her go." Brother Goodwin must have seen the shock come over my face. I had never worked for a minister who would have divided a family for *any* reason. But Brother Goodwin was undeterred and continued, almost as though he was prophesying, "If it's God's will for you and her to stay together she will go back to Louisiana. She will fall on hard times and she may even have to enter prostitution to survive. But she will come back and you will be in the driver's seat. If it's not God's will for you all to stay together God will give you another wife and another son." Brother Goodwin could tell I wasn't buying his explanation so he picked up the Bible on his desk, rose from his chair and joined me on the loveseat. He then held the Bible open and turned to Matthew 19, verses 23–30, and read them aloud:

> Then said Jesus unto his disciples, Verily I say unto you, That a rich man shall hardly enter into the kingdom of heaven.
>
> And again I say unto you, It is easier for a camel to go through the eye of a needle, than for a rich man to enter into the kingdom of God.
>
> When his disciples heard it, they were exceedingly amazed, saying, Who then can be saved?
>
> But Jesus beheld them, and said unto them, With men this is impossible; but with God all things are possible.
>
> Then answered Peter and said unto him, Behold, we have forsaken all, and followed thee; what shall we have therefore?

> And Jesus said unto them, Verily I say unto you, That ye which have followed me, in the regeneration when the Son of man shall sit in the throne of his glory, ye also shall sit upon twelve thrones, judging the twelve tribes of Israel.
>
> And every one that hath forsaken houses, or brethren, or sisters, or father, or mother, or wife, or children, or lands, for my name's sake, shall receive an hundredfold, and shall inherit everlasting life.
>
> But many that are first shall be last; and the last shall be first.

The words from verse 29—one who forsakes a wife or children inherits everlasting life—hit me with the force of a lightning bolt. Back in Louisiana, I had preached from that verse dozens of times but with Brother Goodwin's reading it seemed as though Jesus approved of dividing families. But I took the verses one step further—I felt that if I left Goodwin's ministry then I would no longer be part of the "one body" of Ephesians 4:4. Brother Goodwin's reading of Matthew had the effect of a flashback after a life-threatening car wreck. There, on the loveseat in his office, I instantly recalled every step along the path in my life as a preacher, the Pentecostal churches where I ministered, the revivals where I delivered hopeful messages, my journey to Arizona to become inspired by the Branhamites, learning from the wisdom of Brother Robertson at Six Mile Pentecostal, the Goodwinite convention in Kingsport and then, finally, the move to Des Moines to join the Gospel Assembly Church. What I realized then was that all of these moments represented my attempts to find the right people—with the right doctrine—to preach to and that this quest had led me right to this very seat in Brother Goodwin's office. Then, an awareness of a very different sort came to mind. *The damn Bible,* I remember thinking, *has been my problem all along*. The problem wasn't my failed attempts at finding the right people—it was the Bible itself. Thanks to Brother Goodwin's reading of Matthew, I realized that there was a side to Jesus—indeed there was a side to Christianity—that I was simply out of sync with. If God taught that one should sacrifice his wife or children for faith, then I was more compassionate and humanistic than even Jesus was as represented through the Bible. In a sense, the problem also lay with me: I had been studying *at* the Bible but I had not been studying the Bible itself. With that realization, suddenly everything about my mission was on the table again. As I encountered everyone, from the Branhamites to the Goodwinites, I'd only modified my mission, adding to it like building blocks. All of the pieces fit together nicely but they all rested on an appreciation of the Bible and a belief that the Bible was divinely inspired. But what if the Bible was not divinely inspired? If that was true, my search for the people with the right doctrine was the wrong mission. So cracking the code of the Bible, which I believed was possible under the doctrine-driven Brother Goodwin, would not yield the revival I had sought. I knew then that I was going home. But in order to ease my exit, I told Brother Goodwin that if I left I wouldn't leave until after the May convention.

After making a hurried exit from Brother Goodwin's office, I raced home to make sure that Kelli and Paul were not already gone. When I arrived at the apartment, I told Kelli about my conversation with Brother Goodwin and that we'd need to leave quickly before the convention began that Monday. In the meantime, we'd have to keep up appearances at church so as to not tip anyone off that I was breaking my promise to Brother Goodwin. During Wednesday-night services I took my seat behind Brother Goodwin on stage, just as I always did. But during his message he preached that those who did not obey the order of his church were losing out on the one true ministry on earth—a clear, unmistakable jab at me. Brother Goodwin then thundered that anyone foolish enough to leave his ministry did so because they were possessed by the devil and that once they left they were no longer under God's protection. The idea that I might be possessed by the devil sent me into a tailspin of anxiety far worse than the panic attack that had gripped me at the Lake Charles airport. I desperately tried to hold it together because I was on stage but I was visibly upset to the point where Brother Glen Goodwin, Brother Goodwin's nephew, who was seated to my right, reached over to my right hand and said, "Brother, are you okay?" I was shocked that he could tell that I was so upset. "I'm going to the bathroom," I stammered and then exited out the door behind the stage and hurried into a bathroom stall. I shook so hard that it was difficult to even close the latch on the stall. Insane thoughts raced through my mind–*I'm having a nervous breakdown, I'm possessed by the devil*–so I knew that our departure from Des Moines could wait no longer. I broke out of the stall, rushed out of the bathroom and then into the hallway and, finally, into the Gospel Assembly Church parking lot to the Aerostar.

Back at the apartment, Kelli urged me to stick it out for just a few more days. The best possible moment to leave would be Sunday morning, the day before the May convention when all of the church members were attending a big Sunday service. I told Kelli that she was right and promised to do my best to hang on. So when Saturday night services arrived, instead of sitting on the stage, I sat in the pews among the congregation. When I took my seat one of the ushers spotted me and said, "I'll walk you to the platform, Brother DeWitt." I waved him off. "I'm not feeling well," I lied. "I'm just going to sit here in the audience." But when services began I truly was unwell–I was so uneasy that I felt that at any moment I was going to jump up from my seat in the pews and let out a glass-shattering scream. I began to agonize over the decision to move back to Louisiana. Yes, I loved my wife and my son but we were going back home with no promise of anything; not a job, not a house, *nothing*. Perhaps, as Brother Goodwin had warned in his message, my exit from the Gospel Assembly Church meant that I was possessed by the devil. At the very least, outside of the one true ministry of the Gospel Assembly Church, God would no longer protect me, which would lead to a life more aimless and filled with broken promises than the one I had already led. Wracked by panic and doubt, I quietly slipped out of Saturday-night services before they concluded.

"Let's do this," I told Kelli back at the apartment. "Let's get out of here." Just before sunrise the next morning, Kelli and I packed the Aerostar completely full. What did not fit in the van we left behind, which included all of our furniture and much of the donated food from the "pounding." We took only a few boxes of canned goods, which we squeezed under Paul's seat. As the sun finally came up, we gunned the Aerostar's engine and pulled out of the parking lot so as to avoid one of the owners of our apartment building who, we learned later, had been assigned to spy on us. It felt like an escape, like we were literally running for our lives. But I didn't feel exhilarated. I was left torn and confused and as I tightly gripped the blue-colored steering wheel of the Aerostar, I rehashed my decision to leave Des Moines yet again. *Did God really tell me to come up here and if so what was the point?* I was heartbroken because I felt truly felt abandoned by God. I truly felt like Jesus of Psalm 22:1: "My God, my God, why hast thou forsaken me? Why art thou so far from helping me, and from the words of my roaring?" My thoughts circled back to my realizations in Brother Goodwin's office about the Bible. I was becoming painfully aware that I didn't understand the Bible, the bedrock that everything in my life was built upon. I had investigated concepts like eternal punishment but I had never broached the idea that the Bible might contradict itself or promulgate ideas that I didn't believe in. So as we made the long trip back to Louisiana, I felt as though I wasn't driving home but to a desert landscape empty of all the belief systems that had once given so much meaning to my life. It was like a tornado had torn down every structure I inherited and built upon. I was not even standing on a slab but on bare dirt.

CHAPTER TWO

God Saves Everyone

I cannot face with comfort the idea of life without work; work and the free play of the imagination are for me the same thing, I take no pleasure in anything else.

—Sigmund Freud

NO MATTER HOW UPROOTED I was in my life it was family that provided a spiritual, and physical, grounding for me. My grandfather was perhaps the most grounded man I'd ever known and when, long ago, he skewered the tribalism of Pentecostals, he offered a dose of skepticism about religion that stayed with me throughout my life. My grandmother, meanwhile, was so warm and welcoming that she housed Kelli and me after we were married and had nowhere else to go. So when Kelli, Paul and I returned to Louisiana from Des Moines in May of 1996, it was family that came through for me once again. When I called my mother from Des Moines to tell her that we were coming home, she evicted renters in a trailer that she owned in Rosepine to make room for us.

It was an act of profound generosity on my mother's part because it was a huge, two-bedroom, one-bathroom singlewide trailer with amenities—luxuries to us, really—such as a washer and dryer and window air-conditioning units in every window. The trailer also had significant sentimental value to me. It was my on-and-off home when I was growing up and the dents on its exterior brought back warm memories of the many times I'd pull our family trampoline too close to the trailer in order to pull off silly stunts. I'd haul the trampoline right up to the trailer, often bumping into it, and then dive out of the bedroom window so that it would catch my fall and then bounce me skyward.

Living in my mother's trailer also gave me a freedom from financial woes that I had not experienced since Kelli and I lived for free at my grandmother's. So faced with few job prospects in the secular world and in the church and feeling as though my dream of a revival had been dashed in Des Moines, I hunkered down in the trailer for Bible study. Indeed, I was feeling so raw and hungry for God after the disastrous Des Moines experience that when we arrived home, Kelli and I traveled to Alexandria to see a passion play staged by a group of Pentecostals in town. When the play began and the auditorium was still pitch black, the actress playing Mary came running from the back of the auditorium until a spotlight shone on her. "Jesus! Jesus!" she wailed. Mary had just lost Jesus. I looked at Kelli and she stared back at me—we were both sobbing like babies. We were both feeling so frail in our relationship to our faith that just hearing an actress calling out to Jesus moved us forcefully. Back in our trailer, I immersed myself in the history of the Bible with the passion and zeal of the original apostles. I learned about the process by which the Bible was canonized, the cultural influences on its writers and even the great book's contradictions. I essentially threw myself out of the ministry—and into the Bible. I discovered that the canonization of the Bible had a political story behind it. It was man—Roman emperor Constantine—not God, who was the architect behind the rise of early Christianity through his Edict of Milan in the year 313, a political pact with rival Licinius that granted religious freedom for Christians throughout the Roman Empire. This historical fact is well known to students of Christian history, but it was an eye opener for me. Up until that point I had accepted hook, line and sinker the idea that the Bible was hand delivered to Christians. I believed that God had written the entire book with his own pen. But studying the history of the Bible made me realize that specific books were accepted and rejected based on politics. I saw a human hand behind the writing of the Bible and I saw a human hand holding the pen–not a divine hand. Suddenly, the book had human authors. I also noticed very human contradictions and errors in the Bible. In Kings 4:26, Solomon had forty thousand stalls of horses for his chariots but in Chronicles 9:25, Solomon had four thousand stalls for horses and chariots. I also read about doctrinal disputes within the New Testament itself that made parts of the Bible much more evocative of a debate than the word of God delivered from on high. The debate that had perhaps the most profound effect on me was the circumcision versus uncircumcision debate between apostles Peter and Paul. Peter preached a hybrid of Christianity and Judaism, arguing that Christian doctrine requires an adherence to certain aspects of Mosaic law, such as being circumcised in order to be part of God's family. Paul's doctrine, conversely, was a complete liberation from almost all things Jewish. He advocated a devotion to faith and a sacrifice to Christ alone with *no* adherence to Jewish traditions. As Paul traveled Mediterranea, his fellow Christians rebuffed him because he didn't teach the Gentiles to obey the laws of Moses. The debate between circumcision and uncircumcision reached a fever pitch in the book of Acts, when Paul appeared before the Council of Jerusalem to defend his position. Peter, surprisingly, rose in Paul's defense and preached that the Gentiles were also saved because he himself had once preached before the Gentiles. "Men and brethren," Peter addressed the Council of Jerusalem,

> Ye know how that a good while ago God made choice among us, that the Gentiles by my mouth should hear the word of the gospel, and believe.
>
> And God, which knoweth the hearts, bare them witness, giving them the Holy Ghost, even as he did unto us;
>
> And put no difference between us and them, purifying their hearts by faith.
>
> Now therefore why tempt ye God, to put a yoke upon the neck of the disciples, which neither our fathers nor we were able to bear?
>
> But we believe that through the grace of the Lord Jesus Christ we shall be saved, even as they. (Acts 15:7–11)

James then entered the fray by arguing that if the Gentiles abstained from idol worship and immorality, then the Jewish-Christian church would be able to tolerate them. To me, the doctrinal dispute between Paul, Peter and James demonstrated that human hands had written these books within the Bible–and these were the hands of humans who were disagreeing with each other and occasionally even had political motivations to do so.

The very humanity of the Bible that I discovered connected to my earlier, humanist reservations about concepts like eternal punishment. So where I was once skeptical of eternal punishment–or, more importantly, searching for doctrine that rejected eternal punishment–I became convinced such concepts could have been created by humans and that I could feel safe in rejecting them. The recognition of human authors, in turn, who created the Bible from start to finish meant that I was no longer trapped within concepts such as eternal punishment or the six-day creation story. Being freed from these ideas forced me to understand just how stuck I was philosophically within them and just how mightily I struggled to find a doctrinal fix for everything that I believed to be wrong or inconsistent in the Bible. It was a relief to feel that I didn't have to fix the contradictions or disputes within the Bible because flawed, human hands had created them. Perhaps the human authors of the Bible weren't necessarily possessed by the Holy Spirit; given the Bible's flaws and contradictions, they may have been *inspired* by the Holy Spirit, which made the Bible's human authors even more human. I, too, could be inspired by the Holy Spirit. The Bible's authors, then, were no different from me.

That I was no longer limited to finding truth from entirely within the Bible led to a reassessment of my Christianity. My faith was no longer about finding a particular people, church or doctrine—it was about my relationship with Christ. Ironically, I believed that it was my relationship with Christ that was delivering me from religion. Yet I was far from a nonbeliever; indeed, I saw myself as more Christian than I ever had been. I was becoming a Christian free of the labels and doctrinal fetters that had tied me down. For too long, I had been trying to make contradictory ideas make sense within the confines of the Bible. But once the Bible was no longer the issue, I was relieved of having to resolve all of its contradictions. I had to come to grips with the fact that my dream of a worldwide revival—a revival that I believed would come through discovering the right doctrine—died right there on the brown-leather loveseat in Brother Goodwin's office in Des Moines. But finding the right doctrine no longer mattered in my search for a faith that would bring me as close as possible to God. The question I asked was no longer who has the most pure doctrine but, *What makes people come to Christ*?

As I immersed myself in Bible study in my mother's trailer in Rosepine, no one—not even Kelli—knew that I was undergoing a profound spiritual transformation. I kept my new, life-altering perspectives on faith a secret. I didn't betray change on the outside because I still saw myself as a Pentecostal culturally, if not a Pentecostal doctrinally. The façade I created was a necessity because the transformation, while deeply painful for me, would have destroyed the image my family and friends held of me. The contrast between my outward appearance—still that of a young Pentecostal preacher eager to grow a ministry of his own–and my internal struggle over my faith was mirrored in the schizoid nature of the struggle itself. On the one hand, my months of Bible study felt like a dark night of the soul–I was totally alone and questioning everything I ever believed. There in my mother's trailer, I truly understood the cliché that the hardest thing about searching for the truth is that sometimes you find it. On the other hand, I was completely energized and enthralled by my revelations about the Bible. It felt like the library of Alexandria had not been destroyed and I was one of the first people to walk through it and discover its scrolls. I had prayed with the Branhamites and the Goodwinites in search of these spiritual truths. But what made this moment different and more exciting was that I could actually *see* these truths on paper, sustained by the weight of actual evidence versus being upheld by the power of a particular preacher's personality. If I came to a historical fact about, say, Paul, I could confirm it through a source outside the Bible, like the *Catholic Encyclopedia*, and find out that, yes, that's just the way it happened.

My faith was no longer centered around an argument or a popularity contest between differing Pentecostal worldviews espoused by charismatic preachers; it was about discovering ideas about God and Christianity that were *provable*. It was heartbreaking to finally break through the last piece of my long-held belief that doctrine was divinely inspired because it had ramifications for *every* aspect of my faith. If the Bible is no longer God's voice into the pen of the prophet but is instead a historical reference of an actual event or person, then the idea of, for example, divine healing seen in Isaiah 53:5–"But he was wounded for our transgressions, he was bruised for our iniquities: the chastisement of our peace was upon him; and with his stripes we are healed"–ceases to have relevance and, more importantly, the whole concept of divine healing comes into question. If the divine Bible verse from Isaiah is what the entire fortress of divine healing rests upon, then if the verse has a human author the structure of divine healing collapses. My faith had been anchored to idea that the Bible was not only divinely written but also had eternal implications. So if the Bible has an eternal author then what he wrote four thousand years ago applies to all of us today. But if, as I was coming to realize, the Bible has a temporal author then that specific idea died with him or soon after. The Bible, then, becomes like literature or poetry–I could be moved by it but I did not have to receive it as eternal truth nor as divinely composed.

With the Bible stripped of its infallibility and Des Moines doomed as the place for the revival I had sought, I began to wonder if I had misinterpreted the meaning of my vision. I'd long believed that I was meant to *physically* find the people in the revival of my vision, but what if the revival itself was a metaphor? What if the reason I'd not been able to bring about a worldwide revival was that I had physically moved somewhere looking for the people of the revival, instead of *moving* into a relationship with Christ and becoming more Christ-like and displaying that Christ-likeness to the world? Yet my ideas about my vision were far from conclusive; I still couldn't find a good explanation for the vision that had driven so many decisions that I had made as a young preacher. Perhaps what I was trying to do was find a justification to hang on to my vision even as my faith was shaken so dramatically. I was still convinced, after all, that it was God who spoke to me and told me to move to Des Moines. So I reasoned that God had told me to move to Des Moines to be completely stripped of religion–and in the process of losing my religion I would gain something far better: a close, personal relationship with Christ. *Instead of tearing my faith down,* I thought, *the move to Des Moines actually built it up.* I was moving from materialism to mysticism, from theism to deism.

But even with my mother's support, Kelli, Paul and I could hardly live on my endless days and nights of Bible study. So in early 1997, I returned to selling life insurance, a decision driven as much by the fact that my only significant work history was in insurance as well as the obvious need to bring a paycheck to my family. The blow of returning to work would have been softened significantly if I was actually a capable insurance salesman–but, in fact, I'm a horrible salesman. I hate asking people for money and I hate being involved in other people's money in any way. It didn't help that the atmosphere at the company I went to work for–Liberty Life, based in my hometown of DeRidder–had a pressure cooker–like atmosphere. Every Friday, we'd have a sales meeting in which all of the salesmen's names were written on a whiteboard. Our district manager, Harold Johnson, would then call out each of our names along with our sales activity for the week. I had usually sold next to nothing. I was so intimidated by the Friday meetings that I would buy a policy myself just so I wouldn't have an embarrassing *zero* next to my name on the whiteboard. I was selling expensive whole-life insurance policies so I'd purchase a cheap, tiddlywink policy–like renters' insurance–just to get my numbers up. To keep the ruse going, I'd put the policy in the name of a family member or friend. My talents in the insurance industry were so lacking that I didn't even know what my paychecks, which were solely commission based, would be every two weeks even though the commissions on whole-life policies were nearly 100 percent of the cost of the policy itself. Worse, because I made sales so infrequently I was lucky to make seven hundred dollars every two weeks. So Kelli and I would be so far behind on essentials like groceries and maintenance on the trailer that even if I'd gotten a seven-thousand-dollar check, it would have been depleted in a matter of weeks because we were so far behind in taking care of our bills.

To Kelli, though, these were far from terrible times. She was thrilled that the horrible Des Moines experience was long behind us and, more importantly, encouraged about our future because I'd put the brakes on my evangelist career, perhaps for good. Paul was heading toward elementary school and Kelli instinctively knew it would grow increasingly difficult for me to get back on the road again. To shut the door entirely on any evangelist aspirations, Kelli issued a threat: "You can go back into evangelism if you want to," she warned, "but I won't be joining you. If you choose that path,

I'll stay home, maintain the house, raise Paul and keep him in school." There was no changing her mind; she was done with evangelism. I had to admit to myself that my wanderlust for evangelism had subsided. The driving force, after all, behind evangelizing was a search for the people who had the right doctrine and that no longer mattered.

But I was not ready to leave my faith behind and soon a pastor with the larger-than-life force of Brother Goodwin would come into my life. One afternoon, I was sitting at my metal office desk in Liberty Life filling out paperwork when the back door swung open and I heard one of the sales agents yell, "Brother Glass!" Without turning around, I knew exactly who the salesman was referring to: George Glass Jr., who once served as the pastor of the First United Pentecostal Church, one of the largest Pentecostal churches in the DeRidder area. Brother Glass was a second-generation preacher. His father, George Glass Sr., was such a beloved pastor that he was known simply as "Poppa George." When I was growing up, Brother Glass's ministry had become so massive that it inspired profound resentment in DeRidder's close-knit Pentecostal community; the sentiment among Pentecostals was, "Surely he couldn't get that popular if he was really preaching God's word." That Brother Glass preached a liberal version of Pentecostalism only intensified suspicions about him and his ministry. Unfortunately for Brother Glass, his many enemies were rewarded when he became ensnared in an extramarital affair and had to leave his pastorship at First United Pentecostal Church. So when Brother Glass walked into Liberty Life that day, to me he was little more than an infamous character who represented all of the failures of a liberal, watered-down brand of Pentecostalism. I was so suspicious of Brother Glass that I didn't even acknowledge him, a difficult thing to do because he was such a big, genial presence. He was tall, with a wide smile and an endearingly round face; he was just everybody's paw-paw. One of Liberty Life's salesmen, Steve, who had a freckled faced and brown-reddish hair and a shit-eating grin all the time because he constantly cracked dumb, smart-alecky jokes, greeted Brother Glass at the back door. He then brought Brother Glass to his desk, which was just behind my own, pulled open the desk drawer and exuberantly raised a Snap-on Tools coffee mug featuring cheesy images of women in scant bikinis. "Brother Glass," Steve said with a childish giggle, "what do you think of my coffee cup?" I couldn't stand Steve's crude humor but this seemed like a fantastically ballsy jab at the once-adulterous Brother Glass. But without missing a beat, and in the most beautiful, lilting Southern drawl that sounded like John Wayne transformed into a poetic preacher, Brother Glass replied, "Son, when you look at the mug all you see is flesh. But when I look at that mug all I see is *souls*." At that moment, I fell head over heels in love with Brother Glass. If he had ordered me to rise from my desk and run outside to the parking lot to wash his car I would have done it in a heartbeat. Brother Glass's response to Steve's sexist, schlocky coffee mug that displayed women like wares for purchase was a pure, unadulterated expression of *humanity*. Ministers like Brother Robertson and Brother Thibodeaux were endearing men but I'd never met anyone who handled humanity with such grace and so cleverly. *What have people been telling me all along about Brother Glass?* I thought. *This guy is a freakin' genius.*

After witnessing Brother Glass's sharp exchange with Steve, I swiveled my office chair around and introduced myself to him. He was quick-witted and just full of stories and it seemed as though he knew the full family history of everyone who had ever attended his church. What I particularly loved about Brother Glass was how humble and self-deprecating he was—he made sure to come across not as a theologian but as a country preacher who loves people. "You know, Jerry," Brother Glass cooed, "I'm not a big Bible person; I just lucked into the ministry. I'm flattered by compliments of intelligent people like you." When Brother Glass left the Liberty Life offices that afternoon, his visit sat in the back of my mind. To me, it was further evidence that I didn't know what was going on in the Pentecostal world I had so long been a part of. Here, after all, was a great guy that everyone in *my* world not only criticized but made out to be the anti-Christ. So resentful of Brother Glass were local Pentecostals that they despised him for even daring to show his face after his dramatic fall. He had the sheer gall of staging a comeback–*How dare he bounce back?* Brother Glass's visit made me painfully aware that, yet again, I had a ton to figure out about my long-held assumptions.

But I had little time to ponder my worldview because I was flailing so miserably at Liberty Life. Jerry Shirley, the company's sales manager, even called me into his office one afternoon and said, "Is this what you really want to do with your life?" I had to admit to him that it was not. I then confided to Jerry, who was from a prominent local family that owned a furniture store and even had a street named after them, the strange place I was in my life as far as my sales career and my growing doubts about religion. Jerry listened to me silently and emotionlessly from behind his desk and then said, "I think your problem is you think too much." Right then and there, my life at Liberty Life was over; my boss considered me a failed salesman and a lost, confused soul to boot.

I left Liberty Life in early 1998 to join yet another sales outfit, Cable Time Advertising. I was trapped in sales because I had no education and no real job experience outside of ministry, excluding sales. There was no doubt that I was doomed to failure in my new job, which was selling thirty-second spots to local businesses on cable TV channels. The job had the added misery of drudge work like picking up VCR tapes and business contracts from the army of retailers who were the Cable Time's clientele, which meant endless days spent on the road. One afternoon, I pulled over to the Vernon Parish library in Leesville to use the bathroom. I'd just picked up my paycheck from Cable Time, and as I opened the door to the bathroom stall I had a queasy feeling that whatever the amount the check was going to be, it certainly wasn't going to be enough. Taking a seat on the cold toilet seat, I tore the envelope open and slid the check out and read the check amount with complete horror: *three hundred dollars* for the entire month no less. I knew that I had to break the awful news to Kelli after work, which brought on a ferocious panic attack that eclipsed my panic attacks in Des Moines. Sitting on the toilet with the crumpled paycheck in my right hand, my body pulsed with anxiety. Sweat poured from my palms, moistening the check so completely that it looked as though it had been left in a kitchen sink. When I attempted to rise from the toilet seat, my legs were so wobbly that it felt as though they would not hold the weight of my body. It took every ounce of willpower within me to push the bathroom stall door open, walk as quickly as possible through the library and then into the parking lot where I'd left my Aerostar van. As I pulled myself into the driver's seat and started the engine, however, I felt little comfort because the van was in such disrepair. Its electrical system was on the fritz, so the power windows didn't roll down and the air conditioning didn't work. The previous summer, I had spent day after day in the sweltering van without even the relief of a breeze from the windows. I drove through Leesville as fast as the beat-up old van would go, with my thoughts screaming, *If I can just get to Kelli* during the fifteen-minute drive to Rosepine. When I finally arrived back at the trailer, I was so weak that I almost fell when I put my foot on ground and had to grab the van's steering wheel to steady myself. As soon as I opened the trailer door, Kelli was so taken aback by seeing me in such a miserable state that she told me not to worry about the check. With the calming words from Kelli, the panic attack subsided.

In the weeks after the panic attack, I attempted to change the things in my life that added to my anxiety. I traded in the Aerostar for a white Oldsmobile Cutlass Supreme that made the trips to advertisers' a lot more pleasant and cool. But the panic attacks stubbornly refused to subside. Unbeknownst to Kelli, I would rise early in the morning for work, get dressed and then leave the house, but instead of heading to Cable Time I would drive five miles down the highway, turn onto a dusty dirt road and then into an area surrounded by tall pine trees where the only traffic was the occasional passing of a hulking logging truck. I'd then pull over to the side of the road and sit in the Cutlass Supreme until five o'clock, when I'd drive home and pretend to Kelli that I had been at work all day. This charade went on for about two weeks until I realized that by missing so much work I was going to face yet another pathetic paycheck. So I confessed to Kelli that I'd been skipping work and, for the whole next month, she rode along with me in the Cutlass Supreme to work to steady my nerves and ward off any potential panic attack.

My family, meanwhile, saw my deteriorating mental state as a potent symbol of the lost spiritual place that they believed I was in. After all, I was not evangelizing nor was I trying to build my own ministry. I wasn't even committing myself to another pastor's church. They insisted that I was sliding spiritually and one day my grandmother came over to our trailer to pray for me. Kneeling in the trailer, Grandma prayed for God to deliver me from the evil spirits that were causing my anxiety disorder. I knew, even then, that a cure for my panic attacks was not going to arrive through prayer; it was a psychiatric disorder that affected my nervous system and it would be science, not faith, that would help me. Sitting on the couch in the trailer watching TV one late night, I saw an infomercial for a series of audiocassettes called *Attacking Anxiety and Depression* from the Midwest Center for Stress and Anxiety. Without a moment's hesitation I reached for the phone, called the 800 number on the TV screen and purchased the tapes. When the tapes arrived a few days later, I popped in the first cassette in the sixteen-cassette self-help series–which was comprised of testimonials from people afflicted with panic attacks–and realized that I wasn't going crazy, that this was indeed a legitimate psychiatric disorder. As I listened to the remainder of the series in our trailer, I began to grasp that my brain could tell me something so convincingly that I had almost no choice but to believe it. During anxiety attacks I actually believed that I was dying. The attacks were so severe that I would have rather known that I was going to have open heart surgery at 9:00 A.M. the next day than a panic attack. *That* was the power of the nervous system: we can think things that aren't true and feel and see things that aren't real. With the *Attacking Anxiety and Depression* tapes suddenly the subjective no longer held the power for me that it had once held. Indeed, what I was learning about the power of the mind just might explain some of the experiences I'd had in the past–like speaking with God or hearing his voice. It was neurologically possible to hear an audible voice when there was no voice there. I began to entertain the possibility that there was an objective way of looking at my experiences, and that this objective perspective might prove those experiences to be false. Up until that moment seeing truly *was* believing, but what did it say about my beliefs if I had not seen or heard anything at all?

> *The search for Nirvana, like the search for Utopia or the end of history or the classless society, is ultimately a futile and dangerous one. It involves, if it does not necessitate, the sleep of reason. There is no escape from anxiety and struggle.*
>
> **–Christopher Hitchens, *Love, Poverty, and War: Journeys and Essays***

My reevaluation of what had been the most cherished moments in my life of faith–my conversations with God–were both energizing and enervating. I was more in control of my life, particularly when it came to the panic attacks that were plaguing me, yet I still believed that I could have a deep, intimate relationship with God. When a minster named Charles Pierce, who had a reputation within the United Pentecostal movement for holding forth over a healing ministry without peer, held a revival at the United Pentecostal Church in Leesville, I felt that I had to attend to revalidate what I had experienced in my revival days. Arriving at the United Pentecostal Church on a cool Sunday morning in the early spring of 1999, I took in its tall, cathedral ceilings, white molding, and color-coordinated pews and carpet with a mix of disdain and envy. Its clean, sparse design reminded me of a funeral home and I had long felt whenever I walked into expensively decorated sanctuaries that it was wasteful of the Lord's money. At the same time, I was envious of–and desperately wanted to be a part of–the upper class of Pentecostalism and could be just as harsh in judgments when I visited a poor church with an old, staticy sound system or an unpaved parking lot.

But when Brother Pierce, a slender, square-shouldered middle-aged minister who wore a clean white suit, began the service and ministered to the congregants individually I was far from impressed. Brother Pierce addressed churchgoers with vague and general diagnoses of their problems–"Sister, are you feeling ill? Brother, are you dissatisfied with your job?"–and he ministered from the distance of the stage, which only added an even more impersonal feel to the proceedings. About halfway through the service, however, Brother Piece walked down the small set of stairs from the stage and into the aisles. To my horror, it seemed as though he was walking directly toward me. *God is using Brother Pierce to chastise me,* I thought nervously to myself, *about just how doubtful I have become and how far I have moved from my evangelizing days.* To my great relief, Brother Pierce passed by my seat to focus on a slender man in his early sixties with scraggly facial hair seated in a pew behind me. The man had a disheveled look about him; he wore a tattered suit jacket that appeared to be about thirty years old with threads poking out from it. There were deep stress lines in his face; he was, as the saying goes, rode hard and put away wet. When Brother Pierce stood three feet away from the man, he asked him to stand up. The man rose from the pew and stood silently before Brother Pierce. "Let's talk about your relationship with God," Brother Pierce said. "I know that you've been closer to God than you are now." The man nodded his head in agreement. "Yes, Brother Pierce," he murmured. "I know that you've bad habits, that you've gone to smoking," Brother Pierce continued, bringing another nod of the head from the man and another "yes." An intensely serious look came over Brother Pierce's face. "Yes, indeed, you have gone to smoking. And you are smoking . . . *Pall Malls.*" Just then, the man's eyes became as big as saucers. He opened his well-worn suit jacket with his right hand, rustled through an inside pocket and thrust out a pack of Pall Malls for Brother Pierce and the church to behold, bringing an ecstatic "Ahhhhhh!" which rose from the congregation and echoed throughout the sanctuary. In those first few seconds after the Pall Malls revelation, I felt that I should get on my knees right then and there and pray and perhaps even bow before God. But as the worshipper slid the Pall Malls back into his rumpled suit pocket, I grew suspicious of Brother Pierce's ministering even though a part of me was shouting, screaming and berating the naysayer inside of me, *Move on!* Steadying my nerves, I realized that what had unsettled me about Brother Pierce was that his ministering seemed too much like a parlor trick; this was far from the personal dialogue with God that I had been seeking when I attended the revival. *Belief,* I thought to myself then, *has to be larger and greater in spirit than a magic trick.*

My feelings about Brother Pierce, unfortunately, did not dissuade my family members from seeking out his healing ministry. Just a few days after the services at United Pentecostal Church in Leesville, Brother Pierce brought his revival to the First United Pentecostal Church in DeRidder. My mother took my sister, Britany, to the revival in hopes that Brother Pierce would heal her of her Down's syndrome. I remember thinking that the notion of Brother Pierce healing Britany was ridiculous because I did not see Britany as being ill—I saw her as genetically different. *If Brother Pierce heals Britany,* I mused to myself, *it truly would be a miracle because God would have to heal her all the way down to the chromosomes.* I didn't have any confidence that Britany's Down's syndrome would simply disappear due to Brother Pierce's prayers and, worse, I worried that the services would make her feel like a lesser person. So I just couldn't bring myself to attend the revival with Britany and my mom. My skepticism about Brother Pierce was confirmed when my mom told me after services that Britany simply got in line and was prayed for. Brother Pierce offered no special prayer for, or individual attention to, Britany and of course she was not "healed" of her Down's syndrome. But what was of no surprise to me was a huge disappointment for my mother. She had been reluctant to attend the revival at first but once she committed to going she had high hopes that Brother Pierce might somehow help Britany. My mother was all too aware of what made Britany different but she still allowed herself to have hope. My grandmother, meanwhile, expressed a quiet disappointment about the revival. "It just wasn't God's will," she said and purposefully left it at that. Neither my mom or grandmother attempted to explain why Brother Pierce's healing ministry had not worked wonders on Britany–it was simply a mistake to not be repeated or talked about.

The disappointment with Brother Pierce brought back the dull hum of doubt in my mind. Brother Pierce's revival had failed to rekindle the feelings of intimacy with God that I'd felt during my early evangelist days. Now I felt completely disenfranchised from the relationship with God that I had held very dearly. I had laid down my life for my personal relationship with Jesus Christ. Until then, even as I had growing doubts on religion and the Pentecostal tradition, those doubts had no ramifications for Jesus and me personally. Even the loss of confidence in the divine nature of the Bible had not affected my relationship with Jesus, which I had compartmentalized. No matter where I was in my spiritual life, Jesus was a constant companion. I continually sensed his presence; it was easy to close my eyes and visually imagine Jesus being there and listening to me, to see Jesus's hand in things that did or didn't work out or feel the presence of the Holy Ghost in the form of goose bumps that were like a breeze coming across me physically or internally, a confirmation of Jesus's tangible, permanent presence in my life. With the panic attacks and my subsequent understanding of the effects of the nervous system on my perception of reality, that special, personal relationship with Jesus was finally challenged. It was a step too far in my reassessment of my faith. I realized I had drawn a circle around my relationship with Jesus. It was like a crime scene tape: an area that no one could enter. As I grew older and more skeptical, I internally debated the authorship of the Bible, the fallacies of man-made religion, or questioned the supernaturalism of a healing ministry like Brother Pierce's; but until that moment my relationship with Jesus had been untouchable. I was truly lost and I remember thinking, *This is what a lost person must feel like.*

As my faith underwent its most potent challenge, my career at Cable Time reached a sad tipping point. With few sales in the offing, I realized that the transition from Liberty Life to Cable Time had changed nothing. I had to accept the fact that I was never going to excel in sales. My attention to work was also diverted by my focus on trying to control my attacks. Through the *Attacking Anxiety* series I became aware that my personality–one of obsessive worry and an excessive empathy that literally took on everyone's problems–was making my nervous system weak and sick. Preventing the panic attacks from occurring entirely was going to be particularly challenging for me, so I had to curb them when the panic cycle began with the trigger of the fight-or-flight response. I realized that there was a very brief moment after the fight-or-flight response was triggered when I could engage in "self-talk"; that is, have an internal dialogue about what I knew about panic attacks. So I told myself, *You're not going insane, you're not demon possessed, you're not dying,* and I supplemented that calm, cool talk with very purposeful changes in my physical state. I took long, deep breaths and tightened–and then relaxed–my muscles. Finally, I directed my attention away from the panic attack itself by engaging in small talk with a friend or a coworker. My ability to stop the panic cycle through rational means, the *Attacking Anxiety* tapes, aroused a curiosity within me: *Where did the fight-or-flight mechanism come from?* Through studying biology on the Internet and in textbooks at the Vernon Parish library, I learned that the fight-or-flight response came from the days when we lived in a predator-prey environment, which instilled within us a safety mechanism that would take over in order to enhance our survival. Being exposed to biology then led me to evolutionary biology, all areas of study completely new to me. Through the study of science I realized that the quest for truth that had always propelled me was never able to be completely satisfied because in theology when you got to the bottom of a question, the answer rested on an opinion. In the realm of science, by contrast, an answer was based in fact, which I found to be extremely satisfying. Pentecostalism, it seemed to me, was a world of debating and selling opinions. Perhaps what was causing my profound doubts was my discomfort with both sales *and* opinions. I loved that with science you could put your hands upon the hard rock of evidence in order to answer a question. After so many years of experimenting with different denominations and dissatisfaction with ministers who had not satisfied my search for the truth, my embrace of evidence and rationality was a profound relief for me. Some questions, I realized, had knowable answers and when those questions were answered you needn't agonize over those answers any longer.

Feeling more comfortable about my transition from an unquestioning faith to an evidence-based worldview obviously did not rescue my faltering career at Cable Time. By the summer of 1999, I was so desperate for a way out of the company that I would have accepted just about any job that came my way. One afternoon that summer, I took a break from work to pay my monthly car insurance to the agent handling the policy, Vincent Labue of Shield of Shelter Insurance. I'd always enjoyed visiting with Vincent because while most guys are armchair quarterbacks or generals, Vincent was armchair *everything*–he had the same loose appreciation for just about everything from technology to sports to politics. As I strode into the tiny house by the side of the road in DeRidder that Vincent used as his office, he greeted me with a big, healthy handshake. "How's work?" Vincent asked. Because I knew Vincent so well, I knew better than to put a shine on my sad-sack sales career. "You know how it is, Vincent," I replied, "It's sales. It's *all* up and down." Vincent ushered me inside his house. "Come back here for a minute," he said with a friendly slap on my back. "I want you to try out for a job." I was immediately interested because I was starving to death in sales. Vincent, who also served as city council president in DeRidder, told me that the city had an opening for a code enforcement officer. I listened to Vincent, quiet and embarrassed, because I had no earthly idea what a code enforcement officer was. "So, what's the deal?" I asked. Vincent was incredulous at my ignorance. "Jerry, you'd be issuing building permits and inspections." I paused and affected a more serious look–I didn't want Vincent to think I was totally out of my depth, which I was. "Well, I've had some side jobs in carpentry," I continued. "If you get the job we'll train you," Vincent replied with a knowing wink. "Put in an application with the public works director and we'll see if it works for you."

At Vincent's urging, I traveled to city hall for a job interview about one month later. My expectations for the interview were rock-bottom low because of my inexperience. But when I parked my Cutlass Supreme outside the city hall building, a Spanish mission–style building with a gorgeous bright-red slate roof with a sign out front proclaiming CITY OF DERIDDER in imposing gold letters, my spirits soared. DeRidder was big-city Manhattan for folks like me who resided in smaller towns like Rosepine and the grand architecture of city hall made the experience all the more magisterial. Despite the imposingly beautiful backdrop for the interview, I was relaxed when I sat down with Billy O'Neal, DeRidder's public works director, in his city hall office. Knowing that I didn't have the slightest chance of getting the job was freeing. That Billy, a dark-haired, handsome man in his sixties who favored expensive suits and brightly polished dress shoes, was such an affable presence soothed me even further. He began the interview by asking about my family and as we talked, we realized that both he and DeRidder mayor Gerald Johnson had worked with my grandfather in the West Brothers era. I was proud that my grandparents had a relationship with the public works director *and* the mayor and began to feel the slightest twinge of hope about my job prospects. When the conversation turned toward the job, I was upfront about not knowing *anything* about building codes. To my surprise, Billy responded by delivering a long, blustery rant about the previous code enforcement officer, who he believed had let the job go to his head. Billy said that he'd come down too hard on the wrong people, a venal sin in the small-town South. Though I listened intently to Billy, I couldn't have cared less about his account of the behind-the-scenes politicking in city hall. I wasn't going to get the code enforcement job, so Billy's stories were like reading about city hall scuttlebutt in the daily paper. I was also pleasantly lost in the shared experience our families had with West Brothers, a Camelot time for the area.

When Billy wound down the interview, he ushered me out of his office. Near the door to his office I noticed an electric shoe polisher leaned up against the wall with large, red-and-black-colored buffing pads. This small luxury carried with it the professionalism I'd admired from ministers but without the pretense of a Brother Goodwin. *Perhaps,* I thought then, *I'd be at home here after all.* In the hallway, Billy pointed to the office directly opposite from his own and told me that if I got the job it would be mine. It was a corner office but with a glass wall that enabled workers walking down the hall to watch its occupant at work, a feature that led city hall employees to nickname it "the fishbowl." That moment, something clicked inside of me. The office was so close to the mayor's office that I felt the prestige and professionalism of working at city hall, of being somebody, of being in the know. By the time I walked to my Cutlass Supreme in the parking lot, I wanted that job worse than I had wanted anything in my life. My yearning for the position was only heightened when I described it to Kelli: nearly thirty thousand dollars per year with the potential for raises, sick days, vacation, a city vehicle. After years of struggling in sales, it was like I'd bought a ticket for a multimillion-dollar lottery drawing—and I simply couldn't wait to see if I had the winning numbers.

It took just two days to get a callback for a second interview but the forty-eight hours felt like several miserable months. My anxiety only increased when I was told that the interview would be with both Billy and Mayor Johnson. So when I arrived at city hall for my interview on a sticky summer morning, the grandeur of the building made me feel like an outsider, a sense of inferiority that I feared would prevent me from engaging in the comfortable conversation I'd had with Billy during the first interview. As I took a seat across from Billy's desk, I had to grip the arms of the chair just to stave off a panic attack. I truly believed that if I didn't hold on for dear life, I would spin like a top and fly out of the chair. Fortunately, Mayor Johnson, a tall, slender man in his fifties with wavy, silvery hair and a salt-and-pepper Kenny Rogers–style beard, sat silently in a chair against a back wall, which allowed me to focus entirely on Billy. Their positions in the office reflected the power dynamics at city hall: even though he was only the public works director, Billy ran the city. We talked about our shared history with West Brothers again and I again confessed that I didn't have any relevant experience for the code enforcement officer job. But toward the end of the interview, I remembered how much time Billy had devoted in the first interview detailing the previous code enforcement officer's flaws. "I understand what happened with the last guy," I said. "I don't know much about construction but there's one thing I can promise you both: I know how to take orders." Billy and Mayor Johnson smiled. It was done. I had sold them on me by appreciating what the problem with the job had been–and promising that I would solve it. "You have the job," Billy said, rising from behind his desk to shake my hand as Mayor Johnson gave me a warm, congratulatory clap on the back.

My career at DeRidder city hall began on a clear, crisp Monday morning just after eight o'clock on an early September day in 1999. When Billy greeted me outside his office and told me about the workday ahead, I knew that the learning curve was going to be especially steep. Billy explained that there was going to be an important public hearing that night about a particularly controversial topic: residents from subdivisions built outside the city limits sought to have their properties placed within DeRidder's boundaries. That night, several residents were set to appear at the hearing to request that their subdivision to be brought into the city and get connected to our sewerage system. In the weeks prior to the hearing, the subdivision had been hit by a severe rainstorm that caused its sewer system to be so backed up that its residents had to use the bathrooms at a nearby Walmart. The cost of joining the city was going to hit the residents' wallets hard, so we had to present them with a detailed rundown of all the costs involved. Billy gave me the task of preparing a thirty-page cost analysis to be handed out that night and he wanted it ready by the close of the workday. "Could you make a booklet about all this on your computer?" Billy barked. "I'm gonna get you the text. I need eighty booklets in all." Without hesitating, I said that I could. After taking a seat by the desk in my new office, I called my old school buddy Randal Jackson, who had grown into a tech-savvy adult, and had him walk me through the software on my computer, Corel WordPerfect, to create the cost analysis. To my amazement, I was able to draft the document with enough time left to print it out on thick, blue-colored construction paper and run it through city hall's hand-operated binding machine. As I stacked the eighty booklets on my desk just before city hall closed for the day, I reflected on the fact that my life as an evangelist had imbued in me a kind of scrappy professionalism. I had spent so much of my life making things look better than they actually were–the revivals I'd held in run-down churches in the Deep South were a testament to that talent–that handling even the challenge of creating a complex cost analysis for a construction project I knew nothing about seemed easy.

That night, the public hearing went off without a hitch though I paid scant attention to the back and forth between the Public Works Department and the residents. I was reveling in a simple, offhand compliment from Billy–"Thanks for getting it done, Jerry"–because I'd always felt gratified by attention and praise from fatherly figures like Billy and Brother Goodwin. After a stuttering sales career, I had finally found something that I was good at. There was also a sense of fulfillment working in the public sector that I'd never felt while making cold calls for insurers. In the following months, I seized on every opportunity to do right by my job and by the city of DeRidder. The computer in my office was one of the first with Internet access, so I insisted that all the computers at city hall needed to go online. My insistence on a more modern city hall yielded a contract with the parish electric company, Beauregard Electric, for buildingwide Internet service. That, in turn, led to the creation of an infrastructure of Internet and servers at city hall. I truly felt like I was ushering city hall into the fast-approaching twenty-first century.

My ambitious ideas for city hall, however, lay far outside my duties as code enforcement officer, a position I knew little about. So just after New Year's in 2000, I had Mike Smith, DeRidder's director of utilities who handled our water and sewer systems, take me out into the field for the first time. After piling into my gray, early-1990s-model Ford pickup truck, Mike and I cruised through the streets and alleyways of DeRidder. As I manned the steering wheel, Mike schooled me on small-town politics. We talked about who is not to be trusted, who is nice to your face but will stab you in the back, who never to cross. Late that afternoon, we drove into a trailer park that had sewer lines visible all over its property, a clear violation of city code. "You see that?" Mike asked. "See what?" I replied. I had no idea what Mike was talking about. "The *sewer lines*," Mike continued impatiently. "You see that?" I peered out the passenger-side window and saw sewer lines snaking across the ground. "Oh, okay, Mike, I do see it," I said naïvely. Mike turned to me and smiled. "No you don't."

As we made the trip back to city hall, I realized that Mike wasn't playing favorites. What Mike was telling me was that in a small town like DeRidder if you enforced code to the letter of the law there would be no way to keep up. I felt comfortable with this compromised approach because I had lived in the ministry for so long, a highly political world in which I had to always pay attention to whose toes I might be stepping on. Even though DeRidder's population was growing at the end of the century–the fights by developers to get their properties into the city limits were proof positive of that–it was a still a place where everybody knew everyone's names. It was an ever-changing world, true, but with *never-changing* people. No one wanted to be treated like a number and it was my job as code enforcement officer to maintain the light regulatory touch the city had not only grown accustomed to but also demanded.

With my work at city hall, I rediscovered a sense of purpose that I'd had in the earliest days of my ministry. I was also becoming ever more comfortable with the idea of *not* being behind the pulpit. It was a relief to be away from the spotlight and to not carry the heavy burden of saving souls or recruiting new ones to the church. So in early 2000, I started attending services at Grace of DeRidder but with no intention of ever preaching there. Though the space was once a grocery store, Grace had the newest and most elegant sanctuary in town: there were brass doorknobs and railings, a beautiful stage with rich woodwork, a glass podium on that stage and gorgeous stained glass in the baptistery. Grace's pastor was the great George Glass Jr.–the man whose humanism made such a huge impression on me when he visited Liberty Life–and I'll never forget attending Sunday services at Grace for the first time. As I watched Brother Glass preach, I thrillingly took in his message of inclusion and tolerance and his appreciation for *all* denominations, and the lovely sense of humor to his humanism. "Now, I know that some of us here might speak in tongues," Brother Glass said that afternoon, addressing a handful of Baptists seated in the pews, "but nobody here is gonna bite you." That first message felt like a fresh breeze blowing across my heart. It was wonderful to be a part of a warm, tolerant church family after the cold, brutally judgmental world of the Goodwinites. Though I was struggling with my faith and could not commit myself to attend every Sunday service at Grace, I knew that the church was going to be my home.

My secular work, surprisingly, also eased my spiritual crisis: it bought me time to work through the issues surrounding my faith that I had been wrestling with without success for so long. It helped that I was fortunate to have bosses who I found to be just as inspiring as the ministers I'd looked up to, like Brother Robertson and Brother Thibodeaux. When Billy retired, he was replaced by a Rodney Nutt, a tall, slender, bald retired lieutenant colonel with the army who treated us like beloved members of his troop and had a worldly, cosmopolitan outlook thanks to his travels in the military, which was all too rare in the rural South. It touched me that when Rodney confessed that his father was suffering from Alzheimer's, he was at once stoic yet unashamed to openly grieve about his father's rapid mental and physical decline. When Rodney told me that he would never allow himself to live out his last days in the horrific state of mental decay experienced by his father, for the first time I was confronted with the idea that the taking of a life could be done not out of depression but of self-choice.

At Rodney's suggestion, I began reading the works of Joseph Campbell, particularly his seminal 1949 book, *The Hero with a Thousand Faces*. From Campbell I discovered that there were similarities between messiah stories in different religions and that throughout human history, civilizations produced religion and the structures of religion, which were human attempts at dealing with the challenges of life. The creation of religion by man was not malicious or deceptive–it was, like the fight-or-flight response, a survival mechanism. Arriving after my realization that the Bible has human authors, Campbell's worldview should have pushed me further into disbelief but instead his stance on religion was a saving grace. By grasping the concept that there were very human motivations for the rise of religion, I could promote religion and spirituality not on the basis of its truth but on its benefit to humans. Perhaps religion was nothing more than mythology but that was acceptable because myth had served humanity so well in human history. I even applied Campbell's ideas to the supernaturalism that was so dominant in Pentecostal practice; perhaps supernaturalism is a metaphor for a specific myth and metaphor is, after all, an effective way of making the abstract understandable. Scrutinizing my faith through Campbell's lens made me reassess my vision of a revival, which suddenly seemed like it, too, could be a metaphor. Perhaps what the vision meant was that I was supposed to spread the *concept* of God's love, because God is the product of human needs. Yet to me the idea of God as a concept did not discount the idea that there could be a God out there somewhere. With my immersion in Campbell's works, I realized that the ministers like Brother Robertson, who I'd for so long found to be so insightful, were merely the smartest people in a very small niche: Pentecostalism. It was like I'd been studying with mechanics who understood how a car worked and had suddenly labored under the tutelage of engineers who grasped the concept of transportation itself. On one level, these new ideas caused a sick, knotted feeling in my stomach–they were so different from what my family and church believed. But I wasn't "backslid" from my faith as some folks I knew supposed. Yes, I held a secular job and, yes, I was not preaching. But I was moving forward–however painfully–spiritually. I knew enough, however, to not share the transformation that I was undergoing with my family. It was better to be a backslid Pentecostal than a liberal Christian or, God forbid, a skeptic.

It was an identity that I felt forced to hold on to, in part because I didn't want to disturb the momentum of my career, a late-in-life success that was finally making Kelli feel settled. With a steady income coming in, Kelli convinced me to buy a new home, a beautiful doublewide trailer with three bedrooms, two bathrooms, a spacious living room and separate dining area, and a master bedroom with a master bath and garden tub for soaking, all for the princely sum of forty thousand dollars. We moved the trailer onto my grandmother's property in Rosepine and though her trailer was just a few feet away from her, Kelli and I felt truly independent for the first time in our lives. The trailer was the first, significant new possession that Kelli and I owned in the history of our marriage. From the trailers we lived in to the cars we drove, for as long as we could remember *everything* we owned had once been owned by someone else. There was no doubt about it: Kelli, Paul and I were at last becoming a family with a stable foundation. It was a nine-to-five life much closer to Kelli's vision of what our lives should be like together and, I had to admit to myself, my original desires long before I was saved at Swaggart's.

CHAPTER THREE

God Is in Everyone

Either God can do nothing to stop catastrophes like this, or he doesn't care to, or he doesn't exist. God is either impotent, evil, or imaginary. Take your pick, and choose wisely. The only sense to make of tragedies like this is that terrible things can happen to perfectly innocent people. This understanding inspires compassion. Religious faith, on the other hand, erodes compassion. Thoughts like, "this might be all part of God's plan," or "there are no accidents in life," or "everyone on some level gets what he or she deserves"—these ideas are not only stupid, they are extraordinarily callous. They are nothing more than a childish refusal to connect with the suffering of other human beings. It is time to grow up and let our hearts break at moments like this.

—Sam Harris

FROM THE VERY BEGINNING, I'd thrown myself into my work at city hall and discovered that I was so intensely curious about how local government worked that I explored its functions far beyond my code enforcement job. By early 2003, one of my great passions became zoning. I'd studied the recent history of zoning in DeRidder and discovered that the city had adopted a hodgepodge zoning policy. A business zone was surrounded by residential zones with no buffer zone in between. The chaos of DeRidder's zoning became clear when the city hired an outside consultant to draw up a representation of zoning within the city, a street-by-street map documenting how things actually were. I took the consultant's map and began a new map of my own. I identified older, more historic areas where it made sense to allow for smaller homes and smaller lots. The more sprawling sections of the city, meanwhile, boasting sprawling subdivisions had ample room so they could accommodate big, new homes. Turning to a residential neighborhood in town adjacent to the Beauregard Memorial Hospital, I remembered a doctor who'd come before the Planning and Zoning Commission to ask to transform one of the older homes into a medical clinic. The doctor's request was rejected because the area near the hospital was zoned residential. It seemed senseless to turn down a progressive idea that could breathe new life into a lifeless residential area. Indeed, the denial of the doctor's request led to the home simply sitting abandoned.

So I zoned this area "transitional" because I believed that this designation would preserve its residential character while at the same time ensuring that a homeowner who sought a similarly purposeful remodel would be spared from the public-hearing process. My decision to designate the neighborhood surrounding Beauregard Memorial "transitional" later yielded a medical district for the city, which is exactly what I'd hoped for by tackling the city's zoning policy. DeRidder's population, many of whom were retirees from nearby Fort Polk, needed better medical access, and it felt fantastic to give older folks the resources that would make a tangible difference in their lives. That I'd revised DeRidder's zoning map during late nights huddled around my kitchen table made the accomplishment all the more gratifying: I could bring about change from the most modest of places. City hall work felt just as purpose driven as my life in the church; I couldn't imagine a secular job that could bring me greater self-satisfaction.

Pouring myself into zoning was surprisingly reminiscent of my immersion in Bible study back during my dark Liberty Life days. I was studying zoning and city ordinances with the same analytical skills that I'd utilized when reading the Bible. I sought to find the purest interpretation of a specific ordinance and hoped that I could implement the ordinance in the manner that was intended by its author. Grasping the similarities between Bible study and city hall work brought back a lingering sense of destiny and obligation to the ministry. The pull back to the ministry was much like a person who is battling an addiction and gets too close to a cigarette or whiskey bottle. Those old, familiar feelings of destiny and obligation to please God and save the world came roaring back. I was content to serve the public but I had to admit to myself that city hall was still a Plan B, a substitute for what I was truly born to do.

So I began attending Sunday services at Grace of DeRidder more frequently for spiritual inspiration. I ended up quickly finding it in the tireless Pastor George Lee Glass, the son of George Glass Jr. Back then, Pastor Glass sought to transform Grace into the premiere church in DeRidder and he put forth a superhuman effort to minister to both the city and the parish. Pastor Glass attended a seemingly nonstop string of funerals and weddings and ministered to the sick at hospitals around the area, all in an effort to elevate the name of Grace Church. Pastor Glass was also a champion networker and he enthusiastically forged bonds with many of the employees at city hall, including me.

In September of 2003, Pastor Glass approached me with an unexpected offer: a position ministering at the Korean Presbyterian Church in nearby Leesville. The church had called Pastor Glass seeking an English-speaking pastor to minister to the husbands of Korean women in the church, many of whom were on active duty or were retired military. The leadership at the Korean Presbyterian Church felt that the men in the congregation would attend church more frequently if there was something for them there; the current pastor ministered only in Korean. At first, I blanched at the offer because I was wrestling with so many different issues surrounding my faith. I was still debating the authorship of the Bible–I felt that even though it was not divinely written it might have been inspired by God–and I was extremely skeptical of the church as an institution. It seemed to me that denominations, and even churches themselves, were little more than a business and were not expressing the sort of pure faith and devotion that I had sought to attain.

So while I was excited that Pastor Glass would even think of me for the pastor's job, I positively dreaded the idea of being back in ministry. I had more questions than answers about my own faith and felt that my unsettled faith made me particularly unsuitable for the ministry. A minister was, after all, the answers guy. But the more I mulled it over the more I realized that I *had* to accept Pastor Glass's offer. I worried that if I refused him I'd lose any standing I had with Grace, which had been on extremely shaky ground from the beginning. When Kelli and I first attended Sunday services at Grace Church back in early 2000, Pastor Glass asked Kelli and me to participate in serving communion, which immediately and very visibly turned Kelli off. After our narrow escape from Brother Goodwin in Des Moines, Kelli wanted to be completely out of the ministry–she had no use for all the responsibility it came with or the scrutiny a minister's wife constantly lives under. Since that uncomfortable first Sunday service, Pastor Glass had implored me to teach at Grace's Sunday school and preach at the church, offers I'd politely ignored or refused with thin excuses like "I'm just too busy with work." I'd never been there for Pastor Glass–and now he really needed me.

It was simply going to be impossible for me to turn down the Korean Presbyterian job: Grace was a true church's church and Brother Glass was a preacher's preacher who truly wanted me back in the ministry. He wanted to save me: Pastor Glass believed that if you are called to be a minister you're not gonna be happy unless you're ministering. So I reluctantly agreed to pastor at Korean Presbyterian Church. I reconciled the decision by believing that I was fulfilling a specific need for Pastor Glass, a man to whom I owed so much. I also have to admit that I took the job because I thought that few in the congregation spoke good English, so I could get away with delivering messages that were vague on doctrine and simply supportive of the church family.

My first day at Korean Presbyterian was on a cool, clear Sunday morning in early September of 2003. The church building, a little redbrick structure sitting on a small hill, was extremely modest. Just behind the church sat a doublewide trailer the congregation had transformed into a fellowship hall. Beside the fellowship hall, sadly, was an uncompleted gymnasium; a local contractor had screwed the church over on its flooring and the church didn't have the funds to finish the job. In the past, when I was a restlessly ambitious evangelist, I would have found Korean Presbyterian far too modest for my needs. But after a long break from the church in which I'd taken a much more personal approach to faith, Korean Presbyterian seemed peaceful and charming. When services began, its pastor conducted services in broken English just as I expected. But I quickly realized that the young people in the church spoke English as well as I did, so my plan to deliver a simplistic, general message on doctrine just wasn't going to work. Yet to my surprise, when I took to the pulpit early that afternoon, I immediately fell in love with the congregation, who were extremely gracious, affectionate and appreciative of my time and willingness to be there. I'll have to be honest and admit that I also liked the folks at the church because they were short, just like me. My message that day was–taking a page from Pastor Glass–grace oriented. I told the congregation that God loves everyone and emphasized the frailty of humanity. It was a "God is love"-driven message that I'd delivered many times before. But standing behind the pulpit that day I realized that my preaching style had changed. I was open and vulnerable and strove to convince the congregation to know that just because I was in the pulpit I wasn't gifted to live for God. That the

Korean Presbyterian Church was an entirely new and unfamiliar world was a relief. I didn't have to hew to the Pentecostal style of preaching. I needn't yell, scream, become red in the face or white-knuckle the pulpit. Instead, my mannerisms were open armed and embracing. I finally had the opportunity to strip away the Pentecostal pretense that I felt had burdened me throughout my career and start anew.

Every Sunday afterward, services began with a ring of the bell and the singing of Korean Christian songs, which had a slow, easy and harmonious sound that was starkly different than the ecstatic stomp and clap of Pentecostal music. Still struggling with doctrine, I approached each service as if I was a motivational speaker who sought to do nothing more than inspire the crowd and make them aware of their own abilities. At the end of services, I'd come down from the stage, take the exit door to the right and walk to the trailer-turned-fellowship hall with the congregation trailing behind me. At the fellowship hall, I led the congregation in Bible study, which I taught from a study guide. I'd give the churchgoers a chapter of the Bible to read one week and then quiz them about it in question-and-answer style the next. It was refreshing to work from the study guide–I wasn't consumed with figuring out my big questions about my faith. Indeed, the sanity of Korean Presbyterian was an oasis from evangelical Christianity with its emphasis on achieving the most fanatical devotion possible. I had been burned–and left burned out–by that approach all the way from Pitkin to Des Moines. My presence at Korean Presbyterian, meanwhile, breathed new life into the church; in the beginning, there were just a handful of American men in attendance but as the weeks went by, the number of Americans sharply increased and they were joined by Korean women and children who'd never attended services before. I was not only fulfilling the church leadership's goal of bringing more English speakers out on Sundays, I was growing attendance exponentially. An unexpected bonus was that the church paid–about six hundred dollars per month. With its high pay and low-pressure atmosphere, Korean Presbyterian was the best gig I'd ever had.

Korean Presbyterian lent a calm to my almost-always turbulent existence. But on a freezing night in early February of 2004, my life was about to be rocked once again. Sitting around the kitchen table at my in-laws' house in Pitkin after dinner, I got a call from my mother who delivered the most devastating of news: my cousin Gary Wayne Walley, his wife, Tammy, and their eight-year-old daughter, Megan, were involved in a horrific car accident in Laurel, Mississippi. The family was on their way to dinner after church when a drunk driver behind the wheel of a hulking truck sped through an intersection, lost control of the vehicle, went airborne and then nosedived right into the cabin of Gary's sedan. Mom said that Tammy was barely injured and Megan had broken a leg but Gary was in the intensive care unit. The steering wheel had caved into his chest, the same fate that had befallen my father in the accident that took his life. I instantly sensed that night that Gary might not make it. I told my mom to let me know when she heard anything new and then hung up the phone. A few minutes later, Mom called back to tell me that Gary's dad, Grover, and his mother, Bobbi, had just set off on the nearly three-hundred-mile drive from Rosepine to Laurel. My hands trembling with fear, I placed the phone back on the receiver and began to pray. I beseeched God to spare Gary's life. Gary and I had both begun our careers in the ministry while we were still in high school, yet he had persevered in his devotion to God and never wavered over decades in the ministry. I, on the other hand, had taken a spiritual journey that led me all over the map geographically and doctrinally and was all too cognizant of my own weaknesses of faith. Though Gary and I were on different pages doctrinally–the last time I'd seen him he'd expressed a disappointment in my affiliation with Grace of DeRidder, which he viewed as promulgating an all-too-liberal, bastardized form of Pentecostalism–I still viewed Gary as perfect, pure and honest. If there was ever a minister who deserved a miracle it was Gary.

So I spent that night in prayer, waiting for a phone call from my mother about Gary's condition. As my night of prayer came to a close, the call finally came. It was my grandmother: Gary had passed. With the news of Gary's death, what immediately came to mind was an image of Grover and Bobbi on the highway to Mississippi in the dead of night. They were driving fast and praying hard while Gary, unbeknownst to them, lay lifeless on a gurney in the ICU. In that moment, I saw an anguished and prayerful Grover and Bobbi as clearly as I'd once glimpsed Jesus in my vision. There was something about the cruelty of that image–Grover and Bobbi praying for Gary, unaware that their anguished prayers were in vain–that knocked me nearly unconscious. That God could allow this sort of suffering snatched from me the final shred of my faith, which was my personal relationship with God. It was a moment that solidified my new, emerging perspective of deism. It became painfully obvious that we're all on our own and that Gary's devotion–which far surpassed my own–mattered little in the end. The prayers of Gary's equally devout parents didn't save him, either. My thoughts raced to the many disillusionments in my own life. I realized that there was no reason to think God had intervened when I had asked him to, even in profound points of spiritual crisis like Des Moines. Suddenly, I saw the great flood of the Bible washing over all of human history. I could see the flood everywhere, from the Holocaust to 9/11. *Surely in these historical tragedies,* I realized, *there were millions of unanswered prayers.* Gary's death truly cast a dark shadow on the very concept of faith itself. After the disappointment in Des Moines, I'd transitioned from preaching a message of a devotion-driven faith to a message of grace through faith. Faith in Christ, I believed, was enough; it wasn't about devotion and sacrifice. I believed that God loved everybody and that all of us should feel complete, deep and secure in our relationship to God. But if God doesn't help us, as he had clearly not helped Gary, then what was the point of the endeavor of attempting to have a relationship with God? If God is not a friend in need, God is not a friend indeed.

That night I went to bed in tears. Just before dawn, I lay awake and restlessly moved to the edge of our bed. At that moment, I truly grasped how much I loved Gary. I cried so hard and so forcefully that my whole body shook. It was like an internal earthquake; I cried even harder than when I'd lost my grandfather. I was inconsolable. My cries awakened Kelli, who moved toward me and put her hands on my back to comfort me. When my crying didn't stop, Kelli got up on her knees in the middle of the bed and wrapped her arms around my torso in order to keep me from shaking. It was like somebody grabbing an old washing machine tub to prevent it from rocking violently across the floor. When morning finally came, Kelli and I prepared for Gary's funeral, which was to be held at the First Pentecostal Church in Melville, Louisiana, on Saturday, February 14, 2004. So beloved was Gary in the United Pentecostal movement that the funeral was more like a tribute than a family gathering: one preacher after another rose to sing Gary's praises. But their words—"Sing songs for the fallen soldier! Our Saint has gone on to be with the Lord! We're gonna push a loss to a win!"—came across as little more than Pentecostal cant to me. I felt completely disconnected from the spiritual atmosphere at Gary's funeral and I paid scant attention to the gushing accolades for Gary coming from the ministers. Instead of feeling a deep emotional bond to Gary during my final farewell to him, a cousin who had been there when I took my first steps into the ministry, the funeral made me feel as though I'd walked onto a Hollywood set where everything looks right but is little but a façade. As the funeral concluded, thick, black sheets of heavy rain poured down violently from the cloudy, gray sky. I was asked to be one of the pallbearers so I had to help navigate the coffin from the long, black hearse to Gary's grave, a slippery and treacherous trail of mud and dirt. As I held the coffin aloft, I watched as the water first covered my dress shoes and then soaked my black dress socks. But we pallbearers kept on marching toward Gary's grave–we would have walked through fire because Gary was so loved and esteemed. As Gary was lowered into the ground, it was as though the casket was carrying everyone I'd ever lost. I was burying Paw-Paw again. I was attending my father's funeral. There at the rainy gravesite for Gary in Melville, hope itself was being buried. I saw no justification for Gary's death–*How could God allow this*? And if there was no faith, then there would be no hope.

When Kelli and I arrived back home in Rosepine from Gary's funeral, it felt as though my entire being had been hollowed out. At least when we returned from the crushing disappointment of Des Moines, I had the comfort of feeling that I was leaving behind a manner of devotion that I had come to believe was completely misguided. I felt that I had moved far beyond the Goodwinites who were far too rigid in doctrine and cultlike in practice and, by coming home to Louisiana, the Holy Spirit was leading me to greater and greater truths. But after Gary's funeral I feared that I was beyond lost–I was so unmoored from my faith that I didn't have anywhere to be lost *from*. The sense of a vast chasm separating me from God was profoundly disconcerting. In the past, no matter what the crisis was that I'd encountered with my faith I'd always found a spiritual fix for it. If I couldn't settle on whether or not the Bible was divinely written, then I shifted my spiritual framework to emphasize my relationship with Christ. Emphasizing a personal relationship with God made any issue–doctrinal or otherwise–fixable. But if I no longer had a close relationship with Christ, then there was no way to engage my faith to fix it. There was truly nothing left for me to work with. It was like I'd gone out to the garage and changed out the parts on an old jalopy but then realized that the vehicle was so decrepit that it would no longer function. After making that discovery, I certainly wasn't going to go out to the garage anymore. So for the first time in my life, I felt jaded and furious with God. A part of me believed that God didn't even care about humanity. It's long been said that religion is man's attempt to reach God, but I had come to believe that through moving away from religion and engaging in a personal relationship with God that God was actually reaching for *me*. That relationship dissolved with Gary's passing. I was divorced from divinity and like in many divorces, there was little left but unanswered questions, bitterly felt blame and hard feelings.

In the months after Gary's death, I'd watch from the living room window of my trailer as Grover pulled his truck up to my grandmother's home. Every time Grover visited, I'd pull the curtains in my trailer closed in order to avoid him. I just couldn't face Grover. At family gatherings, meanwhile, the mere mention of Gary's name sickened me to my stomach. One afternoon, though, I saw Grover amble from his truck and into my grandmother's home and, at that moment, my love for Grover and Gary overcame me. I could no longer abandon Grover. So I marshaled what little bit of strength I had and rose from the couch in my living room, walked down the trailer's steps and over to my grandmother's front porch. After gathering myself for a moment, I strode into the home and into Grandma's kitchen where I pulled up a chair to the kitchen table to join Grover, Grandma and Bobbi. Just as soon as they mentioned Gary, I could feel a panic attack rising from within me, but I forced it back down. I wanted to be strong for my family because my grandmother was recovering from a nasty fall; she'd tripped over a FOR SALE sign that she used at one of her many garage sales, resulting in forty stitches to her shin. As Grover and Bobbi wound down the visit, Grover rose from his chair at the kitchen table, turned to my grandmother and said, "Stella, let's pray for you before we go." With Grover's request for a prayer, the image of Grover and Bobbi's unanswered prayers on the road to Mississippi came rushing back. Since that vision, my whole world spun on the axis of the idea of Grover and Bobbi's unanswered prayers and a cruel, uncaring God who refused to intervene in order to save even the most devout of men. But this time, praying with Grover around my grandmother's kitchen table, the image made me realize that faith is not about what you get; it's about what you do. Faith is not getting prayers answered; it's about continuing to pray whether you get answers or not. With this new realization about faith, I believed that I'd received a second chance at my spiritual journey that had veered far off course in Des Moines and had completely derailed with Gary's passing. I felt saved again. My relationship with God was reestablished and I felt the presence of the Holy Ghost from the top of my head to my bended knees. Feeling completely humbled before God, I lowered further to the ground, lay at my grandmother's feet and continued praying. I asked God to forgive for me being distracted, for allowing myself to push so far away from him. Rising to my feet again, I formulated a new message: in the quest to find God and faith, the believer has to exert faithful behavior regardless of the outcome just as Shadrach, Meshach and Abednego refused to engage in idol worship, even if it meant being thrown into the fiery furnace. God might save them, they told King Nebuchadnezzar according to Daniel 3:12, but even if he did not they would never "worship the golden image which thou hast set up." I knew at that moment that heartache and tragedy were a part of a life of devotion that didn't have to be overcome. Overcoming obstacles was not always a demonstration of God's will–perhaps, I thought then, the act of *enduring* itself was an expression of faith.

> *For unto us a child is born, unto us a son is given: and the government shall be upon his shoulder: and his name shall be called Wonderful, Counsellor, The mighty God, The everlasting Father, The Prince of Peace.*
>
> **—Isaiah 9:6**

With my embrace of a new theological worldview–faith is there to sustain us and help us survive but not ensure that we emerge victorious over life's many battles–I felt truly comfortable with Christianity for the first time since the move to Des Moines. My internal debates about the contradictions in the Bible and my disillusionment with religious institutions no longer mattered because I possessed a faith that made sense of human struggle. It was a faith that overrode my doubts because humanism has always been my motivation; it was humanism, after all, that drove me to Brother Goodwin and his rejection of eternal punishment in the first place. With the skies of my faith clearing, my desire to be back in the ministry intensified. Pastoring at Korean Presbyterian, where I delivered messages about a faith that sustains us through hard times, fulfilled that need. Better still, by rejecting a faith that made huge promises–like healing the sick–I no longer felt bound by how God might, or frankly might not, answer prayers.

But as I finally settled into a kind of détente with my faith, my secular life at city hall suddenly became precarious. It was the spring of 2004 and with an election coming up in 2006, aspiring mayoral candidates began making moves toward elected office. My longtime friend and mentor, Vincent Labue, was being encouraged by friends to make a run for mayor. Vincent and Mayor Johnson had long been political allies and personal friends, resulting in city council meetings that were not just harmonious but something of a love fest. But with Vincent's associates urging him to take on Mayor Johnson in the 2006 election, a simple, unfulfilled question from a constituent–"Why is the vacant lot next to my property still uncleared?"–became cause for war between the city council and the mayor. The hostile atmosphere at city council meetings, in turn, opened up a huge, visible rift between Vincent and Mayor Johnson. Tensions at city hall only increased when there were murmurings that Frances Jouban, a well-connected DeRidder resident from a prominent local family in the retail business, was also going to enter the mayoral fray. As the summer of 2004 began, sides were being taken at city hall and my friendship with Vincent created a rift between me and my boss, Public Works Director Rod Nutt, who suspected that I was loyal to Vincent and not the mayor. One afternoon that summer, I bluntly put the question to Rod: "Is the issue here that I'm still friends with Vincent?" Rod cleared his throat and locked his eyes upon mine. "The bottom line is," Rod told me dourly, "that we just don't know if we can trust you or not."

With clear lines drawn between opposing camps, I was out at city hall–not fired, but increasingly removed from day-to-day decision making in the building. I had loved working at city hall because it was as purpose driven as my life in the ministry. But by being shut out of public service, my ability to minister to the community was disappearing. Secular work began to lose its appeal for me and, at the same time, my discovery of a faith that not only accepted struggle but embraced it made returning to the ministry seem more attractive than ever. So almost as if on spiritual cue, in September of 2004 Pastor Glass of Grace of DeRidder asked me to become the first pastor of Grace of DeQuincy in nearby Calcasieu Parish. This Grace was a satellite of Grace of DeRidder housed in a late Gothic revival–style Episcopalian church built in the late 1800s that, though it was on the National Register of Historic Places, had lain abandoned for years. "I don't know if I'm the guy to do this," I confessed to Pastor Glass on the phone on that September day. "There are more ministers out there more faithful than me. I think the church would be better served with them." I also warned Pastor Glass that the ministers at Grace who had preached at the church more often than me would be upset by the decision to put me in charge at DeQuincy. Pastor Glass allayed my concerns by saying that, like my work at Korean Presbyterian, I'd simply be fulfilling a need requiring such a modest time commitment that I could keep my city hall job.

On an unusually warm mid-September day, I made the thirty-mile trip from DeRidder to DeQuincy for a Pastor Glass–guided tour of the old church that was the newest outpost in the small but growing Grace empire in Southwest Louisiana. Though I was familiar with the DeQuincy area, I didn't have a clue how to get to the church, so Pastor Glass and I met at a church that we both knew, Pleasant Hill Baptist, on the south side of town. After parking my city-owned truck out front, Pastor Glass rolled up in his used, church-donated Audi and we made the short trip together to Grace of DeQuincy. I appreciated the odd, fateful bit of symmetry between its address–200 Hall Street–and city hall at 200 South Jefferson in DeRidder. While its white-painted, wood-frame structure was in somewhat of a dilapidated state, its tall steeple with a bell tower up top and arched doors and stained-glass windows exuded a sense of history and stirred within me a feeling of being connected to the larger story of Christianity. Pentecostal churches were so modern and Pentecostalism itself was so young that only the disconnected present was real. In the more than one-hundred-year-old Grace building, by contrast, a story of Christianity was told in its walls and its stained glass. The structure was all the more appealing because of its former name, All Saints Episcopal Church. Secretly, I was very much becoming a Universalist. I believed that God loves everyone and saves everyone. So I took its former name as a confirmation that the pastor's position was fated because I believed everyone was sanctified. *We are all saints,* I thought to myself as I stood on the sidewalk with Pastor Glass outside 200 Hall Street. With a hearty shake of Pastor Glass's hand, I accepted the job and readied myself for my new spiritual home.

Fortunately, I wasn't forced to take the reins at Grace from the start. Every Sunday that fall, Kelli and I traveled with Pastor Glass to watch him preach. His messages were very much of the Joel Osteen "you can make it" variety but, given the handful of congregants in the pews, were also animated with enthusiastic calls to grow the community. It was difficult for me to pay much attention to Pastor Glass, though, because I was focused on getting Kelli's blessing to take on the minister's job. She had long wanted out of ministry and my city hall job, in which I had health insurance and was plugged into the state retirement system, only reinforced her desires for a secular life. But with my career at city hall in decline, my faith refreshed after Gary's death and a seemingly great opportunity in the church waiting for me in DeQuincy guided by the humanistic hand of Brother Glass, I desperately sought Kelli's approval. Indeed, I told myself that Kelli's was such a significant hurdle that only God could make her agreeable. I turned to God for help once again because I didn't know how to exist outside the supernatural sphere. These were the only tools I had–and I had to use them.

After the final Sunday service with Pastor Glass that September, I walked to the back of the church and kneeled by the last pew in order to make a fleece before God. As I kneeled, my dark two-piece suit felt like a straitjacket because I had grown so accustomed to dressing in work clothes–jeans and rugged, blue Dickies work shirts–during my years working out in the field as a code enforcement officer. I lifted my arms in prayer, resting my elbows on the slatted wooden pews, which had such wide spaces between the slats that one had to be careful not to let their elbows fall down into them. *God,* I prayed, *if this is what you want me to do then make Kelli be for it. That will be the sign.* I rose to my feet and was forced to ask myself, *Am I really doing this? Is this the direction I want to take?* The questions were rooted not in my lingering doubts about God but in the quiet, relaxed atmosphere I'd found at Korean Presbyterian. I'd be trading that job for full-time work in the ministry and I'd have to build Grace literally from the ground up.

As Kelli prepared dinner back in our trailer that night, I approached her with the idea of returning to the ministry. Kelli listened silently at first and then interrupted me as I painfully and haltingly professed my desire to pastor at Grace. "I know you've been miserable at city hall," Kelli said soothingly, "and when you're miserable, I'm miserable. So I'm okay with this if this is really what you want to do." It was a done deal: Kelli's approval was the sure, unmistakable sign that I had asked God for when I made the fleece before him. I spent the next several days combing through Grace's financial records to make sure that there truly was enough money to pay me to pastor full time.

There was, after all, no way to grow the congregation at Grace part time as I had done with Korean Presbyterian, which already had a well-established base. My examination of the church's finances made clear that I could make about thirty thousand dollars per year at Grace–a modest salary that Kelli and I could live on but one without any of the benefits I'd enjoyed at city hall. Grace offered a far-from-promising financial future for me and my family but, as I pored over its financial books spread across my kitchen table, I felt a calling to take up the mantle of my Pentecostal forebears. In that moment, I knew what I was going to do; all that was left was a farewell to city hall.

On a quiet Monday after at the end of September, I sat down with Rod Nutt in the same office in city hall–indeed the very same chair–where I was hired five years earlier. Having already so deeply mulled over the move to the ministry, I was blunt. "I've got to quit," I told Rod, who was seated behind the hulking desk across from me. "I'm going back to pastoring full time." Rod was puzzled and angry. "Jerry," he shot back, "is this about money?" I tried to be reassuring. "It's not about money," I replied. "It's *never* been about money." Rod was clearly dissatisfied with my explanation and prodded me for more. "Is it something about the job that needs to be changed?" he continued. "Too many responsibilities? Jerry, if there's one thing I know it's this: everyone leaves over money." I stood my ground. "It's never about money. I'm sorry, but I've got to go." There was nothing Rod could do but accept my resignation. But in order to smooth over the hurt feelings I offered to train my replacement. To my surprise, I found that I became fast friends with my replacement, an effusive, outgoing Beauregard Parish resident named Ronnie Rich. Yet as I shuttled between city hall and Grace of DeQuincy, I realized that the contrast between my former and future jobs couldn't have been more stark. At city hall, I was a technocrat in a high-functioning bureaucracy. At Grace, I sat in a cramped, makeshift office just off the sanctuary that didn't have a desk or even a phone. I felt like John the Revelator on the isle of Patmos: I was truly in exile. It didn't help that Sunday services brought a crowd that Kelli jokingly described as "three Glasses and three DeWitts," meaning three members of Pastor Glass's family and Kelli, Paul and me.

But behind the pulpit, through my messages, I was discovering perhaps the truest expression of faith–a love for God among humanity that could be so intimate that the church itself might not even be necessary. I preached that we had been taught as Pentecostals that the purpose of prayer was to move God, but what if the point of faith was to move us closer to God? "Instead of trying to change God's mind," I preached, "why not change our minds?" I pressed even further, arguing that expressions of devotion such as church attendance do not gain us favor with God. Better to love–to love God and to love your neighbor as you love yourself–than to go to church on Sundays. My emphasis on the importance of love carried over into the subject of sin. There was a controversy brewing at Grace about a group of congregants who gathered outside the church before and after services to smoke. The smoking horrified certain church members; they fretted that DeQuincy residents would drive past Grace and become so turned off by the smokers that they'd never consider attending services at our church. It was simplistic, slam-the-sinner thinking that was contradictory to where I was at doctrinally. Quoting Matthew 15:11–"Not that which goeth into the mouth defileth a man; but that which cometh out of the mouth, this defileth a man"–I preached that it's not what goes into your mouth but what *comes out* of your mouth that truly matters.

One Sunday afternoon, I put on an elaborate PowerPoint presentation supporting my doctrinal interpretation of what was meant by the defiling of man in Matthew. As the slides changed, I preached that we are all filled with the Holy Spirit and that we should not defile the temple of God, which brought murmurings of "mmm," "yes" and "that's right." The congregation was completely with me as I preached and I could tell that they were eagerly anticipating the moment when I slammed the smokers. But the slides changed to a slide picturing a box of fried chicken. The crowd was stunned into silence followed by nervous laughter. I quickly assured the crowd that I was only joking, but then became serious again. "A whole bunch of us folks leave church every Sunday to eat at Popeye's," I preached, "including me. So we all have bad habits. But it's not about bad habits." I opened my Bible and turned to 1 Corinthians 3. I preached that its well known, nearly clichéd verses 16–17–"Know ye not that ye are the temple of God, and that the Spirit of God dwelleth in you? If any man defile the temple of God, him shall God destroy; for the temple of God is holy, which temple ye are"–had been misinterpreted to mean that the destruction or defiling of the human body (God's temple) would bring about one's destruction. But if you read just two verses earlier–verse 15–then there was a very different, grace-oriented message of becoming saved even if the temple is destroyed. "If it is burned up," it reads, "the builder will suffer loss but yet will be saved–even though only as one escaping through the flames." "This is not about the individual," I told the congregation. "It's about the church. And it is the church–not humanity–that God will destroy if it is defiled. It's about the church body being defiled and not the human body being defiled." Returning to my favorite theme of a faith driven by God reaching toward humanity, I read straight from 1 Corinthians 3:9. "For we are labourers together with God," I said. "Ye are God's husbandry, ye are God's building."

As 2005 began, we began seeing crowds at Grace far surpassing the "three Glasses and three DeWitts" who were the sad hallmark of the earliest days of my ministry there. I lovingly referred to the few dozen devoted churchgoers at Grace as "the first faithful fifty" and promised that when the church grew, I'd have assistants pastor to the new members so I could focus my energies solely on those who had been so critical in the building of the Grace community. The increase in attendance came, in large part, because of my strikingly unique messages. But there was an eventual downside to what I preached; namely, that by advocating that my congregation did not have to seek perfection through devotion I was writing off the importance of attending church. If I was the CEO of Grace, I was instructing the congregation to refuse to purchase my product. Indeed, after one Sunday service, a tall, bald-headed thirtysomething member of Grace who was a professional baker in DeQuincy said to me with a wry smile, "Pastor, if you keep preaching messages like that you're gonna preach yourself out of business." He was right but it was no matter to me. I believed that the requirement of attending church–which in mainstream Christianity meant that one would gain credit with God or become closer to God by doing so–was in conflict with my message, which was simply: you've already got everything because of Christ's sacrifice on the cross. I believed that at the moment of Christ's sacrifice, the father transferred all of the sins of the world to Christ so there was no sin left to see, no judgment to be received and no credit to be earned by acts such as church attendance.

It became obvious that while I was a charismatic speaker and well liked personally at Grace, my messages were conflicting with everything everyone at my church had ever known. During the spring of 2005, a husband-wife team of church elders, the Blackburns, hinted at the air of confusion that they felt pervaded the church. "Jerry," they said, "we don't get where you're going. Where are you going?" I had to admit to myself–though I couldn't yet bring myself to tell the Blackburns–that my vision for Grace wasn't about duplicating the liberal Pentecostalism of the original Grace in DeRidder. What I sought to do was build a *community* and not a church at all. DeQuincy had a horrible drug problem, so I believed that we could truly serve the community–and by serving, truly *be-*

come a community–by building a Grace community center with classrooms where life-enhancing programs were taught. The community center would have a gymnasium to focus on wellness and we'd develop a food bank, too. Though I didn't realize it then, it was a vision that was a major leap from Pentecostalism toward humanism.

But my congregation's skepticism mixed with a reluctant tolerance to my messages at Grace was an exceedingly delicate balance that would not hold. When Katrina hit the Gulf Coast in August of 2005 and the floodwaters submerged much of New Orleans soon afterward, I turned my energies toward working with DeQuincy's mayor to open a relief center in town. Early that fall, as membership at Grace grew to nearly one hundred members and packed our little building out, I provided food and prayer to a steady stream of Katrina refugees in DeQuincy, a decision that upset the burgeoning faction of Dominionists at Grace. Dominionists are extremely conservative Christians inspired by a well-known passage of the Old Testament in which God commands Adam and Eve to have "dominion" over the earth. Some believe in an extremely literal interpretation of biblical doctrine–they're infamous for advocating stoning as a punishment, for example–while others fervently await Armageddon. For the Dominionists at Grace, who believed that they were engaged in spiritual warfare with nonbelievers and the insufficiently devout, Katrina was *the* judgment: the surest sign of the Armageddon to come. At its core, the Dominionist interpretation of Katrina–the storm demonstrated that if you're not living right by God, then he will refuse to protect you–clashed with my message that God loves *everyone*. I didn't confront the Dominionists directly, instead choosing to minister to the sick and hungry New Orleanians who arrived in DeQuincy in Katrina's wake. But inside, I fumed at the Dominionist faction at Grace. Katrina was not about God's judgment; it was about a storm that started as a low-pressure zone that slowly, dangerously grew into a tropical wave of low pressure. Katrina had a natural cause, not a supernatural cause.

What flooded New Orleans and sent its citizenry into exile was not, as the Dominionists at Grace argued, God running spiritually corrupt, lost souls out of town but rather a catastrophically flawed levee system constructed by human hands. Besides, I believed that what we did to help those affected by the storm—not why the storm or its destruction happened—was what mattered. My Katrina-era messages were just blandly positive—I preached that the storm was a moment to prove to God just how loving we could be to one another—but the Dominionists at Grace were furious nonetheless. "Are you really saying," they chided me after Sunday services, "that it doesn't matter how people in New Orleans live? That they can be saved if they're alcoholics?" I was unflinching in my answer. "Yes, " I replied sternly, "that's exactly what I'm saying." The Dominionists simply shook their heads in disgust at my apostasy.

Even though I found a profound sense of fulfillment helping Katrina refugees, my constant clashes with the Dominionists lent an enervating feeling to that fall. I realized that many of the folks at Grace held beliefs that were starkly, diametrically different from my own and that by leading this congregation I'd be associated with ideas that I did not share. There simply wasn't enough time to address every one of their wrong beliefs and by my not shaping the theology of the congregation, they were going about the business of shaping their theology themselves. My liberal, moderate and tolerant qualities had the unintended effect of providing license to radical voices within Grace to create an atmosphere where like-minded voices could flourish. It was as if I'd built a nativity scene in my front yard and allowed all manner of folks with crazy ideas about Jesus to stand beside it and rant. The neighbors would say, "Well, if Jerry built it, then he must support what's going on all around it." That's what was happening at Grace—my openhearted, embracing style was enabling bad spiritual habits in the people I cared for the most.

As the Dominionists became increasingly powerful at Grace at the outset of 2006, back in DeRidder the mayoral election yielded a too-close-to-call result that brought a runoff between incumbent Mayor Johnson and a challenger, Ron Roberts, a third-generation DeRidder resident. The runoff was something of a shock to observers of local politics because Ron was one of the least intuitive politicians to ever run for high office: he had a lecturing, from-the-podium style of speaking that seemed almost intentionally meant to alienate voters. Though I was engaged in building my congregation in DeQuincy, I'd closely watched the election because I wanted nothing more than to see Mayor Johnson out of office. I'd left the code enforcement officer job on good terms, but a comment that Mayor Johnson made during my final days at city hall left a bitter taste in my mouth. One afternoon, I overheard Rod Nutt ask the mayor about retirement plans for the soon-to-be retired police chief. "Gerald, what do you plan on doing for the chief?" Rod asked. "What do you mean?" Mayor Johnson replied incredulously. "The man's worked here for thirty years," Ron shot back. "Doesn't he deserve something?" Mayor Johnson's reply stunned me. "Do you know what it means if a man works for city hall for thirty years?" he asked rhetorically. "It means that he can't find a better job." The cruel remark infuriated me, not only because it denigrated a faithful public servant but because Mayor Johnson was a member of the DeRidder gentry: he'd married into the West family of the West Brothers Department Store. It was a snobby, unhumanistic remark that reminded me of the collapse of the West Brothers where the workers–my grandfather included–were sacrificed by the business elite.

Sensing Mayor Johnson's vulnerability, I approached Ron Roberts through my old friend Vincent Labue with an offer: "I can help you win." Ron's interest was piqued and we met at a Dairy Queen in DeRidder in April of 2006, just one week before the runoff. I told Ron that if he won he'd be an outsider starting from scratch. I'll give you the inside track, I told Ron, I'll be your inside guy. But in order to get to city hall, I said, he needed a winning strategy. "You need to start with the Police and Fire Departments,"

I told Ron. "Once you win them over they'll go out and politic for you. And you've got to hit Mayor Johnson on what he's failed to accomplish from the city's master plan." Ron eagerly scribbled down notes as we talked. But after the impromptu political session outside the Dairy Queen, I didn't get the sense that he was particularly committed to carrying out any of my ideas. Just days before the election, however, I received a surprise phone call from Ron. He told me that he'd been using small trucks outfitted with PA systems to travel into DeRidder neighborhoods to deliver a get-out-the-vote message through loudspeakers. His advisors had told him not to use the trucks on Election Day because in their experience low turnout is always good for the challenger. "So," Ron asked, "should I be listening to my advisors?" I was honored just to be asked the question because his team was far savvier in local politics than me. I told Ron that I'd pray on it and call him back. But instead of praying, I quickly dialed up a longtime friend and minister, Harold Lovelace, for advice. "Jerry," Harold said, "I think Louisiana loves a good old-fashioned, Louisiana-style political campaign. That includes everything from walking-around money to stump speeches. Tell your friend to use 'em. Voters like to feel that they're being courted." I called Ron back but was too embarrassed to tell him how I came to my conclusion; I didn't want to betray my lack of political sophistication. When I hung up the phone, I worried about providing the advice in the first place, which was contrary to what everything his closest advisors were telling him to do.

The morning of the runoff was marked by a record April rain that brought exceedingly low turnout. But hewing to my advice, Ron kept his trucks on the streets of DeRidder broadcasting his get-out-the-vote message to its citizenry. I felt fortunate to be out of town that day–Kelli and I were celebrating our wedding anniversary in Galveston, Texas–because I worried so deeply that I'd given Ron disastrous, down-to-the-wire political counseling. Late that night, as Kelli and I made the four-hour trip from Galveston back to DeRidder, I got a call on my cell phone from Vincent Labue.

"Jerry," he said excitedly, "we won. Hold on, Jerry, the mayor-elect wants to talk to you." I could hear the phone being placed into Ron's hands. "Thanks to you for everything that you've done, Jerry," Ron told me. "We're gonna go to New Orleans for two weeks. When I get back I want talk to you about your future at city hall." A sick feeling came over me; I hoped that he was just humoring me for having helped him in a small way to victory. Driving along I-10 East in the pitch-black night just past midnight, I was overcome with anxiety over Ron's job offer: *Is he serious?* As I tightly gripped the steering wheel, I looked at Kelli from the corner of my eye: *Can she stand yet another change?* I'd forced Kelli to suffer by returning to the ministry and here I was on the verge of yet another transition. I knew that all of my life's experiences–from Swaggart to the Branhamites–represented one opportunity after another, no matter how those experiences turned out. And I was so fed up with the Dominionists at Grace that I practically would have joined the military to avoid them. But no matter how promising a return to city hall might sound, I had to think about how Kelli and Paul would manage yet another life change. *How far,* I wondered, *is Kelli going to ride with me into the void*?

CHAPTER FOUR

God Is Everyone's Internal Dialogue

For I am the least of the apostles, that am not meet to be called an apostle, because I persecuted the church of God. But by the grace of God I am what I am: and his grace which was bestowed upon me was not in vain; but I laboured more abundantly than they all: yet not I, but the grace of God which was with me. Therefore whether it were I or they, so we preach, and so ye believed.

—1 Corinthians 15:9–11

WHEN MAYOR-ELECT ROBERTS returned from his two-week vacation at his New Orleans condo in May of 2006, I was faced with a critical life choice: Would I join his fledging administration? I was both excited and anxious about the opportunity. I was still building my congregation at Grace of DeQuincy and a move back into public service—so soon after I'd convinced a reluctant Kelli to rejoin the ministry—would uproot my family once again. So I decided to put the decision in the hands of Pastor Glass, who I was sure would insist that I put God's work at church first, especially because I had been pastoring at Grace full time for two years now. Though I clashed doctrinally with the congregation, especially with the Dominionists, I loved being so deeply involved in their lives. When a parishioner called me "Pastor" that meant more to me than anything in the world; it felt almost as good and as soul-fulfilling as when my son Paul called me "Dad" for the first time. So a part of me wanted a firm, undeniable "no" from Pastor Glass. Yet I had to acknowledge that my contentment with ministering at Grace stemmed from my relationships with its congregants; the supernaturalism and extremely conservative Pentecostalism of the church, conversely, unnerved my conscience.

On a warm, humid afternoon in late May, I sat down with Pastor Glass at his home in Dry Creek, Louisiana, to hash out my future with Grace. It was my first-ever visit to Pastor Glass's home, a white, wood-frame structure sitting in an open field with a pond behind it. It was a modest residence for a man pastoring such a large church but was kept so immaculately that it was an ideal reflection of the growing Grace empire. Every blade of grass in the front yard was cut to a perfect length and the pond shimmered so brightly in the sunlight that it seemed straight out of a pastoral watercolor. Inside the home, its many white surfaces shone with the cleanliness of a freshly scrubbed-down row of church pews. It was far from an ostentatious display of wealth but in the well-kept home I could sense the depth of his resources that were simply invested in a beautiful and elegantly simple way. "I won't take but five minutes of your time," I said as I took a seat on the loveseat in Pastor Glass's living room, which was decorated in a rugged cowboy motif of horse paintings, cowhide, horseshoes and even small sections of barbed wire affixed to the walls. "I just have one question to ask." Pastor Glass's slim, pretty wife, Karen, entered the living room and then, sensing the seriousness of the conversation, offered a quick greeting and turned back around toward the kitchen. "Ron Roberts wants me to come to city hall as the director of community service," I continued. "It's a job that the city charter has mandated from the beginning but the job's never been activated. It's a chief-of-staff position. So this is big for me. I'm asking you—*you as my pastor*—what you think I should do here." Pastor Glass was warm and easygoing but behind that everyman exterior was a minister with the work ethic of a coal miner. He expected his ministers to never stop working, right down to his instruction that whenever a minister walked from his car to church he should pick up every piece of trash and broken limb on the ground before even *thinking* of opening the door to go inside. So I was certain that he was going to come down hard on me for daring to ask for his permission to leave his satellite of Grace that I was just getting off the ground. "I think you should do it," Pastor Glass replied, seemingly without even a second thought. "Really? Do you really think this is something I should do?" I stammered. Pastor Glass nodded his head. "I do." Shocked by the lightning-fast resolution to what I was sure was going to be a long afternoon of debate over my sudden return to secular life, I simply rose from the loveseat, shook Pastor Glass's calloused hand and then headed out the front door.

When I returned home that afternoon, I called Ron with the good news: "I have the okay of my pastor. I can take the job." "I talked to them before they even talked to you," Ron replied with a hearty laugh. Ron explained that he'd reached out to Pastor Glass—through a close friend, Carol Greene, who also happened to be a finance officer at Grace of DeRidder—to ask for his permission to ask me for the job. They had cut me off at the pass. They'd asked for my pastor's permission before they asked me. I felt humiliated to have been kept out of the decision-making loop on such a major life choice, a decision, it seemed, that was made *for* me. As Ron and I wound down the conversation, it was clear that Pastor Glass approved my return to public service in large part because it would be a savvy political move for the growing Grace fellowship, which counted churches in DeQuincy, DeRidder and Sulphur. But even with Pastor Glass's support I was still uneasy about taking the job. And I was embarrassed by my visit to his home; had I known he would be for it I wouldn't have involved him in the decision in the first place.

Even though I'd given Ron an unqualified "yes" over the phone, my hesitance would not allow me to start my new city hall career. So when I ran into Ron at Vincent Labue's insurance office in early June and he asked me pleasantly, "So, Jerry, what are you thinking?" I shot back that we'd seal the deal only if three conditions were met. I said that I wanted my former boss's city-owned truck, a Dodge Durango; his office, which was quiet and private unlike my old office in "the fishbowl"; and his salary. "Let me think about it," Ron said with a contemplative look that told me that he actually was going to think about my extremely ambitious list of demands. Indeed, I truly believed that Ron would get back to me in a matter of hours to turn me down for the job. But just three days later, Ron called to set up a visit at his house. I arrived at Ron's house that same afternoon and after greeting me at the front door, he led me to a small guesthouse out back that he utilized as a studio space. Ron played the trumpet and sang in a band called Beauregard's Courtesy that played 1940s- and 1950s-era big-band music in churches and concert halls throughout Southwest Louisiana, and was such a serious jazz aficionado that his visits to his New Orleans condo were a musical pilgrimage. "I can give you two out of three of your conditions," Ron said as we took a seat on a pair of desk chairs in the guesthouse. "You've got the truck and you've got the office. But I can't give you the salary. If I did that, I'd max you out at city hall. I don't want you coming in already maxed out." It was a done deal. I was ready to return to public life and, with Pastor Glass's blessing to remain at Grace of DeQuincy part time, I'd be making more money than I'd ever made. Exuberant about the coming era that was sure to be the most financially secure we'd ever known, Kelli and I bought a modest Acadian-style home in downtown DeRidder. The purchase was the realization of a decades-long dream of home ownership for Kelli, especially after living in my grandmother's back bedroom and then a succession of trailers. We loved our new home as though it were part of our family.

My first assignment at city hall during the sweltering summer of 2006 was preparing for Ron's swearing-in ceremony to be held that August. It was the end of a campaign that had become so cruel and juvenile that even Ron's affection for bow ties became fodder for his enemies. The fact that Mayor Johnson had been swept out of office after more than two decades only made the bruised feelings on both sides even more deeply felt. But we on Mayor-Elect Roberts's transition team weren't ready to declare a truce, so I arranged for a bow-tie motif for the swearing in, placing bow ties on the walls all over city hall. I even made lapel buttons adorned with bow ties. It was vengeful behavior, but I felt it was an appropriate response that mocked the vicious campaign against Ron. The day of the swearing in, a brutally hot August day when the afternoon sun bears down on you as if it were being reflected through a magnifying glass, Ron stood beaming and sweating behind a podium placed beneath an expansive red-white-and-blue-colored tent with a banner reading CITY OF DERIDDER: OPEN FOR BUSINESS behind him. Ron told the hundreds-strong crowd packed with everyday DeRidderites and parish dignitaries that the city would launch an initiative called "Project Clean Sweep" meant to clear out the overgrown lots and tear down the crumbling, vacant buildings that had become all too abundant during the previous administration's tenure. "The clean sweep," Ron thundered as he held aloft a gold-painted push broom, "has begun!"

It was an exhilarating start to Ron's reign as DeRidder's mayor, but the sprint to the swearing in that summer left me drained and exhausted. I'd spent the summer alternating between city hall and my duties back at Grace, so by the beginning of September my nerves and patience were completely worn down. Every decision I made–from the length of a Sunday service to the time I'd set aside to prepare a message–was driven by the cold logistics of just how tired that task would leave me. The tensions between me and the Dominionists over the direction at Grace were coming even further to the surface. For the Dominionists, faith was all about spiritual warfare and for them–the warriors in that fight–to live as right and be as devout as possible. I, on the other hand, was proclaiming from behind the pulpit that no level of devotion would make us any more acceptable to God. Worse still, the Dominionists seized on my position at city hall as a sign that a religious takeover of a secular government was possible. To the Dominionists, by accepting the director of community service job I was literally bringing the presence of God to the spiritually empty corridors of city hall, with its secular ways of doing business and a heathen, jazz-loving mayor. The Dominionists' warped view of me only served to illustrate just how disconnected I was from them. Though we worshipped under the same roof, we were on two different planes altogether.

It was a dangerous distance because as their pastor I was not only expected to reflect their beliefs but, perhaps much more importantly, minister to them at their most vulnerable moments. Indeed, that fall, Larry Smith, one of Grace of DeQuincy's elders, asked me to provide not just spiritual counsel but medical advice to his brother who had resisted a doctor's request to undergo surgery for an aneurysm in an artery in his abdomen. Larry's brother had been putting the surgery off for months and, knowing that my father-in-law had just undergone a similar surgery that was successful, Larry urged me to pray with his brother and sway him to accede to it. As I drove out to the mobile home of Larry's brother, I realized just how uncomfortable I'd become ministering in situations in which I was literally addressing life-and-death decisions for my congregation. At city hall, I was Mr. Fix-It but at Grace I was the *cosmic* Mr. Fix-It who was supposed to provide not just solutions to the most profound and personal of my congregation's problems but also assure them that, by the grace of God, my fix would leave them safe and healthy in the end. When I arrived at Larry's brother's home, an old, ramshackle singlewide trailer in such a state of disrepair that every piece of it spoke of extreme poverty, I felt a thick, uncomfortable lump in my throat, the result of the uncomfortable task that lay before me. As Larry, a tall, broad-shouldered man with a protruding Santa Claus belly, stood by his brother who was resting in a porch swing, I explained that my father-in-law had a healthy recovery after the surgery and urged Larry's brother to follow his lead. Then we all bowed our heads in prayer. "Lord, take charge and guide the hands of surgeons," I prayed. "Lord, we come before you today to ask you to minister to the doctors. To the nurses. And to the anesthesiologists. Lord, let your spirit dominate the spirit of the operating room." Despite the prayer, I believed that I was imparting evidence-based experience to the Smith brothers. But when the visit was concluded and I shook Larry's hand outside the trailer, I realized that I was not there representing my father-in-law's experience but the Heavenly Father himself. It was the same profound–and fast-becoming unbearable–weight that I felt behind the pulpit.

That night, Larry's brother consented to the surgery and the next morning he was checked into a local hospital. Later that day, as we waited at the hospital, the doctors told us that that the surgery had been an unqualified success. At that moment I was the man of the hour, the man of God who had talked a member of the Grace church family into a life-saving surgery. That Larry's brother was a somewhat backslid Pentecostal compared to his far more devout kin only heightened the sense of miracle. The next day, however, as Larry's brother sat up in his hospital bed eating a meal, a blood clot made its way to his lungs and killed him instantly. The shock of hearing the news was life stopping. It was as though the earth itself had stopped revolving. We'd all been on such a high because he had come through the surgery so well and the Smiths were ecstatically celebrating the miracle of prayer–*my prayers*–only to have that celebration cruelly vanquished in a split second. The sense of responsibility I felt about Larry's brother's sudden demise was rivaled only by my anguish over my grandfather's death. The gut-wrenching guilt over not administering CPR to him appropriately that terrible day–it was that same weight. This time, however, the pain reached not just every fiber of my being but every corner of my faith. *Who was I to have so egotistically and arrogantly traveled to a stranger's trailer,* I asked myself, *and urged him to make a truly life-changing decision that ended up snatching his life from him? If I had not made the visit,* I thought then, *it's likely that this man would still be alive.* This is the same burden, the same responsibility that all pastors take to heart but having so deeply and critically examined my faith, there was an added sense of responsibility. In the wake of the passing of Larry's brother, I saw grief and mourning but also a scramble by the Smiths and the Grace church family to make it all spiritually okay in their minds. One day it was, "Everyone is at fault but God." The next, "No one is at fault, or fault doesn't matter in the end because he'd made it right with the Lord just before he passed." Meanwhile, I could only obsess over the futile effort we had expended in seeking God's assistance. God had not helped us here, just as he had not helped my cousin Gary's parents when they prayed for his survival.

I had been moving away from supernaturalism and toward a moderate, humanistic message of "faith is what you do and not what you receive." But after the death of Larry's brother, even that seemingly mild, inoffensive message suddenly seemed dangerous. I had wreaked unconscionable damage on a family with a theological worldview that I assumed was a safe harbor of sorts. Then I realized that even if I steered clear of supernaturalism in my messages, I couldn't help but create expectations of divine assistance amongst my congregation. No matter how liberal the theology was that I espoused, I had to confront life-and-death issues with my congregation that went far beyond praying for an unpaid light bill or repairing a broken relationship. Any form of faith required me to make a supplication before God, only to bring brutal disappointment. Worse, I was setting my congregation up for one discouraging moment after another and that–much more so than my struggle with my faith–was what was hurting me so deeply. And in trying to comfort the grieving Smiths with empty, well-worn clichés like "God had a greater plan for him" I felt like, spiritually, I resembled an abused wife who greets the police at her front door after a 911 call. She makes excuse after excuse about why her lip is cut or her eye is swollen shut but the police can see the pain in her face. The police know that none of what she's saying is true–and that she's all too aware that she's not being truthful. I felt the same way. The Smiths' grief brought a stream of excuses *for* God from his representative here on earth: me. So the pain of losing a man so quickly and so tragically was compounded by having to make it all right for his loved ones.

As 2007 began, I was completely despondent. At every service at Grace, I felt the weight of my spiritual duplicity. By embracing a new, tolerant message of a faith based upon good acts by humanity and not the judgment of God toward those he deems insufficiently faithful, I believed that I had righted my spiritual ship. But instead I was doing more harm than good to the Grace faithful. It also seemed wrong to espouse a theological worldview that was so deeply at odds with that of the church's founders, like the Glasses and the Blackburns. It was their house, not mine. And I felt as though I was setting fire to the house of God at a moment when the church so desperately needed me most. Hurricanes Katrina and Rita had caused deep declines in the church's membership and Grace needed an enthusiastic builder of God's house instead of a preacher whose inner spiritual conflicts could only bring it all tumbling down like the walls of Jericho.

I desperately sought an exit from Grace but even with my doubts I could still not yet imagine abandoning the ministry. Then, in October of 2008, I unexpectedly received an offer to pastor at First Community Church in DeRidder. I wasn't interested in starting anew in the ministry but I was encouraged by its name. *First Community.* That's where I had been trying to go at Grace: to put the community first. I told an elder there–Brother Libec, a short, bald-headed man in his seventies who wore oversized, circular-shaped glasses on his pinched face that resembled Mr. Magoo–that I'd attend a service and give it a look. My first service at First Community, a Sunday service marked by quiet, contemplative prayer, was encouraging. The congregation consisted of folks who had left the Presbyterian and Baptist denominations and were nondenominational and independent in spirit. *If a single person speaks in tongues,* I remember thinking when I arrived at church that Sunday, *then I'm gonna run their ass out of church.* But Sunday worship at First Community brought none of the expressions of Pentecostalism that I had come to regard as so gaudy and so bereft of spiritual meaning. There were practical pleasures to be found at First Community, too. They had turned an old metal shop into a sanctuary that fit an intimate congregation of about fifty worshippers. An old dentist's office on the property had been converted into Sunday-school rooms. And, perhaps best of all, First Community was just minutes from my house. In fact, I calculated that both First Community and city hall were a four-minute drive from my home, door to door. As Sunday services concluded on that clear, cool fall day in 2008, First Community's nondenominational style and its proximity to my home made the church seem to practically burst with potential.

This time, however, the career change didn't need the approval of Kelli–we were already back in the ministry–but instead her advice on what moving to a church that was one-third of the size of Grace of DeQuincy might do to our family's bottom line. "Can we do this financially?" I asked Kelli one night after our first visit to First Community. Kelli said that we could–but the truth was that we could not. It was a white lie: Kelli had become a discontented pastor's wife and wanted to smooth over the transition from Grace to First Community if it was going to help our marriage in the end. Late that fall, I preached twice at First Community and it felt like a good fit. I was not under the pressure that I felt at Grace to hew to supernaturalism and I could, without fear of the wrath of the Dominionists, preach a liberal Christian message. First Community truly felt that it was going to be easier on my conscience and better for my marriage than Grace. So in early 2009, I broke the news to a small crowd consisting of Grace's elders and the Glasses and the Blackburns: I was leaving. I tried to soften the blow of the bad news with promises that I'd bring Presbyterians into the Grace fold and that I was only taking the job to be closer to home. But Pastor Glass and the church leadership were obviously unmoved and clearly unhappy. When I turned my keys over to the Blackburns on a chilly Sunday in January, the meeting was extraordinarily tense and uncomfortable. They were not just disappointed that Grace was losing its pastor–they were disappointed in me.

But I felt a huge sense of relief by leaving Grace behind. I had come to believe that the congregation at Grace saw their beliefs–even their most extreme, Dominionist beliefs–*in* me, no matter what I preached in my messages. Grace's membership simply believed that I was someone who I wasn't. In doing so, they had forced an identity upon me, which led to an identity crisis. It was not an identity crisis in the traditional meaning where you internally wrestle with who you are, but instead in the sense of feeling as though you can no longer carry the weight of an identity created *for you*. Gone from Grace, I returned to the idea I had held in my dark, post–Des Moines days immersed in Bible study in which I viewed Christianity as an intellectual pursuit, a chance to express everything I had discovered about my faith. What I had learned back then–specifically through the reading of Joseph Campbell–was that Christianity could be a useful mythology, so my messages at First Community could be viewed as utilitarian tools to express that mythology. During Sunday services at First Community, I preached about the tabernacle of Moses–a tent that the Israelites had erected exactly one year after the Passover when the Israelites were freed from bondage in Egypt–as a metaphor for the godlike qualities of humanity. "The table of showbread and the Golden Altar of Incense," I preached, "the laver, the brazen altar; when a person becomes a believer he realizes he possess all of these pieces. These pieces are obtained not through devotion–each and every person is born with that furniture." It was an "ultra-grace" message and the congregants, many of whom were young people in their twenties and thirties, were warmed by my humanistic embrace. The reception I received at First Community confirmed my beliefs when I first started pastoring there: mythology *can* be used to help people. I was having the time of my life there teaching an open, community-driven message of "love thy neighbor as you love yourself," a message that for the most part purposefully avoided doctrine.

But by the outset of 2010, I had fallen into the same spiritual place at First Community that had I had found myself in during my final months at Grace of DeQuincy. Despite the congregation's Presbyterian past, they, too, embraced a supernaturalism that I was far from comfortable with. And once again, the messages I preached were being tolerated but not truly heard. "Things just aren't working out for me," I told the church's elders during a board meeting early that spring. Just as I had done at Grace of DeQuincy, I attempted to ease the shock and pain over my departure with excuse making: work at city hall was all consuming, I said, and by splitting my days between the ministry and public service I was fast losing standing with the mayor. Though the First Community board was deeply dissatisfied with my sudden resignation, for once the excuse had more than just a shade of truth to it. I'd come on board at city hall to be the mayor's number two, and while my position was mandated by the city charter, it was never implemented. So after the hard work of heading up Mayor Roberts's transition team in the summer of 2006, there was little for me to do at city hall. With few responsibilities, the balance of power shifted back to where it historically had been all along: with the director of public works. To assuage my fears about a job that was essentially being negated, Ron engaged me in after-work pep talks about how he'd support me for a mayoral run in 2014. But I doubted that I'd last at city hall that long and, with Ron running uncontested in 2010, I decided that it was time to go.

Squeezed out of city hall and disaffected with the ministry, it truly felt like my life options had run out. But on a quiet Monday that spring, the mayor's secretary sent a salesman to my office and it seemed as though I wouldn't be leaping into the void again if I departed from city hall. But not in the beginning at least: the meeting with the advertising sales representative from a publishing company called Village Profile just seemed like more of the work I'd been saddled with at city hall, which was taking meetings with visitors who nobody else wanted to deal with. The guy was a classic salesman; he was a rotund, middle-aged man with the faint smell of cigar smoke on him and an all-too-enthusiastic demeanor given the product he was pitching, a community publication that is sponsored, published and delivered to over fourteen hundred chambers of commerce across the country. He was at city hall to see if the city of DeRidder would buy ad space with Village Profile. I said that we were interested and asked him to tell me about his job. The ad sales rep, naturally, relished the opportunity to talk about himself; he said that he spent his days crisscrossing the country pitching mostly small, local governments on purchasing Village Profile ad space. With my finances halved because of the loss of income from pastoring at First Community, I pressed him further on details of his sales job. "Who do I need to talk to?" I asked. He seemed surprised that a city hall heavy would express any interest in his line of work. "Are you serious?" he replied. I told him that I was. "Okay," he said, "let me put you in contact with my sales manager."

Two weeks later, I was hired. When I walked over to the mayor's office to deliver the bad news, he sat behind his sprawling desk, folded his hands on his chest and made a teepee with fingers. "I expected that," Ron said. "You going back to preaching?" I could only stammer a reply. "No sir," I said, "I don't think I'm ever going back to preaching. I'm taking a sales job." Ron looked hurt but relieved. I was unhappy with my steadily declining authority at city hall and my unhappiness made the brass displeased with me. "Good luck, Jerry," Ron continued. "I've always believed that there's only three ways to be wealthy: you can inherit wealth, get it through professional work like doctoring or lawyering, or sales. But know this: there's always a place for you at city hall."

Having sold life insurance for years, I was under no illusions about what a depressing grind work at Village Profile would be. Just as I expected, I spent lonely weeks on the road in far-flung towns in neighboring states such as Arkansas and Texas. I'd stay in a city or small town for one week at a time and then cold-call its city council members and, if my luck played out, would set up an appointment with them to sell advertising in Village Profile magazines. But where I'd once just gotten by financially on sales work, this time the inconsistent income plunged Kelli and me into deep poverty again. We'd become accustomed to living on my steady salaries preaching and working at city hall, which amounted to about six thousand dollars per month. At Village Profile, by contrast, I averaged far less than half that. Poor and perpetually out on the road, my sense of self-worth took a brutal beating. I realized that I had become the guy who shows up at an office unannounced who is made to sit in the lobby for hours until *somebody* finds a minute to meet with him. It was a dramatic reversal of fortune that I could barely contemplate without feeling utter hopelessness; in just a matter of weeks, I'd gone from the second-most important person in Beauregard Parish to the least important person waiting out in the lobby of a barbeque sauce company in the Arkansas sticks.

By the fall of 2010, I was so emotionally and spiritually broken that during a sales meeting with a pastor in a storefront church in a mall in El Dorado, Arkansas, I felt a sudden, irresistible urge to not only preach but start a revival. When the church's pastor and I talked about my background, he asked me if I'd consider preaching at a Sunday service. I jumped at the chance. That Sunday, I planned on preaching that the congregation should reach out to the community with food banks and clothes for poor children. But just before I took the stage, I found myself bathed in bright, rock star–style lighting and with ecstatic Pentecostal music over the PA pumping up the crowd for my arrival. I was thrust back into a charismatic environment and, for the first time in years, I preached as though I was standing before a crowd assembled for a revival in rural Mississippi. "You can do anything!" I thundered. "Every one of you here, you all are God's conduit. Devote yourself to your pastor and to his ministry and God will recognize your devotion and bring you closer, with each Sunday here, to him."

The one-shot ministry at the mall church just left me enervated. I had taken the stage simply to try–in vain–to reclaim the ecstatic feeling of my days as a charismatic preacher. But my blind, unquestioning faith was never coming back. And I had to admit that my decision to preach came from the sheer desperation of the sales life. There wasn't a second that went by at Village Profile that I didn't feel that I was the scum of the earth. Then, out on the road again in early January of 2011, I missed a call on my cell phone that I suspected was important. When I checked my voice mail, it was Ronnie Rich, my replacement as code enforcement officer at city hall. Ronnie said to call him back–he didn't tell me what he was calling about–but even before the end of his message I knew what the purpose of the call was. Ronnie had left city hall and started a company of his own called the Building Inspection Group (BIG) only to have his business partner, David Morrison, die after a long battle with cancer. Kelli had just told me about David's passing and I knew that Ronnie was on his own at BIG and very likely looking for a new partner. Sure enough, when I called Ronnie back he offered me a job at BIG and at a salary–four thousand dollars per month–that would get the bills paid at home.

Because building codes had changed so drastically since I had worked as code enforcement officer, thanks in large part to the successive Hurricanes Katrina, Rita and Gustav, at first I just rode along with Ronnie and watched him work. We'd pull up to a job site–like a brand new school being built southeast of DeRidder–in Ronnie's white Nissan pickup and then don rubber boots, reflective vests and hard hats and trudge through the midwinter slush to inspect the construction. Because I was new to the job, I would snap photographs of a project on a digital camera while Ronnie did the actual inspecting. During these long workdays, Ronnie and I shared everything about our lives–bills, kids, our marriage–but I made sure to never venture into the subject of religion. Ronnie had once been a preacher so I knew that we weren't going to agree on much of anything doctrinally. But that didn't matter because I had a job that I loved that was not only paying me well but helping me dig out of the financial hole I had dug for Kelli and me at Village Profile. And it felt great to finally be out from under the preacher identity that had become such a profound spiritual weight at both Grace and First Community.

But in April of 2011, I got an offer I found hard to resist: my father-in-law's nephew William Ivan Swain, who was a Pentecostal preacher in Cut and Shoot, Texas, a tiny town of about a thousand residents near Houston, asked me to preach at his church. A full-throated Pentecostal, William and I were not at all on the same page doctrinally. He'd also known me from my days in the healing ministry, which was so far from what I'd become spiritually that I might have well been another person. And I worried that preaching in Cut and Shoot would lead to an experience similar to what had transpired in Arkansas–caught up in the moment, I embraced a form of faith I no longer believed in. It was a spiritual relapse. But because William was family, I reluctantly agreed to travel out to Cut and Shoot. Somewhere inside me was a spiritual itch that wanted to make a difference in people's lives after months of working in building inspections. As I made the three-hour drive from DeRidder to Cut and Shoot, I became increasingly convinced that preaching at William's church was the right thing to do. *I've got to try one last time to make it work in the ministry,* I said to myself. *There's got to be a way.*

Soon after arriving in Cut and Shoot on a quiet, late Friday afternoon in mid-April, William put me up in a little hotel in town. That weekend I preached in William's tiny wood-frame church. In my messages, I implored the congregation to free themselves from their religious constraints. "Don't leave it to someone else," I told them, "to tell you what the truth is." Because my messages were delivered in my Southern-fried style, they didn't push anybody's buttons but they certainly didn't move anyone either. As I was driving off from Cut and Shoot that Sunday afternoon, it was apparent to me I still hadn't found the right message. No matter what I said to the congregation, they were still hearing something else. I had not found the fix that would bring me back to the ministry. It was disingenuous of me to engage with a world that I felt so disconnected from. I had to admit that I felt a huge amount of pity for Pentecostals—for how their faith affected them day in and day out, the limits it put on their self-expression, how it made their talents go unrealized, how it limited their experiences. I *hated* that pity. That pity was like an impenetrable barrier between me and my former Pentecostal family and the very existence of pity undercut my empathic worldview, in which I believed that God loved everyone and that we all possess God's gifts.

As I turned east onto Highway 190 heading toward DeRidder that Sunday, I realized that what I'd attempted to do in my last days in the ministry with Grace and First Community was the spiritual equivalent of Ted Turner's colorization of old black-and-white movies. There was so much life and color missing from the Pentecostal experience—a color I was desperately, and fruitlessly, trying to restore. So I decided to table the whole notion of the ministry even though I knew that a return to Pentecostalism was fast becoming an impossibility. The sense of awe I now felt at life was a natural and explainable experience, not a divine experience. I cherished that newfound sense of life, which was rooted in science and rationality, and it was hard to imagine turning back.

CHAPTER FIVE

God Is a Delusion

And not only so, but we glory in tribulations also: knowing that tribulation worketh patience; And patience, experience; and experience, hope.

–Romans 5:3–4

FOR THE FIRST TIME since I'd entered the ministry, I settled in my mind that the spiritual fix I sought in order return to preaching was unlikely to be found. I was going to have to live my life without a spiritual resolution. I needed to face the cold fact that I would not be back behind the pulpit anytime soon. Preaching at a somewhat traditional Pentecostal church like William's in Cut and Shoot was going to be impossible and I'd even been unable to make the liberal Pentecostalism of Grace of DeQuincy or First Community work for me. But I could not completely let go of the ministry: I had been ministering for nearly twenty-five years and from the very beginning it was not a career but a mission. *Perhaps,* I reasoned to myself then, *I'll find a mentor in the church and quietly work under him—or maybe I'll pastor to the faithful individually.* But as the spring of 2011 began, I had to push my spiritual crisis even further back into my mind. I was just emerging from the training period with Ronnie, which meant that I'd soon assume real responsibilities at BIG. The promotion would be a big boost to Kelli and me financially as we were just beginning to rebuild from the near financial collapse of my Village Profile period. With a happy, contented wife and a boss who treated me as both a business partner and a brother, life was good again. I couldn't allow my questions of faith to consume me.

But just after midnight on a still-cool night that May, I was thrust right back into the crisis of faith I had labored so hard to avoid. The roar of a box fan in a corner of our bedroom had finally lulled me to sleep when my cell phone, which I'd just silenced, lit up brightly with an incoming call. As I groggily reached over to the antique, rectangle-shaped wooden nightstand where my phone rested, my heart raced. I'd taken dozens of late-night calls over my more than two decades in the ministry and I knew that good news never arrived at this time of night. When I focused my bleary eyes on the phone, I saw the name of the caller and my spirits sank. It was NaTosha Davis, who ran the soundboard at Grace of DeQuincy. NaTosha was truly like a part of my family; I'd even entered her phone number into my phone under the name "NaTosha Davis/DeWitt." Though she stood at just barely five foot tall–we'd lovingly nicknamed her "Lil' D"–her huge smile, quick-wittedness and willingness to assist the church with everything from the sound system to our youth group lent her an outsized presence at our church. As a pastor of a small church like Grace of DeQuincy, *anyone* who wants to help is appreciated but a strong talent and vivacious spirit like NaTosha is an absolute treasure. "NaTosha?" I whispered as I picked up the phone so as not to wake Kelli. "Yes," NaTosha stammered. Even though she barely said a word, I could tell that she was already in tears. I slipped my shoes on, headed down the staircase, walked silently through the foyer and then into the tiny bathroom of our guest bedroom so as to let Kelli continue sleeping. I stood uncomfortably between the baby-blue-colored bathtub and the bathroom sink, which was illuminated by a strip of round lightbulbs above a mirror that made the bathroom–which we hadn't had the money to renovate–resemble a tacky backstage dressing room in a theater.

As I steadied myself at the sink, NaTosha told me that her brother had been severely injured in a motorcycle accident in the Lake Charles area. NaTosha tearfully explained that the ER physicians had failed to revive her brother and that specialists were on the way. Listening to NaTosha, I envisioned her standing outside the hospital and having reached that moment that we all have journeyed to in our lives, when inquiries to nurses and doctors about a loved one's health have been exhausted and our ability to make the situation any better is depleted. It's at that moment when you call your pastor in hopes of bringing God's grace and, perhaps, a resolution to a moment that is steadily speeding toward tragedy. I knew that she wanted me to pray for her brother's condition to improve and for her to have the strength to weather the storm. To pray that she was able to do the right things and not lose it amidst her family's tragedy. But NaTosha didn't say any of this. She didn't even say, "Will you pray for me, Jerry?" She didn't have to. Any pastor worth his salt won't let the conversation go that far. The second that anguished call arrives, it is the pastor's job to pray. It's just like when a friend or family member initiates a hug–an embrace is understood and instinctual between two people who care for one another–so asking for a hug renders it meaningless. I had no doubt in my mind what my role was as I listened to NaTosha's tearful telling of her brother's motorcycle wreck. Yet I could not pray. And every second that went by without my prayer for NaTosha and her brother felt like an eternity, a profound span of time when NaTosha, one of the most beloved members of my former congregation, was left hopeless and without the spiritual reassurance she so desperately and rightly craved.

I struggled to pray because all of the conflicts that had existed inside me about my faith, which I'd temporarily resolved time and time again through my motivation to remain in the ministry, suddenly fused into an awareness that there was no God. But I *could not pray* for NaTosha because I loved her so deeply and could not bear setting her up for the kind of crushing disappointment I'd witnessed with Grover and Bobbi's unanswered prayers over my cousin Gary, or my own prayers for Larry Smith's sick brother. If I prayed for NaTosha and her brother didn't make it it wouldn't be me who would have disappointed her–it would be God who let her down. I didn't want to initiate in NaTosha the long, painful journey of doubt that I had experienced.

For the very first time, I turned to reason. "NaTosha," I said in a calm, reassuring voice, "it sounds like everyone at the hospital is doing everything they can. Your brother is a young man and a strong man. They're bringing in specialists, so we're going to just have to wait this out and see what happens. But, NaTosha, I'm telling you it sounds like he's going to be all right." NaTosha thanked me for taking the call so late at night and for the encouraging words. Then, just before we made our goodbyes, NaTosha said, "Keep him in your prayers." I paused for a moment and then replied, "Of course, NaTosha. Of course." When I hung up the phone I was heartbroken. I knew that I'd deeply disappointed NaTosha. I realized in that moment that if I could not pray for a person who was so near and dear to me then my dream of returning to the ministry was over. I'd given up on preaching after Cut and Shoot but the ministry remained a far off, remote possibility. Now there was no ministry left. I stared into the bathroom mirror. I was in tears. *DeWitt,* I angrily said to myself, *who the hell are you*? It was done. It was over. I couldn't continue to fool myself into thinking that I'd one day find some form of Christian ministry to participate in. I'd bounced from denomination to denomination, from a literal Bible interpretation to an embrace of Christianity as metaphor and I'd finally reached the conclusion of that quest: I was looking at an atheist standing there looking in the mirror. It was a painful realization but the next moments literally tore my soul apart. There, in the guest bathroom, I said three final goodbyes to my loved ones: my cousin Gary, my grandfather and my father.

"Gary," I began, "I loved and respected you so much. You were a huge influence in my life. I'll never forget you, Gary, but I will never see you again. I love you." Nearly overcome with tears, I steadied myself on the bathroom sink again and moved to my granddad, my beloved paw-paw. "Paw-Paw," I said through the tears, "you know how much I love you. You know that if there was any way to see you again I would do it. But this thing–it just isn't true. I thank you for being such a huge part of my life. I'm so sorry that I failed you that day by not being able to do CPR the right way. Please forgive me. I love you." After my farewell to Paw-Paw, I grasped that so much of my spiritual quest was driven by the loss of my father. I didn't possess a single memory of my father; all I had was photographs. One of my earliest memories was of me asking Mom about where Dad had gone. "Where's my daddy?" I'd asked. "He's in heaven," she replied. "How'd he get there?" I continued. "By airplane," Mom replied. So I looked in the mirror and I said, "Dad, I've tried to find you but it's just not gonna happen. I'm sorry." And that was it. My journey through faith was done.

I went back upstairs and quietly rejoined Kelli in bed and opened my laptop computer. *Who in the world,* I thought to myself, *can understand what an ex-minister is feeling?* In a flash of inspiration, I remembered seeing *Losing Faith in Faith: From Preacher to Atheist,* a book by preacher-turned-atheist Dan Barker, on a shelf in a bookstore in the 1990s. I googled Dan's name and found his contact information. The next morning I called his office and left a message saying that I was an ex-minister in need of help. The next day Dan called me back; I was honored just to get the call because I couldn't imagine that a published author would have time to speak to a nobody like me. I told Dan just a little bit about my story–I was still feeling too vulnerable to open myself up completely–and to my relief he was sweet and instantly reassuring. "I've encountered a lot of people like you," Dan said soothingly. "I've helped form a group–would you be interested in joining?" Dan explained that the group, the Clergy Project, was a safe haven for former clergy. The idea of a finding a new home after losing my church family was so appealing that I said yes without asking a single question about the organization. The wisdom of my unreserved leap into the Clergy Project quickly became clear after Dan set me up with a user name and password for its online forum. Soon after logging on for the first time, I found myself feeling hopeful again. It was a hope far outside of my hope of finding a spiritually fulfilled life in the ministry. But by communicating with other ministers and sharing my story and hearing their stories, I felt that familiar sense of fulfillment that came *with* the ministry. *Through these forums,* I thought to myself, *I can help people. My life can have hope—and purpose—again.*

With the Clergy Project, I was back where I'd always been most comfortable: in the lives of others. There were only about fifty of us with the Clergy Project back then but the online conversation was always spirited, inspirational and heartbreaking. I'd share my story and empathize with my online friends about just how hard it is to continue in the ministry when you're questioning your faith, a spiritual struggle compounded by very earthly, practical problems. I remember one minister, who had not yet left the ministry, confessing to me that he had stayed with the church solely for health insurance. His wife had a chronic health condition that required expensive medication and his decision to remain with the church was literally keeping her alive.

Fortunately, there were no such crises in my home, despite my new embrace of atheism. Kelli and Paul had always been just a few steps behind me in my spiritual journey, so the fact that I'd come to a conclusion that rejected supernaturalism didn't surprise either of them. In fact, Paul, who'd grown into an independent-minded eighteen-year-old, had already publicly expressed an atheist worldview and left the church. We didn't even hold a family meeting to discuss the cataclysmic changes to our household. Instead, there was an excited, almost buzzy feeling in our home as Paul and I explored the works of atheists like Richard Dawkins, Dan Barker and Daniel Dennett. That one of the movement's most important thinkers, Dan Barker, was communicating with me by e-mail was such a huge point of pride that whenever I got an e-mail from Dan I'd print it out and read it to Paul over breakfast around the kitchen table. But while Kelli wasn't surprised by my embrace of atheism it nonetheless made her uneasy. I'd gone from a spiritual mission in Christianity to a quest to find out everything that I could possibly know about atheism in a matter of days, and the downtime between these journeys was negligible. Regular, normal life for our family had lasted less than a week. But I felt born again; it was like a salvation that I stumbled across. I could minister to people, I could be in their lives, all without pretending that I was someone who I wasn't or pretending to know all the answers. For me, religion had become like embracing people with a hazmat suit–every emotional connection had occurred with that bulky suit on. Now I could help people without any layers of pretense. I was elated.

With Kelli's awkward embrace of my new beliefs, I knew that the next task ahead was to break the news to my boss, Ronnie. My hands were clammy and slicked with sweat as I maneuvered my car to Ronnie's house on the outskirts of DeRidder on a humid afternoon in June of 2011. The visit, after all, wasn't just about my faith but my future with BIG. Ronnie had hired me with the promise that I would take over the reins of the company and because he was about five years away from retirement he'd already put my name on BIG's bank account. So I was wracked with guilt about my involvement with the Clergy Project; I didn't want Ronnie feeling like he was giving the company he'd worked so long to build to a man he no longer knew. It just didn't feel right to keep where I was at spiritually a secret. It was true that Ronnie knew me as charismatic preacher who was no longer preaching but atheism was something else entirely. Sitting in Ronnie's back porch that afternoon, I laid out my newfound views about God and religion. "Even if the whole world calls you an atheist," Ronnie replied, "it won't change us. And it won't change your place in the company." In that moment, I'd achieved something I hadn't been able to make happen in the twenty-five years since I'd entered the ministry: I resolved my work and faith. My family was fine, my finances ever better, and my boss said that he was okay with atheism. Things had finally come together.

That summer, while talking with my fellow ministers online at the Clergy Project, I learned about two major upcoming events in the atheist community: a banquet to be held by the New Orleans Secular Humanist Association (NOSHA) in September and the Texas Freethought Convention set for October, in Houston. Both events had enormous significance for me that far surpassed mere stops on the atheist convention circuit. I'd been asked to briefly address the NOSHA banquet, which would mark the first time I publicly declared that I didn't believe in God. At the Freethought Convention, meanwhile, Dawkins himself was going to present the Richard Dawkins Freethinker of the Year Award to a gravely ill Christopher Hitchens, who had become something of a hero of mine thanks to his book *God Is Not Great*.

Even though the NOSHA banquet was held at a small, 1970s-era Italian seafood restaurant in the New Orleans suburbs, I was so nervous when I stood before the crowd that I could see only the flash of cameras. Fortunately, when I got behind the podium I slipped easily back into preacher mode. "Reason and science," I told the crowd that day, "have done more to ease human suffering in the last two hundred years than all the sermons put together have done in the last two thousand." The line brought a standing ovation and when the MC took the stage to introduce the next speaker, Dan Barker's wife, Annie Laurie Gaylor, he said with a laugh, "I don't know how she's gonna follow that." After the banquet, I toured the French Quarter with Annie Laurie and felt a profound sense of belonging and inner peace. My public "coming out" as an atheist had been received rapturously and now I was walking down Bourbon Street with Dan's family. Life simply couldn't get any better. But as we took in the honky-tonk Bourbon Street bars,

Annie Laurie asked if I'd be a guest on Dan's Freethought Radio podcast and my serenity was shattered. Speaking to a small assembly of humanists in New Orleans was a private affair, a moment shared by NOSHA members and the few who later happened upon pictures of me from the organization's newsletter. Dan's podcast, by contrast, was on the Internet, where the audience was potentially limitless. With the podcast invite, I had to admit to myself that what I'd found so exciting about my transition to atheism thus far–which was composed solely of poring over atheist books in my kitchen and addressing a tiny group of atheists in a city far from my home in DeRidder–was how easy it had all been. I felt like I was getting away with it. The consequences I feared, such as becoming shunned by my friends and my community, had not come to pass, but I hadn't even begun to *face* the consequences. That led to a realization that my greatest fear in embracing atheism was not a loss of meaning or hope after faith but of rejection–I was consumed with what my wife, son and boss all thought of me.

The night before the podcast that September, I sat awake in bed with worry. *On the Internet,* I thought to myself, *there's no taking it back.* To relax my nerves, I put on my headphones, fired up my iPod and Christina Perri's "Jar of Hearts" washed over me. The song, about a final turn away from an obsessive love ("Now you want me one more time . . . / but I have grown too strong / To ever fall back in your arms") perfectly captured the moment. My religion, my history, my tradition all whispered to me, telling me to refuse to do Dan's show–to give in to religion just one more time. I knew that if I participated in Dan's podcast the next day, my love affair with Christianity would once and for all be over. Late that night and early into the next morning I put "Jar of Hearts" on repeat. I must have listened to the song dozens of times and its chorus–"I have grown too strong / To ever fall back in your arms"–brought tears to my eyes every time. Yet when I did Dan's podcast the next day, to my amazement it turned out to be as without consequence as the NOSHA banquet. I didn't hear a word about it from any of my friends and family in DeRidder. *I'm truly getting away with it,* I thought then.

It was a high that lasted into October when Paul and I drove to Houston to see Hitchens at the Freethought Convention. That fall, Hitchens was being treated for esophageal cancer at the MD Anderson Cancer Center in Houston and nobody knew if he would actually make it to the Freethought Convention. There was an air of raw excitement and anticipation surrounding the event, which was held at the Hyatt Regency on October 8. Hitchens hadn't appeared in public for months and for Paul and me it was our very first encounter with the great public intellectual. When the banquet began that night, a group of staffers walked onto the dais, followed by Dawkins and then Hitchens, who wore a loose, rumpled blue-and-white dress shirt and khaki pants, both of which seemed to envelop his slender, sickly frame. As Hitchens walked into the auditorium, the attendees stood one by one and began clapping. Before long, the entire room, which was packed with well over a thousand people, was on its feet and clapping ferociously for Hitchens. In that moment, if a speaker took to the podium and announced that we could save Hitchens's life if every person donated at least one year from their own lives, the entire room would have granted the request without a second thought. This moment of such pure love for a dying man instantly ranked as high spiritually for me as finding my faith at Swaggart's. "Hitch is in a foxhole," Dawkins said in his short speech honoring Hitchens, a pointed allusion to the well-worn cliché that there are no atheists in foxholes, "and he's dealing with it with a dignity that any of us would be proud to muster." Hitchens then rose to the podium slowly and though his voice was raspy and his speech was labored the clarity of his ideas was astonishing. The speech was quintessentially Hitchens, with its sharpest barbs directed at Jewish settlers in Israel and Islamists alike, those who "look forward to the common destruction of our species with relish."

When Hitchens was finished, he took a seat next to Dawkins on the stage. It was beautiful to witness Dawkins's tender treatment of Hitchens. Dawkins doted on Hitchens's every need and when Hitchens said that he'd like to stay a little longer if that was okay, we all felt that the frailty of that remark, coming from the most pugilistic of polemicists, was heartbreaking in its humanity. It touched upon a truth that we felt: all of us in the auditorium that day were wishing he *could* stay a little longer. Toward the end of the question-and-answer session, an eight-year-old girl rose from the audience and asked Hitchens what books he'd recommend for her to read. Hitchens told the girl that she and her mother should meet him in the hallway later and, sure enough, when the event was over there was Hitchens, surrounded by well wishers snapping photos on their phones and digital cameras, sharing his reading list with the little girl. As Hitchens conversed with the girl and her mother, the crowd surrounding them grew so overwhelmingly large that a young female staffer shouted herself hoarse trying to disperse it. "We're trying to get Hitchens to the hospital," she told me in a sandpapery voice, "and no one will listen to me." I straightened my suit jacket and stood, like a preacher at the pew, on high atop a chair. "May I have your attention please," I shouted to the throng, "the hotel needs everyone to vacate the corridor." The crowd dispersed and Dawkins and Hitchens made a fast escape to the hotel elevators. It felt great to make even a small connection with Hitchens, who would leave our world just two months later.

When I returned home to DeRidder in mid-October, I posted a photo on my Facebook page of me and Paul standing with Dawkins at the Freethought Convention. Because I'd "liked" the likes of Dawkins and Dan Barker on Facebook without any blowback in DeRidder, I didn't think anything of uploading the photo. But unbeknownst to me, an elderly cousin of my grandmother's, Grace Roberts, saw the photograph and forwarded it to several of my friends and relatives. Then, on December 1, 2011, my boss Ronnie texted me and asked if we could meet at the Waffle Shoppe, a popular place in DeRidder for coffee. Because our workdays usually began with a text from Ronnie with the address of our next project, I was suspicious. I texted him back and said that Kelli had come home for lunch. Can we meet in thirty minutes? I texted. He replied that we could.

I arrived at the Waffle Shoppe, a white stucco building at 623 North Pine Street in DeRidder that was once a Mexican restaurant, at around noon that day. I met Ronnie, who had just piled out of his white Nissan pickup truck, in the parking lot. He appeared ready for a workday, wearing a white, long-sleeve work shirt and blue jeans and carrying his leather-bound ledger. "Do I need to get mine?" I asked, gesturing toward Ronnie's ledger. I was hoping that we might be meeting about our next project. "No," Ronnie replied solemnly, "you don't need anything." It was a beautiful, unusually warm December day but Ronnie's dismissive "no" chilled me to the bone. We walked into the Waffle Shoppe and took a seat together in the very last booth. I made several attempts at small talk–"How's your day?" I asked cheerily, but Ronnie was silent. He opened his ledger book and unfolded two pieces of paper tucked inside: printouts of the home pages of the Clergy Project and a related group where I'd just taken a nonpaying position, Recovering from Religion. "I got hit with this this morning," Ronnie said as he slid the pages across the table. "The Pentecostals at the Police Jury"–in Louisiana, some parishes are governed by a body called the Police Jury–"aren't happy and want something done."

In that moment I knew that I was about to be fired but I desperately tried to change Ronnie's mind anyway. "I came to you and told you what was going on with me to the best of my ability," I pleaded. "I didn't know," Ronnie replied, angrily tapping the printouts with his forefinger, "that you meant *this*." Tears welled up in my eyes. "If you do this," I told Ronnie, "Kelli is going to leave me." This was no exaggeration: Kelli had endured nearly a quarter of a century of upheaval in our life together and there was little or no chance that our marriage would survive this latest and greatest moment of turbulence. "I'm going to lose my home, Ronnie," I continued. "I'm going to lose *everything*." Ronnie was not only unmoved by my pleas, he was angered by them. "I don't like being bullied," Ronnie said, referring to the Police Jury. "Like I told you, I have to do this. You're gonna destroy my business." Tears rolled down my cheeks. "Please don't do this," I cried. Ronnie straightened up and a stern look came over his face as though he was about to deliver a final, crushing blow to my hopes. "I prayed about this on the way over here," Ronnie said, locking his eyes with mine. I couldn't help but think about all of the times that I believed God had spoken to me and how those moments steeled my resolve about a decision I was about to make. "God told me that this is your Road-to-Damascus experience," Ronnie continued. I was stunned. Not by the fact that Ronnie's conversation with God had resulted in the loss of my career but that Ronnie would think that *I* of all people was in need of a road to Damascus experience. *This man doesn't have a clue about my spiritual experience,* I thought. *He doesn't know how many Road-to-Damascus experiences I've already had.* But Ronnie wasn't through with me just yet. "When there's nothing left but you and death," he lectured, "God will be able to reveal himself to you in a way that you'll be able to appreciate." That remark, which eerily echoed the atheists-in-foxholes cliché that I'd just seen Dawkins demolish in Houston, lent the dismissal an inarguable finality. All I could do was ask for my last paycheck. "Of course I'll pay you for December," Ronnie replied, "but I need all of my equipment back." I took a moment to absorb the news and then prodded Ronnie again. "You've got me scheduled for inspections this afternoon," I said. "Do you want me to handle them?" Ronnie stared at me, unsmiling. "No," he replied, "I'll do them." Ronnie then picked the printouts up off the table, stood up straight in the booth and, without shaking my hand, turned around and walked toward the Waffle Shoppe's entrance. Near the glass doors toward the entrance, Ronnie stopped by a table to talk with a group of diners, purposefully oblivious to me. I simply pushed open the Waffle Shoppe's doors and headed to my car in the afternoon sun, leaving my friend, mentor and my career all behind.

Fearing that my marriage would be the next victim of my ostracism in DeRidder, I drove over to see Kelli at her clerical job at a local power utility, Cleco, just a few blocks away on North Pine. I didn't even have time to formulate a plan to break the news to Kelli; the task of letting her know that my career was finished was too urgent. So I strode into Cleco and told Kelli that we needed to talk outside. "Ronnie just fired me," I told Kelli out on the sidewalk. "Over all this stuff?" Kelli replied. "I'm so sorry." To my surprise, Kelli hugged me and told me that everything was going to be all right. I was comforted by the fact that at the very least Kelli might be okay. But I knew that everything was absolutely not going to be all right for our family. Outside of preaching and building inspections, I didn't have any idea how to make a living. And Ronnie's remark about pressure from the Pentecostals on the Police Jury was no lie: I discovered that Grace Roberts had also shared the Facebook photos with members of the Police Jury, which would make it virtually impossible for me to land a job anywhere in the parish.

It was a disaster that arrived at the worst possible moment in our lives. Kelli and I had been in financial distress since I'd left Grace of DeQuincy and the consistent pay from Ronnie, which had lasted about a year, merely enabled us to begin the process of catching up with our mounting bills. By the time Ronnie fired me in December, Kelli and I were still far behind on our obligations. The end of December, when I received my final paycheck from BIG, was followed by the new year, in which my income was a terrifying *zero*. Kelli's job at Cleco, meanwhile, brought in about a thousand dollars per month, just enough to cover our mortgage but nothing else. Our home was a dream come true for Kelli after having lived in a series of not-quite-homes such as my grandmother's house and two successive stays in trailers. Now my beliefs were jeopardizing a dream that had been decades in the making. So during the spring of 2012, I took on speaking engagements thanks to my role with Recovering from Religion in hopes that the cross-country gigs might serve as fund-raisers for the organization and for me, as the monies taken in could be used to pay me a small salary for working with the group. But instead I found myself speaking before local groups of atheists who regarded fund-raising as an anathema. Fund-raising, these atheists believed, wasn't just repellent–it resembled the passing of the hat at church. My dashed hopes out on the road led us to only get further behind on our bills.

The monthly note on our house was just one of the many bills we were unable to keep up with. But assurances from friends about the slow, grinding pace of foreclosures kept our worries about losing our home at bay. Then, on a warm afternoon in May of 2012, I saw an unfamiliar vehicle, a late-model, red-colored, four-door Buick LeSabre, pull into our driveway. Since I'd been outed as an atheist, strange vehicles near the house seemed to be commonplace: one day, I saw a middle-aged woman in a boxy, blue compact car pull up into the driveway, stare at our house for several moments and then back away. So the sight of the LeSabre brought a feeling of unease but also a sense that I was simply being harassed again by the locals. But when I sped up to our driveway, my heart sank. It was a sheriff's deputy from the Beauregard Parish sheriff's office. Having worked with sheriff's deputies when I was at city hall I knew exactly why he was at our home: delivering a foreclosure notice. "How ya doin?" said the gray-haired deputy who was clad in an equally gray sheriff's deputy uniform as he rolled down the driver's-side window of his car. I said I was fine. "I've already given the paperwork to your wife. Have a good day." The walk from my car to the front door that day was like taking step after painful step on your way to being handed a death warrant. Indeed, when I arrived at the front door, Kelli's skin was a pale, ghostly white and she shot me a look that was at once stoic and detached. She passed the paperwork to me in an almost "I told you so" kind of way. But I couldn't blame Kelli for being furious with me. With the sheriff's sale set for August 29, 2012, I had just three months to save our home from the auction block.

Incredibly, looming foreclosure proceedings were just one head of the hydra of serious financial problems afflicting our family. Kelli and I were so broke that when we celebrated our wedding anniversary that April, we'd scoured the house for loose change just so we could pay for gas for a trip to Holly Beach, known as the "Cajun Riviera," in nearby Cameron Parish. That summer, when Kelli prepared a garage sale to make some extra cash, one of our neighbors cornered her in our carport and remarked, "I'm sorry that everyone is talking about you and how you're married to an atheist." This was the last straw for Kelli. We were shunned by our parish, our city and now we weren't even welcome on our own block. Kelli insisted that we move away from DeRidder, an idea I angrily shot down. "We can't move," I told Kelli. "Every preacher who comes out as an atheist shouldn't have to move five hundred miles away. We've invested our lives in this community." To me, moving felt like pleading guilty to a crime or like being a convicted child molester who is forced to leave the community. I also believed that my coming out as an atheist had already cost my family so much that giving up our home was a price I was unwilling to bear. And I hoped that if anyone could overcome the struggles of a life as an atheist in a deeply religious community like DeRidder, it could be me. I'd experienced so many hardships and profoundly divergent life experiences–from life on the road working revivals in Mississippi to ministering under Brother Goodwin in Iowa–that I felt strong enough to survive the judgments of my community. Kelli was not convinced by any of my arguments for remaining in DeRidder and replied with an ultimatum: she was going to leave with or without me. Paul was just turning twenty at the time and the dissolution of our marriage wouldn't cause anywhere near the sort of pain it would have caused in his adolescence, so I reluctantly agreed to separate. Though we separated on June 29, I still wasn't ready to give up on our lives in DeRidder just yet. I furiously researched the foreclosure process and quickly discovered that by filing under Chapter 13 of the bankruptcy code, I'd have a shot at stopping foreclosure proceedings and perhaps even resolving my delinquent mortgage payments. So on August 1, 2012, I filed for Chapter 13 bankruptcy in US District Court for the Western District of Louisiana. The foreclosure was stopped. Our home was saved. But it still wasn't clear if Kelli and I would ever enjoy our home together again.

With the bankruptcy, the dissolution of my marriage and the rejection of our family by our own community, the summer of 2012 was a traumatic period without peer in the already turbulent lives of Kelli and me. In the beginning, the crises–spiritual, marital and financial–took me lower in regard to my self-image than those darkest of days working in sales for Village Profile. I had endeavored for so long to have an esteemed place in the community that to suddenly to be at the very bottom of the community was truly crushing. But as the summer progressed, I began to see that I could survive rejection, a revelation that nearly matched the power of my realization that I was a nonbeliever during the phone call with NaTosha. I had never known that I *could* survive rejection. I'd experienced different levels of religious rejection but had always been able to create a buffer: when I knew that an experience was moving in a direction that might end in rejection, I'd move churches or move my home. I always made sure that I had more people for me than against me. Now so many in my community thought so little of me, a first in my life. The rejection was initially overwhelming but, to my surprise, I didn't buckle under the torrent of rejection I faced on a daily basis, and that made me proud of myself. I was overcoming my biggest fear: the fear of rejection.

My coping mechanisms were brand new, too. In the past, I dealt with fear, anxiety, depression and rejection through faith with an internal dialogue that said, *I can do all things through Christ who strengthens me.* But as a nonbeliever, I realized that all of those times I believed that it was Christ who strengthened me, it was actually me who strengthened me. Now that I knew that I could rely on myself as a source of strength, my internal dialogue shifted to, *I can do all things through the strength that I possess.* As an atheist, doing all things doesn't mean doing *everything*–it means doing the most that I am capable of, which allows me to clearly identify with myself as the flawed human being that I am. With faith, I expected to be superhuman, to put on a happy face all the time. Without faith, I'm allowed to be human. If that means spending the weekend in bed wallowing in sadness or self-pity, that's okay. My post-faith mindset allowed me to not only embrace my humanity but reality as well. I realized that I could work with reality instead of supernaturally trying to change reality. A reality-based worldview does not mean surrendering to hopelessness–in fact it's exactly the opposite. Indeed, I came to realize toward the end of the horrible summer of 2012 that hope actually flourished as my expectations about my life became steadily more realistic. Freed from unrealistic expectations, hope became more like a foundational stone in my conscience versus a fluffy, floaty cloud. I hoped for the things that truly matter, like the health of my family or friends or simply for the sun to rise the next morning, and when those things happened I was fulfilled. Faith, by contrast, had locked me into impossibly high hopes–like divine intervention into my everyday life–a sort of anxiety-ridden hope that a gambler has staring at a roulette table. It's hope against impossibly high odds.

I began to see reality not as the enemy but as a partner in dealing with the struggles of being a modern *Homo sapiens.* A kind of virtuous cycle emerged from that summer; as my expectations grew more realistic, disappointments diminished and hope continued to grow. I was becoming a happier person; I was no longer expecting the creator of the universe to step in and change the rules. Suddenly, I was much more interested in learning what the rules were in the first place. At the outset, life felt much less colorful because I'd seen the Holy Spirit behind everything. But again, just as the embrace of reality led to a more hopeful life, shaking off the shackles of such an everyday spiritual battle brought about a nearly instantaneous feeling of contentment. I was no longer at war spiritually and no longer at war with reality. Everything from relationships to rocket science now rested on the foundation of reality, which brought with it a hope that I could learn the rules of life and one day get better at playing the game.

As the fall of 2012 began and as the separation from Kelli was no longer so new or stung so deeply, my reality-based worldview allowed me to truly, finally grapple with Kelli's dissatisfaction with our life together; I'd asked so much of Kelli during our twenty-two years of marriage yet had provided her with precious little in return. I deeply empathized with her perspective, which allowed me to let Kelli, and our marriage, go. So even though it was just me and Paul at home in DeRidder that fall, I hardly felt alone. I was scheduling speaking engagements at atheist conferences across the country, which brought about the energizing, ecstatic feeling of my revival days. Through the Clergy Project and Recovering from Religion, I was ministering again but this time to people in transition *from* faith. It felt like there was more ministry in my life than there had ever been.

The fulfillment I found out on the road, however, did not mask the struggles I faced as a nonbeliever in DeRidder. The very smallest acts of everyday life, like shopping at Walmart for necessities, became freighted with fear and anxiety. Walmart is *the* mecca for Beauregard Parish—there is literally nothing else to do in town. So I knew that it was close to a certainty that a Walmart visit would result in encountering a member of my former congregation or a churchgoer who went to one of the many churches attended by a member of my or my wife's large families. I realized that I could no longer run to Walmart when I needed something; I had to think, *Who am I going to run into there?* It wasn't merely awkward encounters that I was concerned about. Since coming out, I'd received threatening voice mails and e-mails and the thought was always in the back of my mind that there could be somebody out there who wanted to harm me or even my son. Then there was the frightening prospect of running into someone at Walmart who would not resort to violence but would be bold enough to be ugly to me in this most public of places. One early evening in the fall of 2012, I gathered the courage to make the Walmart trip and, sure enough, within moments after passing the greeter by the sliding doors out front I saw a man from my grandmother's church by the grocery aisle. This was a man who, in the past, never failed to greet me at Walmart in the most friendly fashion. He'd actually *cross* an aisle to shake my hand and ask, "How's Britany? How's Sister Stella?" These weren't just pleasantries–he was deeply interested in the lives of my sister and grandmother and truly wanted to know how they were faring on a particular day. No matter what was going on in my life, or in his life as well, I could always count on him for a warm handshake and questions about my family that were imbued with a completely genuine sense of empathy. So that evening at Walmart, I saw him out the corner of my eye by the grocery aisle and had the opportunity to avoid him but intentionally went straight toward him. He was a vendor in town and that evening he was stocking potato chips on an end cap on the grocery aisle. As I neared him, he looked over his left shoulder and his gaze clearly and unmistakably met mine. But instead of a handshake or even a hello, he nodded his head at me and then turned away and returned to stocking the end cap. I was humiliated. It was that red-faced feeling you get when you slip and fall in public but worse–I felt like I'd *emotionally* slipped and fallen.

But as I left Walmart that night tightly gripping a gaggle of plastic bags, I realized that in order to not be emotionally crushed by such encounters, which carried the weight of running into a former love, I had to step back and reevaluate my relationship to these folks who had once been so dear to me. I grasped that I was so hurt and disappointed by his behavior because I considered him family. He was a member of the church family and during my twenty-five years in the ministry that may well have been my family. Driving home from Walmart that night I understood that we weren't as close as I thought we were. The person he no longer loved was not the real me. And the person he believed he was rejecting–a loveless, bloodless atheist–was also not the real me. Suddenly, the encounter became not as personal as it initially felt. He had rejected a false identity. I should not take it personally because he never knew me as a person.

Walmart, of course, was far from the only place I feared in DeRidder. The idea of visiting the local post office just horrified me because one of its employees was the pastor of the church where my grandmother and grandfather met, God's Temple of Refuge. But I couldn't avoid the post office for long–like Walmart, a visit to the post office was a necessity I couldn't function without. One afternoon in the fall of 2012, I ended up in the pastor's line at the post office. I trembled with fear and anticipation at seeing him for the first time since I came out. But fortunately my fears were allayed when he calmly, politely and wordlessly took my order for a book of stamps. I realized as I stood at the counter that he wasn't making an issue out of my presence because he was at work. Just as importantly, because of the smallness of the post office we were a captive audience to one another; unlike Walmart, there was no bread aisle to hide in. There in the post office I realized that the sort of public ugliness I feared would likely never come to pass because such behavior would bring about awkwardness and discomfort to both parties.

As the holidays approached, I began to steel my resolve about not only staying in DeRidder but remaining a presence in town. I realized that the anxiety I felt about my life as an atheist in a town dominated by Pentecostals in Southwest Louisiana did not spring from a choice that I had made–it came from a realization that I'd had about myself. So there was no way to be wrong about it. I realized that no matter how wrong these many encounters felt, I had to continuously remind myself that there was nothing to be wrong about. And I was clear on the options I faced. One option was to pretend to believe something I didn't believe and I obviously couldn't do that; I could also avoid the subject of religion altogether, which was an oppressive way to live. The third and only true option was to live as who I am and express my right to be an individual in a balanced way.

The clarity about my life as a nonbeliever in DeRidder, surprisingly, made the trips to Walmart, the bank and the post office get better and easier every time I made them. Where once the everyday trips brought about such profound anxiety that I literally trembled when I made them, which left me physically and mentally spent, I now calmly approached them without fear. The fear dissipated by making a conscious effort to be myself, to be just as kind and just as open as I had always been. If I'd opened doors for folks in the past, I opened them now. If I'd allowed someone with more groceries in their basket to take a place ahead of me in line, I did the same now. Questions like, *Will I be able to defend myself?* or *Will I be able to explain atheism?* no longer mattered. Indeed, I remained in DeRidder not to provide answers about atheism but rather to pose questions. Questions like, "How did a minister become an atheist?" or "How can Jerry be so nice and be an atheist?" or perhaps "How is it that I can't tell the difference between Jerry the minister and Jerry the atheist?" By viewing my presence in DeRidder as one that stimulates questions, I no longer went to Walmart or the bank with armor on in the battle for atheism. I didn't have to *answer* anything–I am me and that's all the matters.

Though I was becoming more secure in my life in DeRidder, Christmas of 2012 posed the greatest challenges–personal, emotional and philosophical–for me since becoming a nonbeliever. Kelli was coming home for Christmas to see Paul and to visit with our families and we were set to have Christmas dinner at Kelli's family home in Pitkin. Christmas dinner presented me with deep, multiple layers of unease and awkwardness, with my embrace of atheism at the root of it all. My separation from Kelli was first and foremost on my mind but I also had the secondary concern of how my in-laws would respond to our separation, which was due to Kelli leaving town *because* of the town's response to my atheism. Then, there were less frightening but still important questions about Christmas dinner: What were we going to do when it came time to pray over the meal? Kelli's family had a huge circle of friends, so I had to wonder: Who was going to drive up for a holiday visit? Just down the road from my father-in-law's home was a lifelong friend of his named Harvey Ray Johnson, a staunch Pentecostal. Would Harvey show up? I was confident that my in-laws would treat me with kindness and respect because they had always been so loving to me over my many years of marriage to Kelli. But I had no such confidence about their visitors, who could be everyone from Harvey to their pastor and my former mentor in the ministry, Brother Robertson.

Christmas day started off inauspiciously. Just before noon, I drove from DeRidder to Pitkin by myself while Paul made the trip with Kelli in her truck. In the past, the twenty-five-mile drive would have been unremarkable but this time it made me feel truly alone. I reflected on the pain felt by Kelli and Paul about the dissolution of our small family and the alienation from our community. I arrived in Pitkin for the early Christmas dinner, which was actually just a very late lunch, and met Kelli and Paul on the battleship-gray front porch of Kelli's parents. Inside, we took our seats around the large, wooden dining room table flanked by a long bench and straight-back dining room chairs joined by my mother-in-law, Betty, my father-in-law, Donald Ray, Kelli's brother Mark and his wife, Missy, and their son Ty. I was comforted by the sight of the dining room table, which was so crowded with turkey, ham, casseroles, rolls and pasta salad that there was barely enough space for our dinner plates. But before I could relax the moment for the prayer over the meal had arrived. It was the first time in my twenty-two years of life as the Swains' son-in-law preacher that I wasn't asked to pray. I reflected on the fact that even during my time-out period from the ministry I happily passed prayer duties to Donald Ray. But now, not only was I not in the lineup, I wasn't even in the dugout. In fact, I was truly in the stands. "Dear Lord," Donald Ray began, bowing his head, "thank you for this meal today." To my surprise, he lifted his head—the prayer was complete without so much as a reference to Jesus's birth.

As we dug into our turkey, ham and heaping portions of sides like pasta salad, the conversation around the table stayed lighthearted, hewing to innocuous gossip about friends, family and the church. When everyone around the table had their fill of Betty's cooking, we all broke out into smaller units. Paul went onto the back porch with Mark and Ty, Kelli took a walk with Donald Ray, and I ended up with Missy and Betty in the dining room. We talked genially about how things were going at my in-laws' church and, for a moment at least, the familiar sense of familial ease pervaded the room. But then Mark signaled that he had to leave. Because there was so much uncertainty surrounding my separation from Kelli, which was heightened by a sense that my new life as a nonbeliever would make such gatherings very different in the future, the winding down of Christmas dinner felt like I was attending my own funeral. Indeed, as Mark and Missy opened the front door there was an air of finality to their exit. "It was good to see you," Mark said, shaking my hand. "We still love you, brother-in-law." *We still love you*—I had to admit to myself that the remark related as much to my atheism as to my separation from Kelli. And because the two were intertwined, Mark and Missy truly didn't know if they would ever see me at a family event again. Standing at the door and saying a goodbye to them, I reflected on not just the real pain the separation caused but the fact that the separation was the product of my atheism. I had to wonder, *Was it worth all of this? Has it been worth disturbing so many people's lives?*

The ride home to DeRidder with Paul late that afternoon was rough. I had to pull myself together mentally and emotionally so that I wouldn't cry. Back at home, I reflected on that great Dr. Seuss quote: "Don't cry because it's over, smile because it happened." I had to smile and be proud of my transformation because what I'd done was not just for myself but for the many folks just like me who were transitioning from faith. I hoped I'd somehow softened the landing for them. And I had to embrace my new life. It was a life with a less encumbered lease. I'd come to believe that life is something we're all leasing; we never truly own it because we have to surrender it back to the dealership in the end. The difference between the lease I have now versus the lease I had when I was in religion is that the expectations are too numerous to count and there are literally thousands of instances in which you violate your lease agreement. The lease I have now has far fewer restrictions, much less small print. That doesn't mean that I'm less responsible for the lease. Indeed, I feel greater ownership for my actions because I am no longer dependent on an imaginary friend. I'm the only real dictator of my actions. Now my actions come from me–and the committee deciding my actions is a committee of one: myself. Just because I'm central in my decision-making process doesn't mean I ignore the needs of others; now, I reflect on the needs of a much smaller group: my loved ones and my community versus the church hierarchy and a supernatural being.

As Christmas night arrived, I remembered my drive to Pitkin to take Kelli on our first date. I had no idea then just how clouded my judgments were by the expectations that my church, my pastors and my God had of me. My thoughts were anything but free–they were in bondage to a myriad of personalities and ideas. Now I could live my life in a manner that was coherent with the real me. As midnight neared, I became saddened by the realization that I had reaped what I had sown thanks to twenty-five years in the ministry–a life that was not really mine. But then I was hopeful. I was just starting to chart a course in my life that was true to me so that twenty-five years from now, I'll live a life of my own choosing that represents who I really am. That's the hope. It's a hope for the future that fits me where I can make decisions based on my family and community and not what the Bible says. Freed from religion, which forces me to sacrifice my own identity and values, my values become my own. That's the hope. By forcing my way to freedom, I'll set a positive example for the next generation, and I'll feel a hope for them that they will not live an existence characterized by cultural servitude but instead walk into a life of true individual freedom of self-expression.

Epilogue

We must let go of the life we have planned, so as to accept the one that is waiting for us.

—**Joseph Campbell**

AFTER TWENTY-FIVE YEARS, I left the ministry literally kicking and screaming. I did everything that I could intellectually and emotionally; I worked with my conscience in every way possible to not only stay in Christianity but to also remain in the ministry. I truly couldn't envision my life any other way. What was so difficult about leaving the ministry was not leaving a career but a life of *meaning* behind. I believe that ministers are meaning machines. That's what ministers crank out twenty-four hours a day. That is their connection to the lives of the people whom they love so dearly. When I use the phrase "meaning machines" I'm not referring to the televangelist or the megachurch pastor. That's not me or my experience. My experience is the local church, those with a few hundred congregants or less. I recently read that 70 percent of the churches in the United States have less than a hundred members; that's the church I'm talking about. I'm talking about the ministers of small churches who come to your house whenever you call them. I'm talking about the ministers who travel to emergency rooms in the middle of the night or stand by the hospital bed holding the hand of the surviving spouse as his or her loved one leaves our reality. My contention is that these ministers are there in people's lives to provide meaning. So I spent twenty-five years not just in a profession but engaged in a mission to help people find meaning in their lives. I wish that I could say that I love my new, global nonbelieving family more than I loved my church family but that's just not the case. The truth is that I love my new friends with all of my heart, just as I loved the thousands of people to whom I ministered. I loved them through every trial and every struggle that they went through. Theirs was *my* trial and *my* struggle. Their every heartache, every heartbreak, every sickness. All of it belonged to me.

When I came to the crossroads of my faith and realized that my conscience would no longer allow me to be a minister, I believed that my life was over. I truly felt that I would do nothing more than work a secular nine-to-five job, come home every night and watch *American Chopper* on the DVR, wait for old age to come and then get moved into a nursing home to die. I thought the end of my world had arrived because I had no idea how to carry on in my life without being deeply involved in the lives of other people. My entire identity–every bit of pleasure, every bit of excitement that I derived from life–was completely wrapped up in loving other people and in sharing in their experiences. And I had no idea that that kind of meaning existed outside the church.

So when I attended my first free thought convention in Houston in the fall of 2011, where I took that fateful photo with Richard Dawkins and witnessed Christopher Hitchens make his last and perhaps most beautiful and vulnerable public appearance, I was so naïve that when I walked into that room and there were one thousand people in attendance I thought that religion was dead. I really believed that there should be an epitaph somewhere engraved with the words RELIGION: RIP and that we'd all attend religion's funeral the next week. I was so naïve, and so fresh to the idea that there was another way of living that I didn't know there was any other way to exist. Dr. Darrel W. Ray, the author of the great book *The God Virus,* approached me at the Texas Freethought Convention in Houston and told me about Recovering from Religion and asked me if I'd be the organization's director. Recovering from Religion is for faithful folks who find themselves in a transition, who are asking, just as I had asked, "How does a person find meaning in their lives after they leave religion?" This is such a critical question because meaning is one thing religion does well. Very often, religion provides meaning through answers. Whenever you have a question, religion has an answer. When I was a pastor, if I didn't have an answer then I felt forced to make one up. That's what I was paid for: to supply meaning to my congregation. I was a meaning machine.

But since I left the ministry I have not lost the ability to find meaning in my life. In fact, I refuse to describe my embrace of atheism as a loss of faith. I don't feel like I have "lost" anything. I've lost car keys, I've even lost a couple of cats, but I didn't lose my faith. I believe that I *graduated* from religion after over twenty-five years of study in which I applied myself to the best of my ability and took my fellow students deeply to heart. But I don't think that I was a uniquely curious or skeptical presence in the ministry. What I discovered in my decades in the church is that ministers are not only meaning machines but are also deep critical thinkers who are engaged in their own form of free thought. How can that be true? Well, if there's a Pentecostal minister he has probably examined the Baptist doctrine and discredited it. He just hasn't examined his own Pentecostal doctrine with such a critical eye. If there's a Protestant minister who thinks that Protestants are the only true Christians then he has probably stepped back and used a little bit of critical thinking to make an analysis of the doctrine of other Christian sects.

So free thought actually does exist within the ministry. I'd go even further and argue that the majority of ministers who I have learned to love over the last twenty-five years of my life in the church are actually agnostic but don't really know it. They really are—they just don't understand what the word "agnostic" means. They're afraid to allow their doubts to fully surface. But they have doubts. When you stand by the bedside of someone who's leaving this world and it is your responsibility to minister to that dying man or woman—you're ministering to a tithe payer, a husband or a wife who never failed to show up and bring something to the bake sale, a person who had your back when other people in the congregation were being critical, a person who is devoted to God, devoted to the church and devoted to you—you're God's representative standing right there in the valley of the shadow of death and they're looking to you for answers. The greatest tragedy that they can experience is happening—the doctors have done everything they can do—and the situation is completely out of their control. Now it's all up to you to provide meaning, to provide answers. At that moment, I promise you, *every* minister on the planet with a heart for his congregation is agnostic. Because he doesn't know what's going to happen. He doesn't know whether the sick man or woman he is praying for is going to live or die. He's going to pray as sincerely as he can and pull every tool out of his theological toolbox. He's going to use all of the weaponry in his arsenal against this horrifying event. He's going to try everything he can to uplift and console. But when that beloved member of the congregation passes and the minister walks silently down the hallway of the hospital, there are hidden tears. There is a silent breaking of the heart and that man or woman of God who stands amidst the tragedy and heartbreak is going to ask themselves, *Where are you God?* and *Why have you forsaken me*?

In that moment, with the pastor feeling the enormous weight of a life lost, the very thing he or she is taught to do—and indeed the humane thing to do—is to convey hope: a hope *through f*aith. So that man or woman of God takes a deep breath, pushes the sadness, mourning, doubts and disappointments back down inside and walks back into the hospital room to comfort the grieving. That man or woman of God says, "We know God is a healer," "We know God can do anything," "We know that God loves us," "We know that by his stripes we are healed." That man or woman of God is not faking it or pretending. These words are meant to provide solace, peace and meaning to the lives of his congregants at the most desperate juncture in their lives. In that moment, the minister's doubt takes a backseat to the role he or she must play: the meaning machine.

After decades of studying religion, I was awakened to the idea that because skepticism was my nature I had more questions than answers about religion. I realized that free thought had been the methodology with which I explored my theological questions and that agnosticism was the conclusion to an investigation into the question of religion that spanned twenty-five years. But what really brought me to atheism—and I believe that atheism is an opinion because the existence of something outside of our reality is neither provable or unprovable—was humanism. In all of my endeavors, from the ministry to city hall, humanism has been my motivation. It is humanism that gives me hope. And what I now know is that by embracing humanism as fully as I once embraced God, there is hope after faith. What I realize is that—like the minister who has doubts but cannot, either out of ignorance or fear, truly be agnostic—when I was in religion I was a humanist who didn't know what humanism was. Once I shed myself of all the trappings of religion and freed myself from its supernatural thinking, the first thing that happened is that I began to understand humanity at its fullest. And by freeing myself from the shackles of religion and my relationship to supernaturalism, I embraced true hope: the hope that can only be enjoyed by humanists as they serve humanity. It is this true hope, ironically, that is found in religion not because it is divinely inspired but because humans instinctively know that the highest purpose is serving one another.

The reality is that the secular movement provides the only real consolation for humanity. For what I love about being free from religion, what I love about having graduated from faith, is that I still feel a sense of awe at the universe whenever I open my eyes. But now, when I stand outside my home in DeRidder on a starry night and I take in the beauty and vastness of the Milky Way, I know it is not the divine or a supernatural being at work and that the meaning of the great universe laid out before me isn't trapped between the leather-bound covers of a book. Yet it is not the stars or constellations that move me most when I gaze into the sky, but humanity. Humans are so special because as far as we know we are the only part of the universe that can see and appreciate ourselves. That the universe can look back at itself is the most spiritual act imaginable. It's a oneness that provides far more meaning than the oneness doctrine of my Pentecostal days, and it provides a hope for humanity and the universe in all of its complexity that cannot be found through faith.

Acknowledgments

> *Many seem to have absolutely no awareness of how fortunate one must be to succeed at anything in life, no matter how hard one works. One must be lucky to be able to work. One must be lucky to be intelligent, physically healthy, and not bankrupted in middle age by the illness of a spouse.*
>
> —**Sam Harris, *Free Will***

I, for one, know actually how lucky I've been.

Fortunately the *New York Times* article about me, "From Bible-Belt Pastor to Atheist Leader," by the insightful and compassionate journalist Robert Worth brought both Ben Schafer of Da Capo Press and my literary agent, David Patterson of Foundry Media, into my life. The interest and understanding that Robert, David and Ben have demonstrated for my plight has been heartwarming and has given me great confidence for a much brighter future.

Robert, I thank you for introducing me and my story to the world in a truly fair and balanced way.

Ben, your willingness to go so far out on a limb will forever have me in your debt. Thank you.

David, you have not only fought to protect my interests but you've also been interested in the very thing I fight for, individualism. I thank you for that.

My luck continued as David introduced me to Ethan Brown, who would become not only my cowriter but my friend as well.

Ethan, the appreciation I express here will hopefully come as no surprise to you. The skill set you brought to this project was perfectly suited for my story. You've been sympathetic and more than patient. Your tolerant personality combined with your tactful writing process allowed me to cry through the retelling of the sad times and to laugh about the good times. Even more than appreciating your tireless work on this project, I truly thank you for hearing me out. You made this memoir a reality, and in so doing you made me a healthier and happier man.

The story told in this book details some of the many spiritual lessons I have learned over the last few decades, without always having enough space for the names of the many teachers of those lessons. There are dozens who will unfortunately remain unnamed but I would be even more ashamed if I did not at least list these few:

Rev. Gary Amirault
Revs. Mike Williams and Jeff Robertson
Rev. Robert Rutherford
Dr. Harold Lovelace
Bishop Carlton Pearson

I sincerely thank each of you for the direct contributions you made to my life and your indirect contributions to this book. I am lucky to have you in my life.

Long before the publication of the fortuitous *New York Times* article in August of 2012, I already had the support of a faithful team of dear friends, from the brother I never had, Randal Jackson, to my secular mentor, Duane Foshee. I was truly fortunate to have them as friends, even if it was only geography that originally brought us together. As they say: *location, location, location.*

Randal and Duane, I both acknowledge and appreciate the fact that you've both been better friends to me than I deserved. Thank you.

Last but far from least in the friends category are Kelly Thompson, Brad James, the Reverend Tommy Lester and my former church member Kenneth Marcantel, all of whom have never wavered in their fellowship with me regardless of the public sentiment around them.

Kelly, Brad, Tommy, and Ken, not only am I grateful for your faithfulness, I'm also encouraged by your bravery. Thank you.

I'm also fortunate to have added to my network of support some of the very individuals who taught me so much about reason and science before they had ever heard my story or learned my name:

AronRa
Matt Dillahunty
Jacob Fortin
Rich and Diana Joy Lions
Brother Richard Haynes
Sarah Morehead
Seth Andrews
Ray and Sarah Morehead
Philip and Steve Wells
Greg Epstein
Sam Singleton

All names worth Googling.

Not to mention my Clergy Project sisters Catherine Dunphy, Teresa MacBain and Linda LaScola.

Finally I come to the richest, sometimes bittersweet, but always endearing examples of just how lucky a man can be: my family.

Maw-Maw, regardless of how my life's course may have discouraged you, I still and always will think that the sun both rises and sets with you. Thank you for every cent you have spent on me financially and every second you have shared with me emotionally. Your support has always been the bonding force within my turbulent life far more times than I can count. I thank you, love you–and don't worry: a promise is a promise.

Britany, you've been the dearest sister that a brother could ever ask for. You're the only person I know who has never said a curse word while having more right to do so than anyone I've ever met. I'm so proud to be your brother.

GW, thank you for not only accepting me as your own but, more importantly, for loving my mother. You have never failed to support me to the best of your ability. I'm thankful to have been lucky enough to have you in my life.

Mama, the examples of your sacrifices for me and mine are far too numerous to fit within this limited space, but please rest assured that each and every one of them have been noticed and appreciated. Thank you for a lifetime of support that was only topped by the support you've given over the last year. Thank you. I love you, Mama. You're who I want to be when I grow up.

Kelli, thank you for sharing twenty-two years of your life with me. While I was trying to teach the world about soulful matters, you were trying to teach me that being soul mates is what matters. Thank you for trying so hard to fix the unfixable. Thank you for wanting my happiness more than your own. Thank you for being my friend. Thank you for being you. Thank you for bringing our son into the world.

Paul, in ways you will only fully understand much later in life, this book is as much about you as it is about me. The last year has been the hardest year ever for our little family, yet you have handled it with grace and maturity. Thank you for being a stellar example of courage for the sake of individualism. Thank you for sticking by me during the darkest of times and for traveling with me to the most remote places in the country. Thank you for being my hero. Thank you for being the perfect son. I'm lucky to have you.